Circa 1700

STUDIES IN THE HISTORY OF ART · 66 ·

Center for Advanced Study in the Visual Arts

Symposium Papers XLIII

Circa 1700:
Architecture in Europe
and the Americas

Edited by Henry A. Millon

National Gallery of Art, Washington

Distributed by Yale University Press

New Haven and London

This volume was produced by the Center for Advanced Study in the Visual Arts and the Publishing Office, National Gallery of Art, Washington. *www.nga.gov*

Editorial Board
JOHN OLIVER HAND, *chairman*
SUSAN M. ARENSBERG
SARAH FISHER
THERESE O'MALLEY

Editor in Chief
JUDY METRO

Series Editor, CASVA
THERESE O'MALLEY

Program Assistants, CASVA
KIM RODEFFER
NICOLE ANSELONA

Managing Editor
CYNTHIA WARE

Production Manager
CHRIS VOGEL

Design Manager
MARGARET BAUER

Editorial Assistant
CAROLINE WEAVER

The type is Trump Mediaeval, set by Princeton Editorial Associates, Inc., Scottsdale, Arizona.

The text paper is Biberist Matte.

Printed in China by Everbest through Four Colour Imports, Ltd., Louisville, Kentucky

Distributed by Yale University Press, New Haven and London

Abstracted and indexed in BHA (Bibliography of the History of Art) and Art Index

Proceedings of the symposium "Circa 1700: Architecture in Europe and the America," sponsored by the Center for Advanced Study in the Visual Arts, National Gallery of Art, and the Andrew W. Mellon Foundation. The symposium was held 15–16 September 2000 in Washington.

Library of Congress Cataloging-in-Publication Data

Circa 1700 : architecture in Europe and the Americas / edited by Henry A. Millon.
    p. cm. — (Studies in the history of art ; 66. Symposium papers ; 43 / Center for Advanced Study in the Visual Arts)
    Proceedings of a symposium held at the National Gallery of Art, Washington, D.C., Sept. 15–16, 2000.
    Includes bibliographical references and index.
    ISBN 0-300-11475-3 (alk. paper)
    1. Architecture, Baroque—Congresses.   2. City planning—Congresses.   I. Millon, Henry A.
II. Studies in the history of art (Washington, D.C.) ; 66.   III. Studies in the history of art (Washington, D.C.). Symposium papers ; 43.
    N386.U5S78 vol. 66
    [NA590]
    724'.19—dc22   2005018274

ISSN 0091-7338

Frontispiece: Andrea Pozzo, *The Admission of Hercules to Olympus*, ceiling of the Great Hall of Liechtenstein Garden Palace, Vienna, 1705–1708
Photograph Sammlungen des Fürsten von Liechtenstein, Vaduz-Wien

Contents

Preface

The preface to each volume in Studies in the History of Art usually concludes with a statement of the mission of the Center for Advanced Study in the Visual Arts at the National Gallery of Art. This is to foster study of the history, theory, and criticism of art, architecture, and urbanism through programs of meetings, research, publication, and fellowships. In this preface that statement is more properly made first, for *Circa 1700: Architecture in Europe and the Americas* brings together all aspects of the Center's programs under the less frequently visited general topics of architecture and urbanism. The papers gathered here derive for the most part from a symposium held at the National Gallery of Art on 15–16 September 2000. This symposium brought intense scholarly attention to the exhibition *The Triumph of the Baroque: Architecture in Europe 1600–1750*, for which Henry A. Millon (then dean of the Center) served as curator, and which was jointly organized by the National Gallery of Art; the Palazzo Grassi, Venice; the Montreal Museum of Fine Arts; and the Musée des Beaux-Arts, Marseille. That exhibition, which included works in many media in addition to twenty-seven architectural models from the period 1600–1750, in turn provided a sequel to an earlier exhibition, also organized by Henry Millon, and presented in Washington, Venice, Paris, and Berlin in 1994–1995, entitled *The Renaissance from Brunelleschi to Michelangelo.*

Each of these initiatives stands alone, but together they represent the culmination of a lifetime of scholarship and epitomize the productive, combinatory effects of programs of research, scholarly meetings, publication, and fellowships in a creative setting. Especially notable in *Circa 1700* is the geographical breadth of the topics considered, from Lima and Quebec City to Saint Petersburg and Cádiz, and including London and other English sites, Rome, Amsterdam, and Vienna, in addition to Naples, Stockholm, and Lisbon. Many of the architects, planners, and patrons under discussion never saw the actual models to which their own inventions referred, relying instead on paper plans and designs, and the circulation of ideas is shown to be as important in these essays as the movement of people. The volume complements both exhibitions and their catalogues in a methodological sense by setting the new architecture represented by the models within the context of a new urbanism and of the physical transformation of major administrative centers of various types.

The symposium "Circa 1700: Architecture in Europe and the Americas" was sponsored by the Andrew W. Mellon Foundation, and its publication has been supported by the Center's Paul Mellon Fund. The Symposium Papers series within Studies in the History of Art is designed to document scholarly meetings at the Center for Advanced Study in the Visual Arts. These meetings and their publication are the responsibility of Associate Dean Therese O'Malley, who has guided this project from the beginning. A summary of published and forthcoming titles may be found at the end of this volume.

ELIZABETH CROPPER
Dean, Center for Advanced Study in the Visual Arts

7

HENRY A. MILLON

National Gallery of Art, Center for Advanced Study in the Visual Arts

Introduction

The decades before and after 1700 witnessed considerable changes in the politics and culture of states and principalities, chiefly in England, Spain, Saxony, Poland, Brandenburg-Prussia, Sweden, and Russia. The Glorious Revolution of 1688–1689 brought Willem III of Orange to England as William III with his consort, Mary Stuart. The death of the last Stuart, Queen Anne, in 1714 ushered in George I (1714–1729) and the Hanoverian dynasty. Charles II, the last of the Hapsburgs in Spain, died in 1700 without an heir, igniting the thirteen-year War of the Spanish Succession between the French and the allies of the Hapsburgs. The Treaty of Utrecht in 1713 awarded the throne of Spain to a Bourbon and Sicily, together with a regal crown, to Victor Amadeus II of Savoy. In 1697 the elector of Saxony, Frederick Augustus I, became king of Poland as Augustus II, acknowledged as one of the outstanding cultural patrons of the age. In 1701 the elector of Brandenburg-Prussia was elevated by the Holy Roman Emperor, a Hapsburg, to kingly rank for siding with the Hapsburgs against France. Although the papacy had by then lost much political clout and with cultural leadership shifted to France in the late seventeenth century, Rome nonetheless remained a mecca for all with cultural interests and aspirations. In 1700 the Pignatelli pope Innocent XII was succeeded by Clement XI Albani, who, during his lengthy reign (1700–1721), did much to invigorate cultural activities in Rome. It was also in 1700 that Peter I of Russia initiated the Great Nordic War against Charles XII of Sweden. The Treaty of Nystadt in 1721 confirmed Russian occupation of much of the southern coast of the Gulf of Finland, with opportune sites for the newly founded Russian navy and the new city of Saint Petersburg.

The major competing powers, France and the Hapsburg realms of Spain and the Holy Roman Empire, with interests in Italy and northern Europe, through their restless diplomatic and military maneuvering often heightened tensions and threatened fragile truces and terms of standing peace treaties. To ensure feeble autonomies, the smaller independent states sought to maintain peace and a balance of power by adroit shifting of alliances with the principal players.

Permanent military and naval forces required construction of naval stations, ports, shipyards, foundries for artillery, barracks, warehouses, supply sheds, and fortresses to protect ports and frontiers. Centralization of state judicial and fiscal administrations necessitated structures for burgeoning ministries and councils. As royal and princely courts grew, existing residences were enlarged or remodeled, new palaces mandated, and royal hunting lodges and villas built or augmented, each structure certain to contain the latest attributes proper to regal or princely status.

Architects of ability, some from northern Europe with training in Rome and in Italy

Burgerzaal (Citizens' Hall), Town Hall (now the Royal Palace), Amsterdam, by Jacob van Campen and Daniel Stalpaert, 1648–1665, marble inlay on floor
Photograph Stichting Koninklijk Paleis op de Dam

(Johann Bernhard Fischer von Erlach and Johann Lucas von Hildebrandt in Austria and Germany), some from Italy and France working abroad (Domenico Trezzini and Charles Lenormand in Russia, François de Cuvilliés and the Zuccalli family in Bavaria and Austria), sought commissions for new representational structures. Royal and princely palaces were remodeled or built anew to reflect the sober late baroque classicism of Gian Lorenzo Bernini (the Palazzo Chigi-Odescalchi, Rome) or Louis Le Vau and Jules Hardouin Mansart (Versailles and Marly). Ideas, however, for palatial interiors that would open new architectural possibilities in the early decades of the eighteenth century were under way by the 1690s in interior renovations of the Trianon at Versailles and of the dauphin's château at Meudon. Innovations that would usher in the rococo were realized there in the interior designs of Jean I Bérain, André-Charles Boulle, Claude III Audran, and others. The architect of record was Jules Hardouin Mansart, with the young architects Pierre I Cailleteau de L'Assurance and Pierre Lepautre in his studio.

By the end of the seventeenth century the transformational achievements of Francesco Borromini, Guarino Guarini, and Andrea Pozzo in Italy, rarely embraced in the remainder of western Europe, were more readily appreciated in central Europe, particularly in Austria, in the works of Fischer von Erlach and Hildebrandt. In the succeeding century a Borrominian strain from Italy surfaced in central Europe in the work of Matthias Daniel Pöppelman, Balthasar Neumann, and Johann Michael Fischer in Germany, as well as in that of the Dientzenhofer family in Bohemia. The competing architectural currents around 1700, together with shifting political, social, and religious associations, afforded patrons an array of opportunities to realize an appropriate theater of display.

The symposium "Circa 1700: Architecture in Europe and the Americas" was organized to complement *The Triumph of the Baroque: Architecture in Europe, 1600–1750*, an exhibition held at the National Gallery of Art in 2000. It would have been possible and profitable to direct full attention to the implications for architecture of the aggrandizement of military and naval centers, or of centers for production of armaments, silk, tapestry, porcelain, and stemware, or of workshops of painters, sculptors, silversmiths, and goldsmiths. "Circa 1700" instead principally examined the physical transformation of urban centers wrought by centralization of state administration in capitals and major centers. The amalgamation of royal and princely courts with centralized military, commercial, judicial, and fiscal administrations was a notable stimulus to the economy, social structure, cultural development, and building activity within those centers.

Fifteen scholars were invited to write about architectural programs realized in political capitals or major centers of activity in their countries. This volume includes resulting studies of Naples, Rome, Vienna, Stockholm, Saint Petersburg, Great Britain, and Amsterdam, followed by centers on the Iberian Peninsula (Cádiz and Lisbon). The volume ends with capitals in the New World (Quebec City and Lima). Four scholars were unable to prepare their essays on Paris, Madrid, Turin, and Rome for publication. Students will be quick to notice the omission as well of Berlin and Prague, of Copenhagen and Warsaw, indeed of Edinburgh, Dublin, Milan, Venice, and Florence, capitals all, with notable architecture. They, and yet other capitals and centers, await attention to the period.

The contribution of Cesare de Seta to the history of Naples spans the period of Austrian Hapsburg domination, beginning in 1707, during a hiatus in the War of the Spanish Succession, when Spain's possessions of the duchy of Milan and the kingdoms of Naples, Sicily, and Sardinia were ceded to the Holy Roman Empire. His account continues from the restoration of Spanish power in 1734 through the reigns of two Bourbon kings who ruled the Kingdom of the Two Sicilies until Napoleon ousted the Spanish in 1798.

The Austrians apparently had little interest in the enhancement of Naples, as de Seta shows, beyond improving transportation through occasional construction of new roads and strengthening of fortifications. Instead, he focuses his attention on extraordinary architectural works of Domenico Antonio Vaccaro (1691–1745) and Ferdinando Sanfelice (1675–1748), citing primarily Vaccaro's churches and Sanfelice's palaces with their beguiling staircases.

In contrast, the advent of the Bourbons under Charles VII (so known from 1734 until he fell heir to the throne of Spain in 1759 and became Charles III) brought a multitude of public projects. Royal beneficence ensured urban development plans for new avenues and roads, the paving of existing roads, construction of an immense royal poorhouse and an equally capacious horse guard barracks, a school in San Leucio, a cemetery at Poggioreale, a palace at Capodimonte, and the San Carlo theater. Charles' successor, Ferdinand IV, continued the grand public works with a granary and grain mills, a university building, a spacious royal villa at Chiaia with renowned gardens, and, as de Seta highlights, the first two city squares in Naples, the Foro Carolino and the Piazza Mercato. The architects called upon by the Bourbons, Ferdinando Fuga (1699–1781) and Luigi Vanvitelli (1709–1773), had earlier distinguished themselves in Rome. They did not disappoint their royal masters in Naples.

Charles VII commissioned Vanvitelli to design a vast new palace and gardens at Caserta north of Naples, a project that was to rival Versailles. After examining a publication that included the Louvre, the Tuileries, and Versailles, as well as Bernini's design for the Louvre, Vanvitelli is reported to have said, "At Versailles there is nothing, and there is little in the rest; Bernini's design has some beautiful things." Charles VII may have enjoyed hearing his architect suggest that he would be housed better than his cousin at Versailles.

Elisa Debenedetti's work has been a notable stimulus for study and publication of the history of eighteenth-century art and architecture in Rome. In her contribution to these proceedings, rather than considering the architectural aspirations of the powerful and wealthy, she draws attention to the housing and residential structures built for the upper bourgeoisie in the first half of the eighteenth century. In these buildings, without lofty intentions or rhetorical posturing, Debenedetti sees an interest in homogeneity and continuity within an urban matrix. According to her analysis, conformity and modesty were already present in Francesco Borromini's late-seventeenth-century additions to the building complex at the Chiesa Nuova and Carlo Fontana's revisions to the Palazzo Ludovisi at Montecitorio. This reserved approach flourished in the eighteenth century with structures designed by Alessandro Specchi, Filippo Barigioni, Ferdinando Fuga, Sebastiano Cipriani, and Filippo Raguzzini.

Debenedetti sees Roman buildings of the early decades of the eighteenth century as reflecting nostalgia for an Arcadian past and the mentality of the rising bourgeoisie. Commissions emphasized social context and function, subordinating decoration to consideration of the larger background of the urban fabric.

The inner city of Vienna in the early seventeenth century was little affected by the baroque, as Hellmut Lorenz reports, but was to be transformed 150 years later. Until the defeat of the Turkish armies in the second siege of 1685, Vienna was a massive fortress, with little government need to stimulate building or sponsor prisons, hospitals, and poorhouses. The persistence of the formidable fortifications meant that baroque churches and palaces were inserted within a dense and irregular urban structure. Lorenz emphasizes that the well-known baroque architecture of Vienna was built by members of the nobility rather than the crown. Examples cited are the building projects of two princes, Johann Adam von Liechtenstein and Eugene of Savoy, who engaged Italian and Austrian architects both for their urban palaces within the walls and for suburban villa or castle garden palaces. The Liechtenstein garden palace, designed by the Italian architects Domenico Egidio Rossi and Domenico Martinelli, was decorated by yet a third Italian, Andrea Pozzo, who frescoed the great hall with masterful perspective renderings. Lorenz also cites the many examples of baroque architecture widely dispersed in Hapsburg lands in Hungary, Bohemia, and Moravia and designed by French, Italian, German, and Austrian architects.

Mårten Snickare discusses the reflection of both Italian and ancient Roman architecture in the transformation of Stockholm during the reigns of Charles XI and Charles XII. He sees appreciation for ancient and modern Roman representations of the virtues of a centralized authority as beginning in Stockholm with the work of Jean de La Vallée. After a two-year stint in Rome, La Vallée prepared designs for the coronation of Queen

Christina in 1650, among them a Roman triumphal arch. Time spent in Rome by Erik Dahlbergh and both Nicodemus Tessins, father and son, furthered the baroque transformation of Stockholm. Snickare describes Tessin the Younger's grand plan of 1713 for central Stockholm as a vision that was to inspire successive building campaigns over the next two centuries. His astute analysis envisions the plan as the embodiment of an imagined ideal state, a baroque utopia that failed to be realized as Sweden's military and political power waned in the later eighteenth century.

Foundations of the architecture and planning of Saint Petersburg began in Moscow, in the early building programs of Peter the Great and even those of his predecessors. Dmitry Shvidkovsky chronicles the collage add-ons of Post-Byzantine and Italian Mannerist elements in seventeenth-century structures built by members of the imperial family, nobles, and courtiers. For what would become a new capital on the Gulf of Finland, Peter the Great proposed new concepts of order, not only in the administrative structure of government, following Prussian examples, but also in urban planning and architecture. Saint Petersburg was to be a grandiose ideal embodiment of the seat of a new empire. Peter's ambitious vision and achievement exceeded that of Charles XII for Stockholm. Architects, planners, and theoreticians were called from Italy, Switzerland, Prussia, Saxony, and France. Mindful of the importance of naval power and maritime commerce, the well-traveled monarch also sought to emulate the naval stations and related architecture of the United Provinces of the Netherlands. From 1703, for over thirty years during the reign of Peter the Great and his successors, the Italo-Swiss architect Domenico Trezzini and his family played significant roles, always under the monarch's direction. In achieving Peter the Great's expectations for Saint Petersburg, the extensive building programs of the emperor and his successors, nobles, and courtiers provided ample opportunities for continuing importation of architects and designers of interiors, among them the well-known Andreas Schlüter, Jean-Baptiste-Alexandre Le Blond, Nicholas Pineau, Nicola Michetti, and Gaetano Chiaveri.

Giles Worsley's "Search for an English Baroque" examines the works of Wren, Vanbrugh, Hawksmoor, and Archer, demonstrating that the relatively few baroque monuments in Britain appeared only toward the end of the seventeenth century after the Treaty of Ryswick in 1697. Notable in this context were the towers of Saint Paul's Cathedral, Greenwich Naval Hospital, and Hawksmoor's and Vanbrugh's country houses at Easton Neston and Castle Howard. In some respects the situation in Britain paralleled that in Vienna as outlined by Hellmut Lorenz. In both cases, building by the crown was limited while the aristocracy generated commissions. Hawksmoor and Vanbrugh were the prevailing architects in Britain in the first two decades of the eighteenth century but between the outbreak of the War of the Spanish Succession in 1702 and the Peace of Utrecht in 1713, there was little architectural activity. Worsley argues persuasively that both church and country house commissions gave the two architects opportunities to develop their own interests. Hawksmoor seems to have concentrated on contemporary interpretations of principles derived from ancient and early Christian architecture, while Vanbrugh appears to have found inspiration in confident Elizabethan and Jacobean examples. Worsley's fresh interpretation sees Vanbrugh searching for a self-conscious English architecture. These later efforts of both architects, whose early work had demonstrated an appreciation and understanding of Continental baroque, were not to be comparably successful. A neo-Palladian respect for classical conventions dominated architecture for the remainder of the century and beyond.

Konrad Ottenheym describes aspects of the flourishing Dutch Republic following the Peace of Westphalia in 1648. The population of Amsterdam tripled during the century to 200,000. Ottenheym calls attention to the government of Amsterdam, an oligarchy of 200 families of merchants and bankers. Vast civic building programs were undertaken for the prosperous, burgeoning city and its expansions, including projects for naval shipbuilding and outfitting, maritime commerce, enlargement and improvement of port facilities for the Dutch East India Company, and religious and social institutions that included new Protestant churches; orphanages; housing for the elderly, the destitute, and widows; and houses of correction. It may have been the structures for the Admiralty and the East India Company and those for the welfare of the population that impressed Peter the Great in the late 1690s. Ottenheym's discussion of the sober brick architecture of the republic and the city government, in contrast to the splendor of the new stone and marble Town Hall, emphasizes that a hierarchy of building types was the embodiment of an ideal of order and harmony in a well-organized city-state.

Fernando Marías chronicles the physical transformation of Cádiz in the late seventeenth and early eighteenth centuries as it became the exclusive port for trade with American and Asian colonies and grew to become the economic capital of the Spanish kingdom. Before concentrating on the checkered history of the extraordinary design for the cathedral of Cádiz by Vicente de Acero y Arebo, Marías calls attention to the immense model of the entire city of Cádiz ordered by Charles III. Made of wood, ivory, and bone, it was built in 1777–1779 at a scale of 1:250. Encompassing an area larger than 1,235 acres (500 hectares), the model measures more than 22 by 41 feet (692 by 1,252 centimeters). It includes areas for future development and shows both existing and proposed military and civic structures, some of which can be opened to reveal their interiors.

Marías uses preserved documentation to tell the absorbing story of Acero y Arebo's role in the design of the cathedral of Cádiz, from the laying of the cornerstone in 1722 to his resignation in 1729. A plan, elevations, and sections of Acero's design were distributed to a number of consultant court architects. The written responses of three from Madrid in 1727 and those of an additional two consultants, one from Seville, in 1728 are considered in Marías' essay. Further documentation exists in three pamphlets published in 1728–1730, two by Acero himself. Acero's daring design for this last cathedral built in Spain was modified by successive architects, and "the profile of the building was entirely reordered."

After Portugal regained its independence in 1640 and finally made peace with Spain in 1668, Lisbon, the capital city of the kingdom and its colonial empire, became the center of a potent European state. Walter Rossa cites politically sagacious marriages of the Bragança dynasty in the latter half of the seventeenth century that welded the interests of Britain, Savoy, and Austria with that of Portugal, ensuring favorable consideration by the papacy. A papal bull in 1716 granted a diocesan division of Lisbon that included the elevation of the archbishop of west Lisbon to metropolitan and patriarchial status, confirmed the integrity and autonomy of the Portuguese Eastern Padroado, and approved the right of the king to nominate nuncios.

Rossa concentrates his attention on the inspired ambitions of John V (1707–1750)—religious, political, and imperial—each with architectural consequences as he, too, sought to fashion a new Rome on the model of a city he had never seen, as his travels were confined to Portugal. Nonetheless, he commissioned many models of buildings or portions of buildings in Rome. His envoy requested plans and projects from Roman architects in contemplation of the aggrandizement and enrichment of Lisbon. The help of Carlo Fontana, who from 1700 had been the royal architect of John V's father, Peter II, was enlisted for decorations in the Portuguese church in Rome, Sant'Antonio dei Portoghesi. Among the Fontana students and followers who sent drawings were Filippo Juvarra, Tomasso Mattei, Antonio Canevari, and Johann Friedrich Ludwig (João Frederico Ludovice in Portugal). All but Mattei were invited to Lisbon. Ludovice would build the palace and convent at Mafra. Juvarra's designs for a new patriarchal cathedral and palace, carefully studied by Rossa, were never executed, and the royal palace and the patriarchal chapel and palace were destroyed in the earthquake of 1755.

Though all the models and other collections of John V's "Roman architecture museum" were likewise destroyed in the earthquake, accounts tell of numerous salons filled with series of large models of buildings, measured drawings, and volumes of engravings of plans, sections, elevations, and views of Rome. Records exist of models of the Lateran Baptistry, the Palazzo del Quirinale, the Cappella Gregoriana at Saint Peter's, and for many more, including a silver model of Bernini's Four Rivers Fountain in the Piazza Navona.

The monarch provided himself and his architects with a collection valuable for both study and illumination.

Marc Grignon sets out to demonstrate that printed, painted, and drawn images of cities, both plans and views, are fashioned to transmit charged information. For Grignon, what may be a recoverable intent is inherent in the choice of point of view, the placement and scale of structures represented, and buildings omitted, misplaced, or minimized within a recognizable representation of a city. Following Grignon's thesis, a portrait of a city is less to represent accurately the location, relative size, and topographical relationships of principal structures than to promulgate a particular political, religious, social, or economic point of view. His contribution is a perceptive analysis of views and plans of Quebec City, the capital of New France in the seventeenth century, for their intended content and record of conflict.

Robert de Villeneuve's plan of Quebec City of 1685, together with contemporary documentation, reveals, under Grignon's detailed and informed examination, a number of instances in which Villeneuve faced alternatives and made choices that expose aspects of the disagreements among successive governors, bishops, religious orders, and merchants within Quebec City as well as conflict inherent in the tenacious oversight of the colony by the ministry and king in France. In Grignon's hands, Villeneuve's plan becomes an informative and eloquent testimonial to the potential physical consequences of political tensions in Quebec City in 1685.

Francisco Stastny chronicles two significant moments in the history of Lima, the capital of the viceroyalty of Spain that occupied much of South America. Lima was constructed on a site chosen by Francisco Pizarro in 1535 for its position on a river in a valley close to the sea and routes to Spain. The moments Stastny has chosen document the erection of monuments to the king by viceroys, emulating a custom well known in Spain, France, and in many monarchies. The first, dedicated in 1651, was the impressive Fountain of Lions and Dragons by Pedro de Noguera, 10 meters (32.8 feet) tall, in the Plaza Mayor. Crowned by an image of Fame, it served as a focus for the square and trumpeted King Philip IV, the Spanish Empire, Viceroy Sarmiento de Sotomayor, and members of the town council. The second monument, an equestrian statue of the Bourbon King Philip V by Baltasar Gavilán (or Meléndez) erected almost a century later in 1739, was in need of an equally worthy site. The general advisor to Viceroy José Mendoza, in an inspired moment, suggested, in emulation of ancient Rome, placement of the statue in a prestigious location atop a masonry arch over a bridge that served as an entrance gate to Lima. Stastny utilizes newly discovered engraved copper plates bearing a representation of the monument to describe the gateway transformed into a triumphal arch crowned by the equestrian statue, its pedestal with arms of Castile and Leon and two rampant lions with flanking obelisks. Sad to say, the monument, the arch, and most of the city of Lima were destroyed by the devastating earthquake and tsunami of 1746, similar to the disastrous earthquake that leveled Lisbon nine years later in 1755.

The papers gathered here bear witness to the tensions among competing political and cultural attitudes of evolving complex societies in the early eighteenth century. Later in the century disquiet and disillusionment with oppressive and intolerant royal policies would gain strength among European political and social philosophers. Theorists of architecture were, in this period, to plant the seeds of a revolutionary new architecture.

CESARE DE SETA
Università degli Studi di Napoli Federico II

The Architecture of Naples in the Eighteenth Century

From 1707, when Austrian conquest related to the War of the Spanish Succession ended a long period of Spanish Hapsburg rule, to 1734, when Spanish rule resumed under the Bourbons, Naples was a possession of the Austrian Hapsburgs. The establishment of the Austrian regime aroused many hopes, but they would, as before, be disappointed. The Hapsburg government soon demonstrated a lack of interest in innovation, espousing essentially conservative policies. Nevertheless, the political and cultural fervor of the time engendered a new era that contrasted with the blandness and stagnation of the preceding years. The inventiveness and insight of the intellectuals who were engaged in debating the major issues of the new century left a lasting mark on the history of European thought. One only need note the judgment of Pietro Giannone on the major innovations of the period.[1]

The Urban Development of Naples under the Austrian Viceroyalty

The essentially anticlerical policies of the Hapsburgs did not stimulate significant programs, especially in architecture, which the regime allowed to continue as the exclusive preserve of the church and of an affluent aristocracy. At an urban scale, the most important initiative was the rescinding in 1718 of municipal building regulations and related tax burdens. Although the city had expanded to the suburbs in defiance of established norms, the growth resembled spreading pools of oil. From one or more points, depending on the suburb, urbanization followed ad hoc development adapted to the morphological and functional necessities of each zone. This growth, in spite of the size and magnificence of many ecclesiastical and secular buildings, was by nature provisional, simply because, in the absence of legal sanctions, it followed neither a plan nor a scheme that supported an organic pattern for new settlement. One might say that the rescinding of regulations brought about a reversal of this trend, but without suggesting that from this moment the city began to develop in accord with a precise building plan. Rather, by fostering public works and by directing urban development along several routes, the state decisively, even if indirectly, determined diverse options for the urban future of Naples. In this period two roads were realized along the littoral zone that led east toward Vesuvius. Via Marinella, which extended along the shore eastward from the Chiesa del Carmine, was virtually rebuilt, and in 1732, somewhat farther inland, Via Loreto was opened parallel to Via Marinella. Farther east, a small fort built at Vigliena on the Vesuvian coast was subsequently enlarged and reinforced several times.

Giovanni Battista Lusieri,
*A View of the Bay of Naples,
Looking Southwest from the
Pizzofalcone toward Capo di
Posilippo,* 1791, oil
The J. Paul Getty Museum,
Los Angeles

The Architecture of Domenico Antonio Vaccaro and Ferdinando Sanfelice

The twenty-seven years of the Austrian viceroyalty, in spite of the minimal interest shown by the government, were a salient moment in eighteenth-century Neapolitan architecture. The architects Domenico Antonio Vaccaro (1691–1745) and Ferdinando Sanfelice (1675–1748) dominated the architectural scene for the entire first half of the eighteenth century. Vaccaro came from a family of artists. Andrea, his father, was one of the principal sculptors of the eighteenth century in Naples.[2] Domenico learned sculpture from him and painting in the studio of Francesco Solimena, the superman of the late seventeenth and first half of the eighteenth centuries.[3] According to Anthony Blunt, author of an important critical volume on Neapolitan baroque and rococo architecture, knowledge of these two arts constantly informed his manner of building.[4] Accordingly, his first great innovation was to transform the sculptural decoration of typical seventeenth-century Neapolitan architecture into a decorative web in which fully round figures play an integral role in architectural design. This integration went much farther than that of Cosimo Fanzago, for whom architectural decoration and sculpture had distinct roles and functions. Light also assumed a fundamental role in Vaccaro's architecture, above all in his religious architecture, where it acquired a strong symbolic significance of purification, emphasized by the predominant use of white stucco for both walls and decoration and the restriction of color to polychrome marbles for altars.

Vaccaro's most notable creation was the Chiesa della Concezione at Montecalvario, a true autograph work of which he designed and oversaw every detail.[5] This structure realizes the unity of the arts celebrated by baroque poetics: decoration, sculpture, and painting are here the work of a single hand. The plan is a central octagon (fig. 1), elongated for longitudinal emphasis, enclosed within an ambulatory that forms the transepts, choir, atrium, and four diagonal corner trapezoidal chapels flanked by triangular spaces. The paired piers that form the corners of the octagon and support the drum and

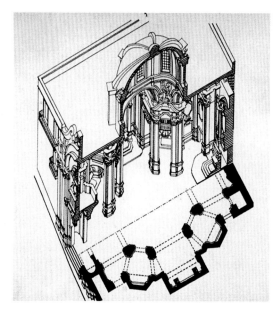

1. Chiesa della Concezione, Montecalvario, Naples, by Domenico Antonio Vaccaro, 1718–1724, axonometric section
From Raffaele Mormone, "Domenico Antonio Vaccaro architetto, I," *Napoli nobilissima* 1 (1961): 145

dome are capped by curved, broken, scrolled pediments (fig. 2). The spaces between the pairs of piers are open below the choir balconies, which are supported by single arches of remarkable profile that contrast with the fully round arches on the cardinal axes (fig. 3).

Another church by Vaccaro that merits citation is San Michele, Port'Alba.[6] Its plan is a central square elongated by two rectangles. One serves as the entrance atrium; the second, with rounded corners for a choir, itself extended by an additional rectangular space with curved sides, contains the main altar. Light, here the prime element of the architectural composition, permeates the interior, both through a high octagonal drum and pierced dome above the central space and through a still taller lantern crowning the altar. One of the most accomplished of Vaccaro's churches, San Michele, Anacapri (fig. 4),[7] is a masterwork based on an octagon (fig. 5), a design in which the influence of Borromini is everywhere evident (fig. 6).

Vaccaro is noted above all for his ecclesiastical buildings, but he also designed a magnificent palace in Naples for the prince of Tarsia.[8] Rather than to the building itself—a sumptuous complex of which today virtually nothing remains—it is useful to refer to the well-known print *Prospetto del gran palazzo di sua eccellenza il signor principe di Tarsia,* which Vaccaro engraved in 1737. In this handsome view the landscape ele-

ments are unified harmoniously with the massive structure. Palace and gardens cascade down the slope, together with a scenographic pair of entrance ramps, toward a large park, with the great loggia overlooking a terraced garden. The grand panorama is lost today, its spectral presence known only through Vaccaro's print. Vaccaro here took refuge in a world of nature in which a perceived exploitation of the site seems mitigated, elegantly, by the pleasure of the picturesque. The sumptuous palace with terraced gardens and its own unique urban character invites comparison, on the one hand, with the architecture of Roman villas with terraced gardens and looks ahead, on the other, to the realization of the later Villa Campolieto.[9]

Vaccaro also planned and designed the decoration of the cloister of Santa Chiara.[10] Here he intended a succinct dialogue between nature and the pictorial, in which painted vine shoots on the majolica that sheathes the octagonal pillars intertwine with real vines that spread on the pergola above the same pillars; or fish, also painted, swim in the depths of the fountain centered in one of the compartments of the cloister. Vaccaro's extraordinary talent is also evi-dent in both the Certosa di San Martino (fig. 7),[11] following the Fanzago model, and in the sober, elegant Immacolatella Maritime Station at the port of Naples. In point of fact, Vaccaro, with his intricate exploitation of plan types—church plans that were actually the result of combining octagonal and rectangular forms—created a refined and distinctive decorative manner with a singular spatial purity that surely ranks among the greatest achievements of this moment in Naples. His enlightened and adroit typological experiments were rarely pursued by other Neapolitan architects. On the other hand, the facade of the church of the Chiesa della Concezione became a model for many Neapolitan churches, much as a web of decorative stucco became the stylistic characteristic of both secular and religious architecture of the century. Vaccaro, therefore, belongs fully to the rococo, in which architecture achieves a lightness of design that seems to contradict the fundamental laws of statics to such a degree that in Santa Maria delle Grazie, Calvizzano—according to the happy phrasing of Blunt in the text cited above—"pilasters and entablature disappear [and] merge . . . into a band of clouds and sky."[12]

The other great protagonist of eighteenth-century architecture in Naples was Ferdinando Sanfelice, a member of a well-to-do aristocratic family from Seggio di Montagna. He built primarily for Neapolitan aristocracy, beginning with his own family. The aristocratic palace was his special area, in contrast to Vaccaro, who put his best efforts into religious structures.[13] Like Vaccaro, he was a student of Francesco Solimena, whose studio was the forge for Neapolitan art of this period: Vaccaro and Sanfelice, Giovanni del Gaizo, and Giovan Battista and Muzio Nauclerio passed through this school.

In his religious buildings, Sanfelice employed unusual geometric plans. In fact, for Sant'Aspreno and the Nunziatella he proposed star-shaped plans. It did not fall to him, though, to build either of them. His final plan for the Nunziatella, which was begun in 1713, gave way to a single nave with side chapels and arches. Even less fortunate was Sant'Aspreno, which was never built. The two-story facade of the Nunziatella has a portal of white marble below a large aedicule at the second level, both framed by paired pilasters. The canted wings are joined to the taller central section by modestly stressed volutes.

Sanfelice's decorative scheme—tectonic and intended to enhance the structural framework, whereas those of Vaccaro were atectonic—may be examined, according to Blunt, in light of classical models of architecture in Rome in the seventeenth century, which, according to Blunt, Sanfelice "could have known through the engravings in Domenico de' Rossi's *Studio d'architettura civile* (Rome, 1706–1721), which became a textbook for baroque architects outside Rome."[14] In this regard I can confirm that the treatise of de' Rossi was widely known in Naples and available in several of the better public and private libraries of the period.

In the realm of secular architecture, Sanfelice's special invention and innovation should be emphasized. In his palazzi, he concentrated above all on designing the courtyard and its connection with the staircase to produce an astonishing scenographic effect.[15] This is particularly clear in the Palazzo Fernandez (fig. 8), where the architect seems to have concentrated his interest on the staircase as a graphic and optical

focal point within the architectural composition, with the aim of generating amazement in the response of the viewer. Beginning from this premise he gave octagonal or oval form to the courtyard and placed the stair not to one side, as in the traditional Neapolitan courtyard palace, but opposite the main entrance, in an empty space which, through large openings in the front and rear walls enclosing the stair, enabled the eye to pass through the architectural material and lose itself in the natural beauty of the garden.

This tectonic and typological skill is clearly seen in the Sanfelice family palace

3. Chiesa della Concezione, Montecalvario, Naples, by Domenico Antonio Vaccaro, 1718–1724, interior of dome
Photograph by Tim Benton

4. San Michele, Anacapri,
Naples, by Domenico
Antonio Vaccaro, 1719,
facade
Author photograph

wings on either side of the courtyard. Sanfelice's innovation lay precisely in honoring
the stair as the element that connects the
courtyard with the entire palace. Thus the
stair is, for the most part, no longer hidden
behind the enclosing wall of the courtyard—
as continued to be the mode in Austria,
Spain, or even in Italy, in Genoese palaces—
but instead is given prominence by detailing
the openings and stringcourses. The widespread adoption of this new treatment of
the stair has raised doubts about more than
one attribution to Sanfelice. A case in point
is the Palazzo dello Spagnolo (fig. 9), in the
Via Vergini. Several documents published
by Alfonso Gambardella in his work on Sanfelice[17] name a Francesco Attanasio, engineer
and surveyor, as architect-builder of the
palace. This is not to deny, however, that
the building was strongly influenced by
Sanfelice, who, being a noble, may have
entrusted the execution of the building to an
obscure engineer. Equally interesting is the
stair he had built in his own palace, but in
a secondary courtyard, to provide access to
apartments off to the left. Confined to a
restricted space that determined its use as a
secondary stair, it is composed of two spiral
stairs joined at each floor by a hexagonal
landing. A similar example is found in the
palace built for Bartolomeo Di Maio on the
Discesa della Sanità.[18] Here, space limitations caused him to design a stair of rhom-
boidal form, with the sides angled toward the
interior. Of this Blunt justly notes, "When
faced with a closed and confined space for a
staircase, Sanfelice was often stimulated to
great ingenuity."[19]

The staircase Sanfelice designed for the
Serra di Cassano palace is without doubt
among the most spectacular and majestic of
the century. The stair opens directly from the
octagonal courtyard without any separating
wall. It is located in a large area that opens
from the courtyard through an arch of such
dimension that the stair is displayed to the
visitor in all its magnificence. The stair is
completely open at the lower level to enable
direct access from the main entrance as well
as from a secondary one on Via Monte di Dio.
It begins with three steps to the right and left
from a central passageway situated under a
bridge that forms the arrival landing at the
entrance to the piano nobile, and continues

in the Vergini district. Here each of the
parts of the stair is defined on the courtyard facade by a different type of opening. A
fully round arch corresponds to the point
of arrival and the intermediate landings,
while irregularly shaped octagonal openings
express, in the angle of their upper and lower
edges, the incline of the stairs. A string-
course on the facade gives additional articulation to the rhythm of the stair. In this way
the wall as a whole acquires a characteristic
V form, which Bernardo De Dominici (the
Vasari of eighteenth-century Neapolitan
art)[16] likened to a large bird that spreads its

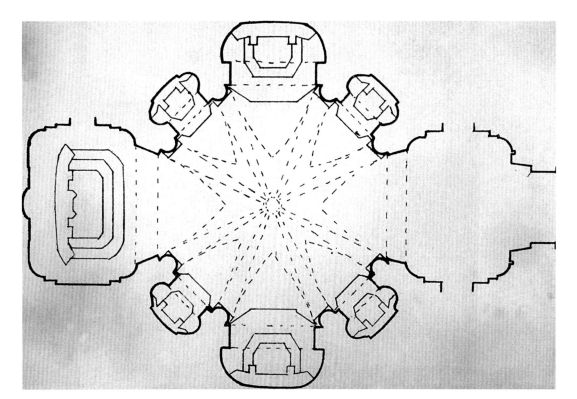

5. San Michele, Anacapri, Naples, by Domenico Antonio Vaccaro, 1719, plan
From Anthony Blunt, *Neapolitan Baroque and Rococo Architecture* (London, 1975), 115

with two flights, perpendicular to the bridge above, that rest on two immense piers. The last flight of the stair is instead aligned with the bridge and is supported by ramping arches that flank the central arch and follow the slope of the stair.

The entrance portal or doorway of the palace of a Neapolitan noble is another architectural element that acquired a significant role over the centuries. Because of the narrowness of Neapolitan lanes, the facades of palaces were not easily viewed; thus the

6. San Michele, Anacapri, Naples, by Domenico Antonio Vaccaro, 1719, altar
Author photograph

7. Certosa di San Martino, Chapel of San Gennaro, Naples, by Domenico Antonio Vaccaro, 1706
Photograph by Tim Benton

8. Palazzo Fernandez, Naples, by Ferdinando Sanfelice, 1740s, staircase from the courtyard
Author photograph

9. Palazzo dello Spagnolo, Naples, by Ferdinando Sanfelice, about 1740, staircase from the courtyard
Author photograph

portal terminate in two prominent reverse volutes, from each of which sprout naturalistic renderings of a branch with spreading leaves.

In summation, one may say that Vaccaro was an artist tied more closely to tradition, while Sanfelice sought with greater resolve to refresh the traditional, grafting new sprouts to the old root stock of seventeenth-century architecture and achieving quite original results that rank among the eighteenth-century's most successful examples of princely palaces.

Architects who should be mentioned in addition to Vaccaro and Sanfelice include Arcangelo and Marcello Guglielmelli and Giovan Battista and Muzio Nauclerio.[20] Marcello Guglielmelli, probably the son of Arcangelo and remembered primarily as a decorative artist, worked on the interior decoration of the library of the Oratorio dei Gerolomini, built between 1715 and 1725, and a new facade for San Giuseppe dei Ruffi, originally designed by Dionisio Lazzari. Here he used a solution, invented by Fanzago, for a stair that enters an atrium (to be repeated several years later by Giovan Battista Nauclerio for San Giovanni Battista delle Monache). At San Giuseppe, the architect

entry portal became the most important feature for catching a visitor's attention. Sanfelice designed new and fanciful solutions. Cases in point are the Palazzo Pignatelli di Monteleone (fig. 10), where he replaced the acanthus leaves of the capitals with human masks, and the Palazzo Bisignano, where two massive volutes are substituted for a pediment. In the Palazzo Bartolomeo Di Maio, on the other hand, the crowning element of the portal is molded in a play of curves that reflect the plan of the balcony above, while the ends of the lintel over the

designed a single stair that enters the atrium through three arches. Their rhythm is articulated farther on by the inclusion of columns that not only emphasize the flight of steps but also support a markedly salient entablature. The gate and terrace of Santi Severino e Sossio have always been attributed to Giovan Battista Nauclerio, while the only work that can with assurance be considered Muzio's is the altar in the vestibule of San Pietro ad Aram.

Ephemeral Decorations for Festivals

Included among the most authentic, original aspects of Neapolitan artistic culture, and an integral part of civic life, are the ephemeral decorations designed for religious and civic festivals, whether for special occasions or as intrinsic elements of the musical life of Naples. During the seventeenth century major architects (Domenico Fontana, Bartolomeo Picchiatti, Cosimo Fanzago, Dionisio Lazzari) were already engaged in this activity, developing a tradition that would have its moment of greatest exuberance during the eighteenth-century civic celebrations for members of the court (baptisms, weddings, pregnancies, saints' days, and funerals), which were occasions for the adornment of the city with unique installations and the decorative sheathing of urban spaces with wood and papier-mâché that lasted all of a morning. Citizens on their own took part in the festival preparations, as did the church on major religious holidays (Christmas, Easter, and major saints' days).[21] Triumphal arches, greased poles, fireworks displays, pools, porticoes, and hundreds of other varieties of festival constructions are credited to the most accomplished names in eighteenth-century architecture and scene design. Naturally these decorations are known to us only through prints or books compiled to commemorate the occasions. An engraving by Francesco de Grado depicts a fireworks installation ignited on 28 August 1724 in front of the royal palace, an area designated for these spectacles, as was the space in front of the Castel Nuovo. For a festival in 1740 celebrating the queen's delivery of a child, Ferdinando Sanfelice built an extraordinary, intricate structure (fig. 11) known to us through four prints

10. Palazzo Pignatelli di Monteleone, Naples, by Ferdinando Sanfelice, 1718, main entrance
Author photograph

and a painting on copper by Tommaso Ruiz.[22] In 1763 Luigi Vanvitelli designed the installation for the fair (a commercial as well as a civic celebration), also held in front of the royal palace and later moved to the oceanfront site of Chiaia, in what would become the Tuileries of Naples. Vincenzo del Re, Antonio de Torres, Nicola Tagliacozzi Canale, Francesco Saracino, and Nicola Fiore are among the artists who became established in this genre of installation, alongside celebrated figures such as Sanfelice and Vanvitelli.

Disegno in prospettiva della gran Macchina Fatta avanti il Real Palazzo Fornita di varie sorte di merci e saccheggi dalla Plebe nel anno 1740. per celebrare le magnifiche Feste della nascita della Sereniss. Reale Infanta, inventato e diretto dal Sig.r D. Ferdinando Sanfelice Patrizio Napoletano.

This aspect of Neapolitan culture has been examined with insight, beginning in 1968 with a study by Franco Mancini,[23] and we shall seize the opportunity, substituting a part for the whole, to discuss a relatively new subject that extends our view beyond Naples, to Rome. For centuries sovereigns of Naples had paid homage to the Roman pontiff, in recognition of his symbolic sovereignty over the Kingdom of the Two Sicilies, with the festival of the Chinea. Installations of papier-mâché and wood, decorated with painting and stucco, were, from time to time, erected in different squares. Whether in fact this custom originated in the Middle Ages, by the eighteenth century the festival had become a significant occasion. The event took place over two days, 28 and 29 June—the feasts of Saints Peter and Paul—with fireworks and accompanying illumination of centerpieces for the solemn ceremony. In addition to a tribute in gold, the ambassador or other representative of the king of Naples presented a white mare—the Chinea—with a silver cup mounted on her back. Having been suppressed for political reasons for more than two decades, the ceremony was revived, with a great display of wealth, under Hapsburg rule in 1722. For the duration of the Austrian domination of Naples, the ceremonies and

the installations took on a special importance, a confirmation of the close rapport the Hapsburgs intended to cultivate with the pope. The procession began in the Roman Piazza Santi Apostoli, site of the Palazzo Colonna; wound its way to Castel San Angelo; and ended at Saint Peter's, where the mare was received by the pope, in whose presence—well trained—she knelt.

The contemporary descriptions of Francesco Valesio and the Chracas *Diario ordinario* are a precious witness, enabling us to follow this occasion, which became a scheduled event, capable of attracting crowds of the faithful and curious, as well as foreign travelers who bear witness in many accounts in their journals. During the eighteenth century the starting point and the itinerary could vary according to contingencies (including *sede vacante*) or the wish of the ambassador. In the first Chinea of the century, in 1722, the ambassador to the Holy See was Fabrizio Colonna, and the ceremony, the first in many years, was especially solemn. The piazza selected was, moreover, the site of the residence of the ambassador and remained as such until 1734, that is to say, until Charles VII Bourbon was seated on the throne of Naples. For many years the architect of the ephemeral constructions was

Alessandro Specchi, among the best known of Roman architects; he was followed by Gabriele Valvassori. Symbolic and heraldic motifs, references to the commissioning sovereign, are evident: a restless white mare symbolizes Naples, a two-headed eagle the Hapsburg dynasty. Vesuvius and the Sebeto River occur frequently in the scenography.

Examination of the prints that record the Chinea gives rise to several reflections. First, the ephemeral architecture represented clearly shows awareness of a mix of cultures that is not simply Roman, but leans toward motifs that may in some ways allude to the Austrian tradition of Johann Bernhard Fischer von Erlach and, above all, to Johann Lucas von Hildebrandt, the two principal architects of the Danube area from the mid-seventeenth to the early eighteenth century. If Specchi, in fact, holds to a stylistic norm marked by an uninhibited classicism, there is no doubt that Valvassori sought with his installations to espouse an Austrian vogue that arrived in Naples and Rome with two viceroys of Naples under Charles VI Hapsburg: Wirich, count of Daun (1707–1708; 1713–1719), and Aloys, count of Harrach (1728–1733). This predilection seems to me evident in the two installations for the Chinea of 1728 (Valvassori, architect, and Filippo Vasconi, engraver), in which a hexagonal temple that rises from the center of a very kinetic base suggests awareness of forms that belong to Hildebrandt. In the second construction, of 1730, designed by Michelangelo Specchi (brother of Alessandro) on the theme of the Capitoline Hill, it is not difficult to recognize composite forms of celebrated Viennese palaces, beginning, obviously, with the Belvedere. But never has there been a Capitoline Hill in Rome so foreign to the indigenous culture as this depiction in rococo fashion. This dissonance in stylistic vocabulary occurs again in the 1731 installation, by Bartolomeo Poli. The triumphal arch that dominates the scene has a decorative lightness enhanced by the concave-convex rhythms of the splendid base. A change, not happenstance, began in 1734, with Charles VII Bourbon as king of Naples, when the entourage of French artists who resided in the Palazzo Mancini captured, so to say, the contract for the management of the festival. The rationalized Piranesianism of Louis Le Lorrain took the

principal role in 1746, 1747, and 1748 with solemn temples, a little powdered, as is appropriate to these installations. During the 1760s, chinoiserie appeared, as did archaeological motifs that referred to the newly excavated remains of Herculaneum and Pompeii and to important sculptural groups from the Farnese collection (the *Farnese Bull*), as well as other themes that derived from the culture of the period.

The Capital of Charles VII Bourbon

With the fall of the Hapsburgs, the age-old problems afflicting Naples were magnified. Although the impediments to urbanization were multiplied, the city continued to have an irresistible attraction for new inhabitants, while uncontrolled population growth progressively worsened congestion and disorder.[24] In 1734 Charles became king of Naples and in 1738 of Sicily as well. The first positive results of new policies would be visible by midcentury. The rebirth of Naples' economy was accompanied by public works intended to prepare the city for a new role.

Transformations of the port of Naples may be examined in this light. They included the rebuilding of the principal wharf and, opposite it, a new, smaller pier flanked by large warehouses. The Tribunale della Salute (public health courts), later called the Immacolatella, were erected in the area between the two wharves. The modernized port was intended to be the principal transformation that would ensure the commercial future desired by the sovereign. Concurrently with the renovation of the port facilities, work was done on the road that connected the port with the Marinella, along the coastline to the Carmine bastion of the city wall. The work included demolishing the southern section of the wall. Port traffic was thereby diverted from the center of the city and steered to the provincial roads, an eminent advantage to the local merchants.

Among initiatives of general interest was the replanning of the Mergellina coast and the road to Posillipo. With the city wall now decisively ruptured, settlement overflowed toward Chiaia and Posillipo, areas that had, in fact, begun to merge with the urban whole more than a century earlier. Nevertheless, it should be said this development was somewhat fragmentary, consisting of a number of stages, some indeed of considerable architectural importance. In Naples it is difficult to identify an eighteenth-century urban quarter because private initiative, at last free to occupy agrarian land, could build independent of preexisting nuclei. Homogeneous areas were, therefore, only rarely realized. The seventeenth-century situation was reversed, and the model for Neapolitan urban development in the eighteenth century became decisively centrifugal. Private individuals, both rich and less rich, tried in every way to isolate themselves, building their residences in the country and on the hills. The architectural-urban initiatives promoted by the court endorsed the tendency, putting self-interest ahead of any concerns for the problems of the capital. In this context, the Albergo dei Poveri (poorhouse), the Palazzo di Capodimonte, the Caserma (cavalry barracks) at the Ponte della Maddalena next to the Serraglio (menagerie), the Granili (public granaries), and the Teatro San Carlo theater became the highlights of eighteenth-century Naples.[25] These grand achievements were located—with few exceptions—outside the metropolitan area, yet at the same time were elements that defined the area and directed the expansion of the city. They are characterized by a scale sufficient to dominate any context rather than blend into it, which explains why the structures—indicative of a European Enlightenment culture—had no influence on urban reality.

For the enlargement of the royal palace, the king called on Giovanni Antonio Medrano and Angelo Carasale, designers of the Teatro San Carlo.[26] Medrano also collaborated on the initial phases of the royal palace at Capodimonte, the first great work desired by the sovereign. After a brief interlude with the Roman Antonio Canevari, he reassumed direction of the building until work was suspended, not to be completed until the nineteenth century. A hunting lodge was the first building at Capodimonte, a pristine site though close to the city. To this beginning was added a project for a palace suitable for housing the Farnese collection, which Charles had inherited from his mother. A close relationship between nature and architecture is the principal characteristic of the palace and its park. In the words of Stefano Gallo, "The view of the building, though distant, nevertheless prominent in the verdure . . . creates an initial projecting axis eccentric to the urban system: as though it had a value as a cultural stimulus for almost half a century, rather than representing a royal proposal for development."[27] If the plan of the building—a rectangle, with five arches on the long sides giving access to three internal courtyards—shows little dynamism in the articulation of its surface and volume, the fan-shaped organization of the park, entrusted to Ferdinando Sanfelice in 1742, is a valuable and original work of landscape architecture.[28] The result is neither a French plan nor an English park, but a bit of each. The landscape, together with the palace—with the addition of the celebrated porcelain factory—is witness to one of the happiest moments of eighteenth-century culture, in which forward-looking ideals are marvelously fused with scenographic taste.[29]

The deaths of Vaccaro (1745) and Sanfelice (1748) marked the first major break with this culture. It coincided, within a few years, with the renunciation of rococo and the espousal of Roman architecture by Charles VII, who called the two principal architects active in Rome, Ferdinando Fuga (1699–1781) and Luigi Vanvitelli (1700–1773), to Naples. Fuga was entrusted with directing the construction of the Albergo dei Poveri, a gigantic structure projected by the sovereign to house 8,000 persons (figs. 12–15). The architect began with a plan for a square structure with four courtyards (see fig. 12) sited on the outskirts of the Loreto district. The site was then abandoned, perhaps because building a structure of that size virtually on the water's edge in this area, which had a clearly defined military function, was less than appropriate. Further, perhaps it was feared that such a structure in an uninhabited area might become a ghetto, cut off from the life of the city. The site on which the poorhouse was finally built had, by contrast, a number of advantages. At its edge rose the Miradois Hill, whose verdant mass supplied an ideal background for the severe volume of the building. Fuga here abandoned the square plan for a rectangle with five courtyards, the central one containing a huge chapel with four radiating arms crowned by a dome (see fig. 13). The reduction of the length of

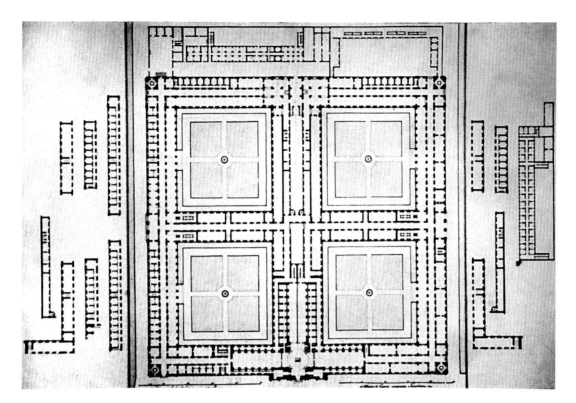

12. Ferdinando Fuga, *First Project for the Albergo dei Poveri, Naples*, 1750–1751
Gabinetto Nazionale di Stampe, Rome

the facade and the greater number of courtyards did little to counteract the scale of the structure, which was fully visible only from an oblique perspective.[30] Via Foria, widened and paved in 1766, in these years became the principal access road to the city. But unexpected difficulties made it impossible to complete the building. The portion constructed is only about a fifth of the projected volume. The work, begun in 1751, continued throughout the eighteenth and early nineteenth centuries.

The Albergo dei Poveri is one of the structures that assumed a weight and prominence of the first order in the cityscape of Naples. Its size and the severe structural scheme that governs its design make it an exceptional unicum. It should not, however, be seen simply as an architectural work of immense dimension. Rather it is a small sector of a city, constructed—finally—on the basis of a single project and planned in all its aspects: functional, compositional, and structural. This first conception of an integrated, self-sufficient community, including, in particular, provision for vocational training of the young (found also in another exurban building project, the school at San

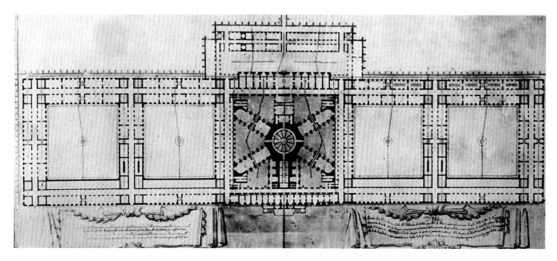

13. Ferdinando Fuga, *Second Project for the Albergo dei Poveri, Naples*, 1751
Gabinetto Nazionale di Stampe, Rome

14. Albergo dei Poveri,
Naples, by Ferdinando Fuga
and others, begun 1751,
aerial view
From Roberto Pane, *Ferdinando Fuga*
(Naples, 1956), 149

building. On the north side, on the interior courtyard, is an exedra containing a domed elliptical chapel. The relationships between the curved lines of these volumes are the only elements that contrast with the severity of the facade—ordered by vertical rectangles—and, more generally, the whole.

The barracks, rising next to the Serraglio, built by Sanfelice in 1742–1748, were left incomplete. In the Duca di Noja plan, the rectangular plan of the earlier building, to which the northwest corner of the Vanvitelli structure backs up, is clearly seen. Several decades after construction of the barracks, the Serraglio was converted into stables.[32] It is likely that the new use—also suggested by the lengthwise addition to the plan—had influenced the choice of site for the barracks. The location of this extremely simple structure outside the Loreto district, along the road to Portici, attests to the expansion of the city toward Vesuvius.

Ferdinand IV's Policies for the Renewal of the Capital

In 1759 Charles VII Bourbon, at the death of his half brother Ferdinand VI, left Naples for Madrid to be crowned King Charles III of Spain. Since Charles' heir, Ferdinand IV, was too young to rule, a regency was formed, headed by Bernardo Tanucci, enlightened administrator of the realm and former prime minister under Charles. When Ferdinand assumed the throne eight years later, in 1767, he immediately indicated a strong desire to continue the policies of his father and foster urban and architectural enterprises.

Construction of the Granili, designed by Ferdinando Fuga, began in 1778. The structure was erected along the road to Portici, which from the time of Charles VII had been chosen as the location for public works that conformed to a new mode of conception and intervention in urban space. The so-called granaries, whose main facade was over 500 meters long, were to serve not only as a storehouse for grain, but also as an arsenal and a rope factory. From Federico Schiavoni's plan of Naples (1872–1880), it is possible to extract an idea of the plan of the Granili. A long, central, double-loaded corridor extends the full length of the building. The internal monotony is replicated over

Leucio[31]) is evidence of an enlightened effort that anticipates in several ways the utopian projects of the beginning of the nineteenth century.

Also to be remembered among the public works fostered by the first Bourbon is the cemetery (Camposanto) just outside the city on the slopes of Poggioreale. Fuga planned the cemetery about a decade after beginning construction of the Albergo dei Poveri. Visible on the Duca di Noja plan (fig. 16, near top right) as a large rectangle enclosing a regular grid of tomb sites, it was part of a larger planning project for the area and the streets that connected it with the city.

The other eminent personality was Luigi Vanvitelli. Around 1757 he began the cavalry barracks at the Ponte della Maddalena, left incomplete in 1772. It is his most bare-bones work, with a battered ground story interrupted along its lengthy extent only by two severe portals with bosses of peperino. The two upper levels are articulated only by simple framing of the windows, stressing by their plainness the military nature of the

the length and height of the exterior by uninterrupted rows of windows of the same size and placement.

These unusual projects mark a complete rejection by the eighteenth century of a late baroque urban vision. The new formal dimension of the city is defined by these fragments of urban fabric—the Albergo dei Poveri, the Palazzo di Capodimonte, the Maddalena barracks, and the Granili—in which all the norms of perspective composition are overturned. They are buildings difficult to capture in a single glance because of their very dimensions. They need to be studied section by section. The perspective foci of the buildings are always beyond the visual field of the viewer. The facades run into the surrounding urban structure, and each of the elements can be read from many viewpoints.

During these same years, in a project of similar scale, the university, the Palazzo degli Studi, was transformed into the Royal Bourbon Museum.[33] The vicissitudes of this building are varied and complex. Begun in 1585 by Fra Giovan Vicenzo Casale, it was to have been the new headquarters of the royal cavalry. However, it was ill-adapted to this role, and much the same may be said about its subsequent remodeling into a university. Many architects had a hand in the reworking: Medrano, in 1735, in a restoration; Sanfelice, in 1742, in an enlargement; and eventually, in the second half of the eighteenth century, Fuga and Pompeo Schiantarelli, who gave it a definitive and more radical transformation. Notwithstanding the continuing efforts, especially by the last architect, who, with the death of Fuga in 1782, was left with the problem of reorganizing the building, the final results were largely undistinguished. Nonetheless, the structure came to have a significant place in the cityscape. Aligned on Via Foria, it stood at an angle to the sloping Fosse del Grano, which connected it, across Via Toledo, with the center of the city. To the north it was linked to the royal palace at Capodimonte, across the Imbrecciata. The building therefore developed in what might be called a barycentric location with respect to the axial streets of Via Foria and Via Toledo and the as yet inaccessible rising slope that led to Capodimonte. Under the Bourbons, both Via

15. Ferdinando Fuga, *Elevation of the Main Entrance of the Albergo dei Poveri, Naples,* 1750s
Gabinetto Nazionale di Stampe, Rome

Foria and the road to Capodimonte became two of the most important axes for development of the city. With this new street pattern, the museum building formed a hinge of sorts between the old city and the development of the hilly area. Aware of the fundamental importance of the new role accorded to this building in the urban environs, Schiantarelli prepared an initial project whose most significant contribution was to establish an active dialogue between the building and the city. But neither this project nor the three that followed were ever realized. The planned enlargement was not carried out, and the only proposal of the architect that was welcomed—although not without numerous arguments—was the addition of a single story. To this proposal Salvatore Palermo, in his commentary to Carlo Celano's guide to Naples,[34] wrote: "The niches between the windows of the first floor as well as the statues have been suppressed in order to have the first level the same as the second level; also removed are all the friezes that enhanced the windows." Thus the building lost forever its recognizably baroque appearance, to acquire another that, in its poorly executed articulation, is not, according to Arnaldo Venditti, to be attributed to Schiantarelli but to his successor, the architect Francesco Maresca.

Another important project realized in these years by Ferdinando IV was the plan-

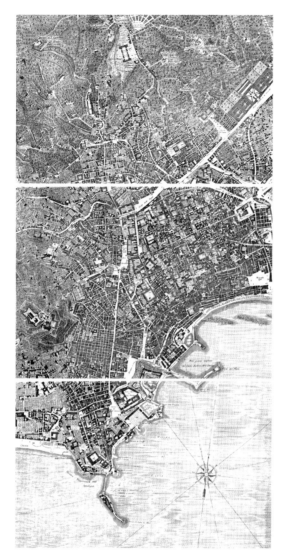

16. Giovanni Carafa, Duca di Noja, *Topographic Map of the City of Naples*, 1775, copper engraving (detail), showing the cemetery at Poggioreale at upper right
Museo Nazionale di San Martino

ning of two piazze. The significance of this achievement is all the greater because Naples had no squares other than the marketplace, the Piazza Mercato, which was really Angevin in origin. The Spanish viceroys who governed Naples beginning in the sixteenth century, notwithstanding their indefatigable commitment to modernization of the city, did not pay any particular attention to this type of development. The places of public, civic, and religious gathering remained those determined by the Angevin plan. They were generally in open areas, not designed or well defined; they were spaces crowded around religious or civic buildings and were ad hoc in both duration and character. Naples on the whole is bereft of squares conceived as parts of an organic whole.

To understand this situation, it should be noted first that Naples retains an urban structure that is, in its general lines, shaped by the Greco-Roman *cardo* and *decumanus.* The buildings, usually three to four stories, form a very compact urban structure, of the highest density of any in Europe. To open a space in this close-packed area of palaces and convents must have seemed a real departure. To create a piazza in this compact urban fabric the authorities would have had to initiate a series of expropriations, measures that would have engaged the central administration in a wrestling match with the powerful noble class and with the even stronger religious orders. Therefore the viceregal power believed, following a centuries-old tradition, that it was more appropriate and practical to organize, on significant occasions, immense scenographic installations that transformed existing sites into true and fitting, sumptuously decorated squares. The scenic backdrops and installations were designed de novo from festival to festival with a richness and largesse of means that no actual piazza could ever have boasted. Moreover, the perpetual renewal of the scenography and installations was a continually persuasive demonstration of viceregal power vis-à-vis all social classes.

Thus, as festival installations became models for the realization of marble obelisks, so also, in the case of the Piazza del Gesù and the Piazza San Domenico, did the religious orders come to recognize the need to transform urban space into true and appropriate squares. The first and important decision was to transform the *largo*, or open space, in front of the Mercatello into a forum in honor of Charles VII Bourbon. The Foro Carolino[35] should, for its urban and design importance, be considered the first true piazza realized in Naples. The space had begun as an important market for animals and fodder and, with the passage of time and development of settlements on the hills to the east, had come to assume an increasingly defined urban role as the hinge between the oldest section of the city, encircled by the viceregal walls, and the new zones of expansion. Moreover, it was positioned along the axis that extended from the Capodimonte Hill to the *largo* of the Royal Palace.

17. Claude-Joseph Vernet,
*View of Naples with
Vesuvius,* c. 1748, oil
Musée du Louvre, Paris; photograph
Réunion des musées nationaux / Art
Resource, New York

The commission was given to Luigi Vanvitelli in 1760 but took more than five years to realize. The adopted plan, a large hemicycle with symmetrical terminations, began at Port'Alba and followed the longitudinal axis of the open space. In the center was a monumental niche designed in neo-sixteenth-century taste, intended to house a bronze equestrian statue of Charles VII. The statue, sculpted in plaster as a model, was destroyed in the revolution of 1799. Reconstructed in plaster again, it fell a second time in 1803. The hemicycle is enclosed by a giant-order Doric colonnade on a continuous base. The regularly spaced columns become pilasters at each end. Aside from a taller central section, the entire hemicycle is crowned by a balustrade with statues.

The eighteenth-century critic Francesco Milizia was not pleased by the piazza, since he considered it deficient on one side. The formal solution devised by the architect was, on the other hand, an excellent choice given the need to bring some decorum to this fragmented urban space. In fact—in a topographic analogy—Vanvitelli's solution was taken up in 1781 by Francesco Securo, who used a hemicycle as the solution to the planning for the Piazza del Mercato, destroyed that year by a fire. The preexisting church of Santa Croce del Purgatorio was inserted at the center of the new space. "The piazza," writes Arnaldo Venditti, "defined to the east by the complex of the Carmine Convent and to the west by the church of Sant'Eligio with its ample hospital, took on a new configuration: Securo's simple arrangement achieved an enclosed space that flows toward artisans' streets of Angevin origin, across five blocks of shops, and at the same time masks the view of the bank of houses behind. Only toward the coast . . . is the piazza lacking a closing element."[36] The attention to the organization of the piazza, focused on bringing order to the shops, underlines the four-hundred-year history of its mercantile function, which dated from the time of the Angevin domination. Thus, within the space of twenty years, Naples had two squares designed and completed in every detail. That of Vanvitelli has a classical dignity and an elegance that Securo was not able to impart to his more modest contribution.

Among the great urban developments of the second half of the eighteenth century is the planning of the Chiaia Riviera at Villa Reale. The old project for transforming the beach area into a tree-lined promenade was picked up again by Carlo Vanvitelli (1739–1821).[37] Chiaia was by this time one of the twelve quarters of the city, resplendent with new palaces. The most developed area was that toward the port of Chiaia, while the zone toward Mergellina continued to preserve the aspect of a fishing village. Villa Reale is a landscape design of notable interest. In the words of Venditti, "The garden . . . with its layout of infinitely long perspectives, is without terminating elements, recalling major French examples. . . . Neoclassical taste seems most clearly apparent in the two small symmetrical pavilions

18. Claude-Joseph Vernet, *View of the Bay of Naples,* 1748, oil

Musée du Louvre, Paris; photograph Réunion des musées nationaux / Art Resource, New York

flanking the entrance."[38] The park was characterized by its division by five long parallel avenues, along which were placed statues and fountains.

These urban developments, in which architecture plays a leading role, were accompanied, also in the second half of the eighteenth century, by road building. Indeed, it may be said that they constitute one of the most important public works of the reign of Ferdinand IV. The roads to Rome, Abruzzi, Molise, Calabria, and Puglia were redone, as well as those to the various royal residences.

Ferdinand IV governed Naples until 1798, when, to escape French troops, he embarked for Palermo on Admiral Horatio Nelson's ship. Thus ended a century that is surely among the supreme moments of Neapolitan artistic life, one in which architecture and urban renewal were especially remarkable because of the presence of architects of international rank, including Luigi Vanvitelli and his fierce rival, Ferdinando Fuga.

Conclusion

In the second half of the eighteenth century Naples was one of the major capitals on the Grand Tour. When the painter Claude-Joseph Vernet arrived, he chose to depict the city from east to west (figs. 17 and 18). In his celebrated view, Naples is shown scattered with churches and monasteries promising secret wonders, dotted with sumptuous palaces and their beautiful gardens. Above all, the view is one of the Bel Paese's most suggestive scenic panoramas.

Goethe, in his *Italian Journey,* does not hesitate to assert that if in Rome it is possible to hold a dialogue with world history, Naples is better for living. Admiration of this sort has been accorded Naples in a rich literary tradition that flourishes in concert with its iconography. Its chief interpreters include, in addition to Vernet, painters such as Giovanni Battista Lusieri (see page 16) and Philipp Hackert.

NOTES

1. Pietro Giannone, *Storia civile del Regno di Napoli* (Naples, 1723).

2. Franco Strazzullo, *Edilizia e urbanistica a Napoli dal '500 al '700* (Naples, 1968); Franco Strazzullo, *Architetti e ingegneri napoletani dal '500 al '700* (Turin, 1969).

3. Anthony Blunt, *Neapolitan Baroque and Rococo Architecture* (London, 1975), 129–158; Ferdinando Bologna, "La dimensione europea della cultura artistica Napoletana nel XVIII secolo," in *Arte e civiltà del settecento a Napoli*, ed. Cesare de Seta (Rome and Bari, 1982), 59.

4. Blunt 1975, 110–178.

5. Raffaele Mormone, "Domenico Antonio Vaccaro architetto, I," *Napoli nobilissima* 1 (1961): 135–150 (hereafter Mormone 1961a); Blunt 1975, 112–115; Cautela, Di Mauro, and Ruotolo 1993–1997, 11: 673–680; in general, see the monographic work by Salvatore Pisani, *Domenico Antonio Vaccaros SS. Concezione a Montecalvario: Studien zu einem Gesamtkunstwerk des neapolitanischen Barocchetto* (Frankfurt am Main and New York 1994).

6. Mormone 1961a; Blunt 1975, 115–117; Cautela, Di Mauro, and Ruotolo 1993–1997, 10: 636–640; Pisani 1994, 105–106.

7. Mormone 1961a; Blunt 1975, 114–115; Riccardo Lattuada, *Il Barocchetto a Napoli e in Campania* (Naples, 1988), 115–119; Pisani 1994, 104–105, 116–117.

8. Raffaele Mormone, "Domenico Antonio Vaccaro architetto, II: Il Palazzo Tarsia," *Napoli nobilissima* 1 (1961): 216–227; Blunt 1975, 119–120; Salvatore Pisani, "Palazzo Spinelli di Tarsia in Neapel: Domenico Antonio Vaccaio und die Kunst des Barocchetto," *Mitteilungen des Kunsthistorischen Instituts in Florenz* 40, nos. 1–2 (1996): 148–211.

9. Leonardo Di Mauro, "La struttura urbana tra richieste private e utilità pubblica," in *Settecento Napoletano: Sulle ali dell'aquila imperiale 1707–1734*, eds. Nicola Spinosa and Wolfang Prohaska [exh. cat., Kunstforum der Bank Austria] (Naples, 1994).

10. See the monograph by Roberto Pane, *Il chiostro di Santa Chiara* (Naples, 1954) and Cautela, Di Mauro, and Ruotolo 1993–1997, 4:196–197.

11. Raffaello Causa, *L'arte della Certosa di San Martino a Napoli* (Cava dei Tirreni, 1973), 76–79; Blunt 1975, 110–111, 118; Lattuada 1988, 50; Pisani 1996.

12. Blunt 1975, 112.

13. See the monograph by Alfonso Gambardella, *Ferdinando Sanfelice architetto* (Naples, 1974); Blunt 1975, 129–158, 187–194; and Alastair Ward, *The Architecture of Ferdinando Sanfelice* (New York, 1988).

14. Blunt 1975, 135–136.

15. Francesco Capobianco, "Scale settecentesche a Napoli," in *Architettura: Cronaca e storia* 8 (1962): 401–417; Magnus Nykjaer, "Architecture and Visions of Space. Some Eighteenth-Century Staircases in Southern Italy and Their Relationship to Contemporary Concepts of Space," *Analecta Romana Instituti Danici* 12 (1983): 149–173; Christof Thoenes, "Ein spezifisches Treppenbewusstsein. Napler Treppenhäuser des 18. Jahrhunderts," *Daidalos*, no. 9 (1983): 77–85.

16. Bernardo De Dominici, *Vite de'pittori, scultori ed architetti napoletani non mai date alla luce da autore alcuno* (Naples, 1742).

17. Gambardella 1974.

18. Blunt 1975, 140; Ward 1988, 225–228.

19. Blunt 1975, 145.

20. Blunt 1975, 107–108; Richard Bösel, "Freitreppen und Treppenvorhallen im barocken Sakralbau Neapels," *Römische Historische Mitteilungen* 20 (1978): 123–142; Cautela, Di Mauro, and Ruotolo 1993–1997, 3:174, 177–178; 12:746.

21. *Civiltà del '700 a Napoli 1734–1799* [exh. cat., Museo e Gallerie Nazionali di Capodimonte and other venues in Naples], 2 vols. (Florence, 1979–1980), 2:341–342.

22. Franco Mancini, *Scenografia napoletana dell'età barocca* (Naples, 1964); Franco Mancini, *Feste ed apparati civili e religiosi a Napoli dal viceregno alla capitale* (Naples, 1968); "Scenografia," in Florence 1979–1980, 2:301–370.

23. Mancini 1968.

24. Raffaello Ajello, "La vita politica napoletana sotto Carlo di Borbone," in *Storia di Napoli*, 10 vols. (Naples, 1975–1981), 4:445–726; Cesare de Seta, *Architettura ambiente e società a Napoli nel '700* (Turin, 1981); Gerard Labrot, *Palazzi napoletani: Storie di nobili e cortigiani 1520–1750* (Naples, 1993).

25. Jörg Garms, "Arquitectura," in *El arte de la corte de Nàpoles en el siglo XVIII*, ed. Nicola Spinosa [exh. cat., Museo Arqueológico Nacional] (Madrid, 1990), 25–36.

26. Gaetana Cantone, "Il Teatro del Re: Dalla corte alla città," in *Il Teatro del Re: Il San Carlo da Napoli all'Europa*, ed. Gaetana Cantone and Franco Carmelo Greco (Naples, 1987), 43–80.

27. Stefano Gallo, "L'architettura in Campania dal rococò al neoclassico," in *Cultura materiale, arti e territorio in Campania* (supplement to *La voce della Campania*), eds. Ferdinando Bologna, B. D'Agostino, and Cesare de Seta (Naples, 1979–1980).

28. Bruno Molatoli, *Il Museo di Capodimonte* (Cava dei Tirreni, 1961), 9; Arnaldo Venditti, "Valori ambientali nell'architettura napoletana," in *Ricordo di Roberto Pane: Incontro di Studi, Napoli 14–15 ottobre 1988* (Naples, 1991), 527–539; Araldo Venditti and Margherita Azzi Visentini, "Antonio Canevari," in *Dizionario Biografico degli italiani,* 62 vols. to date (Rome, 1975), 18:55–58; Garms, 1990.

29. Manfredo Tafuri, "Per una critica dell'ideologia architettonica," *Controcampo* 1 (1969): 33.

30. Roberto Pane, *Ferdinando Fuga* (Naples, 1956), 222.

31. Ferdinando Patturelli, *Caserta e San Leucio* (Naples, 1826); Arnaldo Venditti, *Architettura neoclassica a Napoli* (Naples, 1961), 98–108; Giancarlo Alisio, *Siti reali dei Borboni* (Rome, 1976), 47–65; Luigi Mongiello, *San Leucio di Caserta* (Bari, 1980).

32. Germana Aprato, "Il serraglio di Sanfelice al Ponte della Maddalena," *Napoli nobilissima* 3 (1964): 237–246.

33. Venditti 1961, 76–79; *Da Palazzo degli Studi a Museo Archeologico* [exh. cat., Museo Nazionale di Napoli, 1975] (Naples, 1977).

34. Carlo Celano, *Notizie del bello, dell'antico e del curioso della città di Napoli divise dall'autore in dieci giornate per guida de'viaggiatori, con aggiunzioni di Giovan Battista Chiarini,* ed. Salvatore Palermo (Naples, 1792; facsimile reprint, Naples, 1969).

35. Roberto Pane, *L'architettura dell'età barocca in Napoli* (Naples, 1939), 275–276; Giancarlo Alisio, "L'ambiente di Piazza Dante in antichi rilievi inediti," *Napoli nobilissima* 4 (1965): 185–192; Arnaldo Venditti, "L'opera Naploletana di Luigi Vanvitelli," in *Luigi Vanvitelli architetto,* ed. Renato de Fusco (Naples, 1973), 131–135.

36. Venditti 1961, 87–88; Renato Ruotolo, "Un inedito progetto settecentesco per Piazza Mercato," *Napoli nobilissima* 15 (1976): 48–51.

37. Venditti 1961, 59–74; Arnaldo Venditti, "Carlo Vanvitelli da collaboratore ad epigono dell'arte paterna," in *Luigi Vanvitelli e il '700 europeo: Atti del congresso internazionale di studi, Napoli Caserta 5–10 novembre 1973,* 2 vols. (Naples, 1979), 69–73, 121–169.

38. Venditti 1961, 133–205.

ELISA DEBENEDETTI
Università di Roma "La Sapienza"

Middle-Class Rome: From the Baroque City to the European Capital

An exhibition on eighteenth-century Rome presented in 2000 by the Philadelphia Museum of Art devoted considerable attention to what is known broadly as the Arcadian movement. In this context it is appropriate to call attention to a type of late baroque architecture that is complex, long-lived, and geographically widespread: the houses and apartment buildings of the upper urban bourgeoisie.[1] Although this architecture varies from place to place in dates and in design, especially in the first decades of the eighteenth century, it is common to the major cities of the European continent.

In making a connection between architecture and Arcadian literature, Sandro Benedetti quotes an oration by Nicolò Forteguerri, a notable representative of the literary Arcadians, celebrating the recognition of architectural designs in the Concorso Clementino of 1711. Taking the theme "The Arts Perfect the Universe," he set forth a clear, utilitarian, and rational poetics of architecture, defining it as the sum of the "arts that perfect the universe," since it beautifies the world, makes it comfortable, and turns it to the advantage of mankind by providing protection from the elements and from wild beasts. In 1732, on the occasion of another Clementine competition, the Arcadian poet Ludovico Piccolomini developed a sort of theory of the arts as consisting in "conjunction, harmony, and exchange with math-ematical sciences," to the point of seeing architecture as a servant of mathematics. He then touched on the theme of stylistics and proposed a precise poetics that reconciled reasonable and comfortable construction with formal exigencies, concluding that in architecture, "no differently from the fairest poetry, *number* and *thought* should thus govern."[2]

In the major capitals of Europe, especially in Rome and Paris, the idea of a contrast between monument and urban fabric gained an increasing hold. This concept assumed a homogeneous fabric from which loftiness and rhetoric were excluded. Its adherents included not only Francesco Borromini and Carlo Fontana, but also Alessandro Specchi, Filippo Barigioni, Ferdinando Fuga, and Sebastiano Cipriani, all prime movers in the urban landscape. The application of precise rules led to considering every element that was not monumental as a contribution to the whole. Doors and windows, cornices and stringcourses were to be consistent in height and visually aligned like musical notes on a staff, forming a melodic line only rarely interrupted by elements such as balustrades or French windows opening onto balconies. Borromini, for example, remained faithful to a grammar that went back at least to the *renovatio* of Sixtus IV, by concerning himself only with the plasticity of cornices at corners, where he replaced Antonio da Sangallo's

Giambattista Nolli, *Nuova Pianta di Roma* (1748), detail showing the Piazza Montecitorio and the area south of it, including the Piazza Sant'Ignazio
From *Rome 1748: The Pianta Grande di Roma of Giambattista Nolli in Facsimile* (Highmount, N.Y., 1984); National Gallery of Art Library

37

ashlar with rounded elements, concave and convex pilasters, and plastic accents around windows.[3]

This chapter in the history of architecture brought a new critical reflection on the city as a living organism in which residential structures and monuments interact, each playing its own role, as in a musical score in which the continuo establishes the rhythm and the musical figure is grafted onto it, giving new life to the idea of a reciprocal exchange among the arts in which poetry, music, and architecture find a common denominator in a theme of "good taste." This idea informs much of Arcadian poetics and is embodied in the simple style that Giovanni Mario Crescimbeni called for in his *L'Arcadia* and that Fontana, with his graceful sensibility dictated by simplicity, comfort, and reasonableness, would be the first to adopt in architecture. The poet Leone Pascoli would echo it, with other cultural implications, in the preface to the first book of the *Vite de' pittori, scultori, ed architetti moderni*, published in 1730.[4]

Crescimbeni's poetics, focusing on propriety and gracefulness, on melodious song, elegant realism, and clear and convincing evidence, is, with the moderation that distinguishes it, most relevant to the subject of houses that require no space other than that of the urban background, modestly complementing buildings of greater architectural quality and symbolic importance.[5] Even the great masters, such as Borromini, and, a century later, Giuseppe Valadier, shunned complication in the interest of harmony. Examples are Borromini's Palazzo Falconieri and Palazzo Carpegna and Valadier's Palazzo Poniatowski and Palazzo Lucernari.[6]

Before delving further into an analysis of some aspects of urban residential architecture, it is advisable to examine the historical reasons for the spread of such construction on a large scale. Although the aristocratic palace had, since the sixteenth century, represented the only type of construction in Rome, in the course of the seventeenth century the city, having reached its walled boundaries, began to grow vertically. This trend would become more pronounced in the subsequent century, when the art of the arrangement and decoration of interiors became the principal concern of architects and theoreticians. The organic spaces created by seventeenth-century architects were fragmented into a series of smaller chambers to accommodate the uses and customs of a wealthy society in the avant-garde of fashion. These interiors were decorated with an abundance of luxurious ornamentation that earned the name *rococo*. The style is marked by the abandonment of centralized perspectives, which had prevailed in seventeenth-century architecture, in favor of varied and lively spaces in which ornamentation animated structure, replacing awareness of it with a rhythmic continuity. As Rome expanded with the demolition of its medieval walls and their replacement by broad avenues, and as expansion followed the axes of roads beyond the walls, the clear-cut separation between city and countryside was eliminated. More space became available for building, allowing architects to design splendid residences with vast gardens. The development of the city center was, however, less extensive, taking the form of construction of large apartment buildings for the rapidly growing middle class. This phenomenon was quite similar to what was happening in Paris, where, aside from some individual cases such as the Hôtel de Soubise or the restoration of older structures such as the Palais Royal, from the end of the seventeenth century onward the apartment building, generally of four stories, became a characteristic feature of the urban fabric, contributing, with the refined lines of its street perspectives, to the transformation of the image of the city into that of a modern European capital.[7]

In Rome, some of the rich repertory of apartment houses from the eighteenth century, excluding the monuments, can be classified as influenced by Borromini (about ten instances), or by neo-sixteenth-century examples (seven or eight). Almost none are in the manner of Bernini, although an exception is the Palazzo Rondinini, the work of Gabriele Valvassori (the facade in the Via Angelo Brunetti) and Alessandro Dori (the facade in the Via del Corso; fig. 1). Most of these structures belong to none of these categories. Given their great number, they require the assignment of a historical identity, not so much for stylistic characterization as for interpretation.[8] The few small

1. Palazzo Rondinini, Rome, facade on Via del Corso, by Alessandro Dori, 1745–1749
From Maria Vittoria Mancinelli, "Il Palazzo Rondinini da Gabriele Valvassori e Alessandro Dori," in Elisa Debenedetti, ed., *Roma, le case, la città* (Rome, 1998)

by Sebastiano Giannini, as well as to matters connected with Borromini's plans for the vicinity of San Giovanni in Laterano. Such an interpretation would suggest that the late baroque apartment house was derived from the houses of the nobility and that the progressive dilution of its baroque character was a departure toward a more rigorous and rational approach to meet market demands. The large number of Roman facades conceived with considerations of both architectural decoration and economy offered an ample repertory based also on the persistence of sixteenth-century models. In view of the notable proliferation of these small buildings, which strikes even the most absent-minded wanderer in Rome, key terms can be applied so frequently as to constitute an attempt at interpretation: simplicity, linearity, sobriety, efficient interior arrangement, classification as rented or owned. It is possible to view design in terms of economy, that is, of the search for a decoration that does not entail excessive cost, in terms of new, more "intellectual" demands for a baroque decoration that is rationalized, leading to simplification of the decorative repertory of the masters and to schemes that create order while enriching the overall composition and blending with other rhythms of a freer sort.[10] All of these concepts refer to a specific cultural climate, that of Arcadian literary theory and its application to architecture. The play of rationality, straightforwardness, and decorative forms derived from Bernini, Pietro da Cortona, and Fontana, but with a reduction of baroque grandiloquence, offers an analogy with Arcadian poetics.

Let us consider two earlier examples, from the seventeenth century, which to some extent constitute an exception for their time. The first is two small buildings, demolished in 1885, in Via Larga, at the Chiesa Nuova, in which Borromini's vocabulary is apparent (fig. 2). This investigation could be extended to the entire district near San Giovanni in Laterano.[11] Documents recently discovered attest to the existence of a plan in which the master's characteristic desire to be typical finds a modest outlet in fountains with marble basins enframed by doorways in the sixteenth-century style. But why did Borromini design and construct two buildings for

buildings from the Roman eighteenth century that can be seen as clear expressions of the so-called Borrominian revival—for example, a building of 1737 in the Via dei Crociferi, which represents the clear adherence of Francesco Bianchi to this style—could be interpreted as the use of an antirhetorical language preferred by middle-class clients who were convinced that the profusion of complex stuccos and moldings could make their dwellings resemble those of the nobility.[9] The building is, perhaps, related to the rediscovery of Borromini's designs and to the publication of the *Opus architectonicum*

the Philippine fathers that were based on an earlier building by Paolo Maruscelli, constructed nearby in 1630? Great architect that he was, he seems to have shown his awareness of the importance of this type of architecture, which requires humility, continuity, a sense of measure, sensitivity to surroundings, respect for what has been and what can be foreseen, abandonment of any temptation to complicate when the purpose is to sing in harmony. In a sense, it is giving up the attainment of sublime heights for the purpose of enhancing what might be called the "towers," that is, the monuments.[12] The works around the Chiesa Nuova were "set between the Parione district and Via del Pellegrino, one of the most famous and popular streets in Rome," within which a "broad street was opened with a bit of piazza at great cost to the Fathers." They were part of a plan that followed a long and tortuous path and involved several buildings between the Piazza della Chiesa Nuova, Via dei Cartari, and Via Larga, in a prestigious location facing the new Oratory. In the final analysis, it was no less than an urban plan with which the fathers of the Oratory laid the groundwork for dominating the area around the church. The fathers showed that they were pursuing, in civic architecture, the Vitruvian ideal of homogeneity and symmetry of the parts. The square has later additions (the most recent works date from a century after those of Borromini), but the architecture is homogeneous in combining decoration and rationality. Its sobriety is a statement of intent to achieve new geometric balances to set against the solemn grandiloquence of the church facade, whereas the functional aspect of the new facades intentionally ignores references to the complex chiaroscuro of the Oratory.[13] In this exchange between background buildings and monuments, it is perhaps possible to see embryonic images of the eighteenth-century city.

In contrast to Borromini, whose own buildings contribute to the fabric around the church and the Oratory (which he himself began in 1637), a second master from Ticino, Carlo Fontana, redesigned the Bernini facade of the Palazzo Innocenziano (Palazzo Ludovisi) on the Piazza Montecitorio, used for the judicial bureaucracy of the Papal States, and, in so doing, refined it and played it down.

2. Piazza della Chiesa Nuova, Rome, before the demolitions of 1885, with a house designed by Paolo Maruscelli (foreground), two by Francesco Borromini (center), and one by Camillo Arcucci (background)
From A. M. Racheli, *Corso Vittorio Emanuele II: Urbanistica e architettura a Roma dopo il 1870* (Rome, 1985)

Bernini's design took advantage of the less than grand location to create a facade that is progressively and only obliquely revealed. Fontana, on the contrary, reversed the marvelous angular specificity of that composition and solved the puzzle. He transformed the portal and added an attic but otherwise changed little of the previous composition. He rendered it focused, clear, and legible and gave it a new meaning, canceling the complex baroque play and submitting it to the unified and simplifying domain of a single point of view. This approach was to be enhanced over time with the planning of the piazza and its access on an axis with the papal court (fig. 3), following the chirograph of Clement XII of 1732. Thus a new urban structure was given to the entire complex, which nonetheless still reflects an ambitious program going back to Alexander VII and Bernini. In this new structure, a reasonable, subdued approach imbued with compositional skill prevails. The works of Fontana pursue goals of urban territorial interest to such an extent that the entire area adjoining the palazzo becomes, in its majesty, the protagonist of the surrounding context. It is a rather paternalistic example of classicism, following the example of the Palazzo Farnese, but with a historical validity that qualifies it to be included among the great European examples, as if it were a point of junction or

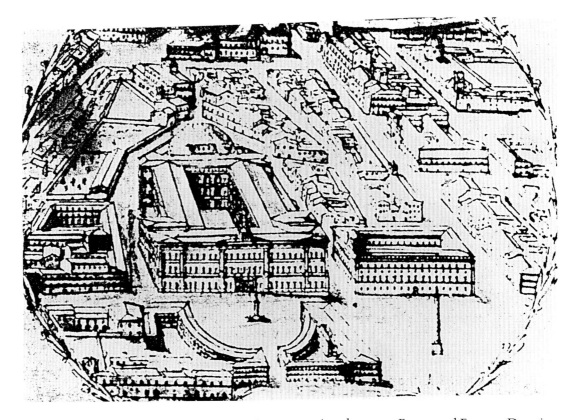

a pivot between Rome and Europe. Drawing inspiration from proportional systems, of which those who converted seventeenth-century grandeur into structures based on functional concerns could not have been unaware, the designers of the eighteenth-century buildings around the palazzo naturally opted for rational models. The decision was made in relation not to an epic or theatrical past, but to a present which, free of both baroque excesses and the rigidity of future neoclassicism, took form in a particular wealth of composition that could redeem and qualify even the severest compositional modes to arrive at great formal achievements, the fruit of a vital artistic stance. Inaugurated by a great architect who gave rise to and developed the Arcadian style, distancing himself from the baroque heritage, the Piazza Montecitorio, with its "antipiazza" (fig. 4) has, in the structures that shape it, been a classic example of the continued presence of an active and intelligent aristocracy that succeeded in turning its way of life into a source of income, creating a sort of social and residential cross section combining shops, small buildings for law courts, hotels, and architects' studios (such as that of Filippo Raguzzini) with noble dwellings.[14] In fact, the middle-class architecture that proliferated in this area can, perhaps as a result of the "historicization" of the location, be seen as avant-garde—as a modernization of the results Fontana achieved a few decades earlier.

The slightly earlier Piazzetta Sant'Ignazio is another admirable example of this phenomenon, which is widespread in European capitals and presents many problems of definition despite its importance as a type of urban planning that involves entire sections of cities. The buildings designed by Filippo Raguzzini for a site opposite the facade of Sant'Ignazio are pleasant and well modeled and pursue a beautiful play of curves. This is the picturesque square in which Raguzzini, conceiving an ideal space to receive the Jesuit church, showed the inspiration of a great inventor and the imaginativeness of a set designer, imparting graceful movement to surfaces in an entirely eighteenth-century manner, this time conforming to the barocchetto style promoted by Pope Benedict XIII. The design, however indebted to the articulations of baroque space, is the ingenious invention of an artist whose achievement, over a long career that lasted until 1730, demanded—to use Virgilio Spada's expression —"great efforts in small things." Not only do Raguzzini's buildings succeed in the monumental task of providing a scenic setting for, and embellishing the space around, the church; they also represent a new entrepreneurial approach of treating buildings as real estate whose revenues could finance the completion of the square.[15]

The problem of the use of space in relation to architectural design arose again in 1727, when Raguzzini, by a commission from the Confraternità Macellai (butchers' confraternity), was engaged to reconstruct the oratory in the Piazza della Quercia, in the same area as the older church of San Nicolò de Curte. The simplicity of the facade as a whole, its harmonious use of pilasters and cornices, is the realization of his complete maturity (fig. 5). Here he perfected a new style, which manifested itself above all in the concurrent reworking of the residential blocks in the square. The scheme is different from that of the Piazzetta Sant'Ignazio, where the apartment buildings extending

out from the church actually form theater-like wings, adapted to the great baroque theater created by the proud facade; but, as with that project, the design of the new urban space respected what already existed and what had been created in the last decade of the seventeenth century. The attempt to reconcile the relationships between the heights of the cornices of Santa Maria and the windows of the two buildings at right angles to it gives rise to architectural associations that are not accidental. The curves and moldings of the facade are perfectly coincident with the cornices of the first level of windows. The continuation of the upper cornice, recalling the two seventeenth-century buildings, conceals the space incorporated into the new building by absorbing a little street parallel to Via dei Balestrari, thereby eliminating a split between two nuclei of the confraternity. A different and more balanced proportioning of the facades also results. The double stretch of cornice appearing on the former block corresponds to the cornice line of the enclosed street, which is interrupted near where the church protrudes, drawing attention to its height. Furthermore, to create additional space in the area previously occupied by the ancient single-nave basilica, Raguzzini inserted the arms of the new, Greek-cross structure into the residential blocks and made the end of each arm a semicircular bay. Even though the footprint of the church was thus enlarged, the new facade, stylistically very similar to the small buildings facing Sant'Ignazio, fit within the dimensions of the piazza as one of the four semicircular ends of the Greek cross. By creating bays, the architect achieved a compact volume. This is a rare example of a modest and adroit integration of secular and religious architecture.[16]

In this alternation of monuments as "towers" and lower-profile buildings arranged around them, the result of the widening of spaces and small squares, the creation of points of view, and the reworking of pre-existing buildings, a new chapter in the history of architecture was written on an urban scale in the first four decades of the century in Rome and in other European capitals. This development perfectly reflects the mentality of a rising bourgeoisie. The buildings

of this period met the needs of the century of expediency. Commissions were related to the social contexts in which projects were to be carried out, and designs were adapted to the functions of the sites and the uses of the surrounding spaces. Decoration was subordinated to the organism as a whole.

Roman urbanism is built on the monument, or history, and on the landscape, or nature. But in Rome and in Lazio, nature is history and poetry and keeps in its forms the myth, or genius, of the past. Hence it is fitting that this new urban architecture originated in Rome and spread later to Paris and then to the rest of Europe.

NOTES

1. Edgar P. Bowron and Joseph J. Rishel, eds., *Art in Rome in the Eighteenth Century* [exh. cat., Philadelphia Museum of Art] (Philadelphia, 2000); Elisa Debenedetti, ed., *Roma borghese, case e palazzetti d'affitto*, 2 vols., Studi sul Settecento romano, vols. 10 and 11 (Rome, 1993–1994); Elisa Debenedetti, ed., *Roma, le case, la città*, Studi sul Settecento romano, vol. 14 (Rome, 1998).

2. Nicolò Forteguerri, "Le arti perfezionanno l'Universo," in *Memorie per servire alla storia della Romana Accademia di San Luca*, ed. Melchior Missirini (Rome, 1823), 181 and following, and Ludovico Piccolomini, "Il trionfo delle tre nobili e belle arti Pittura, Scultura ed Architettura mostrate nel Campidoglio . . . ," in *Atti dell'Accademia di San Luca*, vol. 5 (Rome, 1732); both quoted in Sandro Benedetti, "Architettura in Arcadia: Poetica e formatività," in *Arcadia: Atti del convegno di studi per il III centenario*, Rome, 15–18 May 1991 (Città di Castello, 1995), 358–359 and nn. 7 and 9.

3. Paolo Portoghesi, "Presentazione," in Debenedetti 1993–1994. With this comparison to musical texts, further explored in examples of Bach's transcriptions from Vivaldi and Webern's from Schubert, Portoghesi enters into the typically Arcadian concept of a competition among the arts (poetry, music, architecture), and then applies it to the "minor" architecture, if it can be so termed, of Francesco Borromini.

4. Giovanni Mario Crescimbeni, *L'Arcadia del canonico Giovanni Mario Crescimbeni* (Rome, 1708); Leone Pascoli, *Vite de' pittori, scultori, ed architetti moderni: Edizione critica dedicata a Valentino Martinelli* (Rome, 1730–1733; reprint, Perugia, 1992), 42–45.

5. Crescimbeni, on the subject of good taste, which is embodied in the simple style, recommends: "Do not depart from pastoral custom and simplicity. . . . " "L'autore a chi legge," libro I, avvertimento III, in Crescimbeni 1708, n.p.

6. Elisa Debenedetti, *L'architettura neodamca classica* (Rome, 2003), 176–184.

7. Jean François Cabestan, "La naissance de l'immeuble d'appartements à Paris sous le règne de Louis XV," *Paris capitale des arts sous Louis XV: Peinture, sculpture, architecture, fêtes, iconographie*, ed. Daniel Rabreau (Paris, 1997), 167–195.

8. MariaVittoria Mancinelli, "Il Palazzo Rondinini da Gabriele Valvassori ad Alessandro Dori," in Debenedetti 1998, 231–259.

9. Giuseppe Bonaccorso, "La figura e l'opera di Francesco Bianchi: Precisazioni su una famiglia di capomastri e architetti di origine lombarda," in Debenedetti 1993–1994, 65–91.

10. Elisa Debenedetti, "Le case di Roma nel Settecento," *I beni culturali tutela e valorizzazione* 7, no. 6 (November–December 1999), 13–14.

11. Augusto Roca De Amicis and Elisabeth Sladek, "San Giovanni in Laterano," in *Borromini e l'universo barocco,* ed. Richard Bösel and Christoph L. Frommel [exh. cat., Palazzo delle Esposizioni] (Rome, 1999), 232–233, catalogue entries XII.40–XII.41.

12. Cabestan 1997, 167–195.

13. Francesca Ferri, *La conformazione di Piazza della Chiesa Nuova a Roma: 1630–1748* (Roma, 1993), 31. Ferri explains how an independent artist like Borromini conformed to a preestablished model, making his buildings consistent with those of Maruscelli and other restored ones in Via Larga. The Umbrian architect Camillo Arcucci also adapted to this model in a design for the reconstruction of several small buildings in the Piazza della Chiesa Nuova.

14. Elisa Debenedetti, "Le case della piazza e dell'antipiazza di Montecitorio: Immagine pubblica e proprietà privata," in Debenedetti 1998, 11–37. It should be borne in mind that the definitive plan of the piazza and the program for its renewal were not set until the time of Clement XII, in two chirographs, the first of 1730 and to the second, as mentioned, of 1732. The second ends with the statement, "At Montecitorio . . . it was decided to create a square rather than a street," alluding to the construction of the "antipiazza" on axis with the palazzo. The Palazzo Ludovisi was commissioned by Nicolò Ludovisi and his brother-in-law Camillo Pamphili. It became known as the Palazzo Innocenziano when it became the curia under the papacy of Innocent XII. Now it is known simply as the Palazzo Montecitorio, in the piazza by that name.

15. Dorothy Metzger Habel, "Piazza Sant'Ignazio, Rome in the 17th and 18th Centuries," *Architettura* 12 (1981): 31–65; Joseph Connors, "Alliance and Enmity in Roman Baroque Urbanism," *Römisches Jahrbuch der Bibliotheca Hertziana* 25 (1989): 207–294; Giovanna Curcio, "L'area di Montecitorio: La città pubblica e la città privata nella Roma della prima metà del settecento," in *L'architettura da Clemente XI a Benedetto XIV: Pluralità di tendenze,* Studi sul Settecento romano, vol. 5, ed. Elisa Debenedetti (Rome, 1989), 167–169. On types of decoration in Roman building of the first half of the eighteenth century and their relationship to an international repertory, see Nina A. Mallory, *Roman Rococo Architecture from Clement XI to Benedict XIV (1700–1758)* (New York, 1965). Ferri 1993 quotes Virgilio Spada in the context of the construction of the Chiesa Nuova in the Borromini era.

16. Rosanna Di Battista, "Il progetto di Filippo Raguzzini per le case dell'Università di S. Maria della Quercia," in Debenedetti 1998, 169–179.

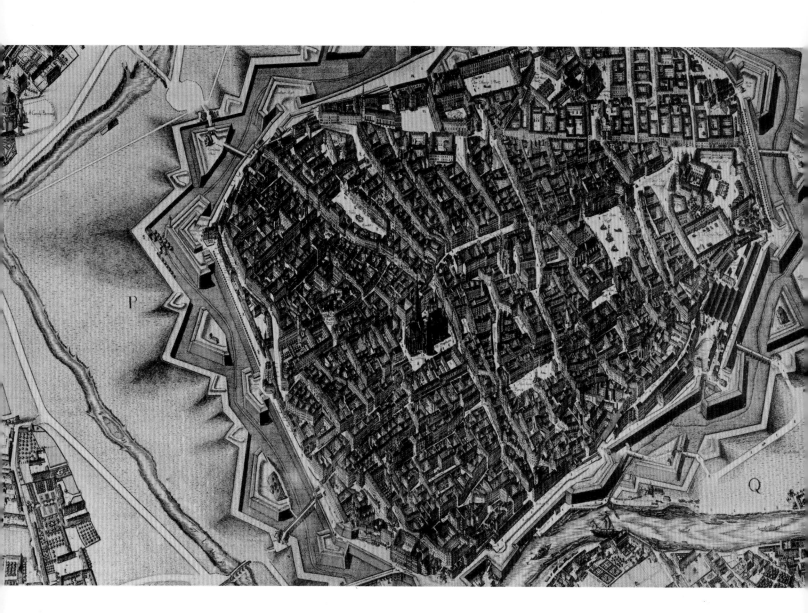

HELLMUT LORENZ

Institut für Kunstgeschichte der Universität Wien

"Vienna Gloriosa": Architectural Trends and Patrons

B oth the exhibition and the symposium to which this volume is related drew attention to the many architectural innovations that appeared throughout Europe around 1700. Among these were new architectural theories and debates, the transformation of urban centers according to new standards of city planning,[1] and the rise of new building types to meet the developing needs of cities and their governments.[2]

In considering the role of Vienna around 1700, however, I cannot for several reasons join in this harmonious chorus on the rise of new concepts and solutions. First, one can find hardly a trace of new theories among the architects active in Vienna around 1700. Second, the center of Vienna, the Innere Stadt, retained in its medieval form throughout the period of the baroque and would not be transformed for another 150 years. Finally, the government of Vienna was neither willing nor able to create or stimulate the development of new building types, even those that met basic social needs, such as prisons, hospitals, and poorhouses.[3]

But there was without doubt a Vienna Gloriosa of the baroque.[4] Many guidebooks of the time refer to the wealth and splendor of Vienna's baroque architecture, and a large number of examples, a series of remarkable buildings complete with rich interior decoration, exist today. They were new in style— that is, in their orientation toward the Italian high baroque—and highly representative of the ambitious demands of their patrons— mostly, as we shall see, members of the nobility.

This essay will first offer a brief overview of the state and general form of the city around 1700, then concentrate on some works for the most important noble patrons, and finally take a short look at the imperial sphere of architecture, including remarks on the late career in Vienna of the Roman virtuoso Andrea Pozzo.

In 1700 the city of Vienna was a fortress that had proved its strength in several wars since the Middle Ages and once again as recently as 1683, during the second siege of the city by the Turkish forces of the Ottoman Empire. Vienna's nearly invulnerable fortification was praised as reflecting the farsighted leadership of the Hapsburg emperors. An engraving from a somewhat earlier work, Daniel Meisner's political treatise *Thesaurus Philo-Politicus* of 1625, shows the walled city and the emperor discussing with a military architect a new concept to improve the defensive works (fig. 1).[5] The inscription emphasizes the preservation and improvement of the city walls as the major achievement of the Hapsburg rulers. The inscription, *SUCCESSORIBUS*, advises coming generations to continue this prudent care for the fortifications, an admonition followed by

47

1. Anonymous, *Vienna in the Early Seventeenth Century*, engraving, 1625

From Daniel Meisner, *Thesaurus Philo-Politicus*, vol. 1 (Frankfurt am Main, 1625; reprint, Nördlingen, 1992); author photograph

SUCCESSORIBUS.

Wien.

Incassum non fit, struere amplas grandibus Urbes   Sumptibus, hoc studium postera secla probant.

Daß ein Regent ein Vestung bawt,
Gschicht, daß man auffs Lands Schutz nur schawt.

Die Nachkömmen sollen sich bevleisen,
Solch werck zu rühmen vnd zu preisen.

succeeding emperors Leopold I (r. 1658–1705), Joseph I (r. 1705–1711), and Charles VI (r. 1711–1740).

Thus, after 1700, when the Ottoman menace had ceased, this somewhat mystical glorification of the invulnerable encircling walls was a major obstacle to any attempt at urban development or expansion. The emperors themselves and their leading military counselors, the Hofkriegsrat, maintained the fortifications—a policy more of symbolic than of military importance. During the entire period of the baroque there was never a serious movement to raze the walls, and they remained until 1857. The normal process in major European cities in the eighteenth century—that of tearing down defensive walls and expanding the city according to modern principles of urban development—was never considered in Vienna.[6] Even Salomon Kleiner, one of the first artists to celebrate the new glory of the baroque buildings of the city in a series of more than one hundred etchings, gave artistic expression to the importance of the walls.[7] In his illustration of the Trautson Palace, one of the major works of Johann Bernhard Fischer von Erlach, he not only showed the architectural qualities of this new building, but

also included a small part of the walls in the left foreground of the composition—just to make clear that all the new splendor of baroque architecture was possible only under the protection of solid fortifications (fig. 2).

The glorification of the walls, strongly supported by the Hofkriegsrat, had severe consequences for the development, or, better, the nondevelopment, of the city. Comparing two maps of Vienna—one by Bonifaz Wolmuet, from 1547, and another by Joseph Nagel, from 1770 (figs. 3 and 4)—we can see clearly that over more than two centuries the city did not expand and the street layout of the Innere Stadt underwent no notable change. Nearly all the streets, narrow lanes, and little squares that existed in the sixteenth century retained their medieval form until the end of the baroque period. Most of them in fact exist in this form today.

Even major monuments had to be inserted into the confined and irregular street layout, as was the case with the parish church of Saint Peter's, the first high baroque ecclesiastical building in Vienna, begun in 1701 by the Italian architect Gabriele Montani and completed by Johann Lucas von Hildebrandt.[8] Most of the architectural qualities

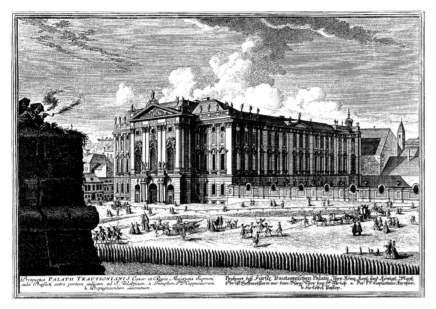

2. Salomon Kleiner, *Trautson Garden Palace, Vienna* (begun c. 1710 by Johann Bernhard Fischer von Erlach), engraving, 1725
Private collection, Vienna

3. Bonifaz Wolmuet, *City Map of Vienna in 1547*
From Max Eisler, *Historischer Atlas des Wiener Stadtbildes* (Vienna, 1919), plate 4; Historisches Museum der Stadt Wien

of this oval-plan structure—for instance, the dynamic articulation of its two-tower facade—are hard to perceive to this day because the church had to be sited on a pre-existing small square.

Thus the story of the *forma urbis* of Vienna in baroque times is far from glorious. The history of baroque urban planning in Europe—characterized by brilliant examples of broad avenues, long axial streets, and scenographic squares—can be written without even men-tioning Vienna, the powerful capital of the Holy Roman Empire.

In any other capital in Europe during the age of absolutism, leadership in the promotion of a new art and architecture representative of the state lay in the hands of sovereigns and their advisors at court. Vienna is an exception to the rule. It was exactly in the years around 1700—a period of significance for further development—that members of the nobility were by far the most important promoters of the innovative baroque architecture of Italy: they played the leading role in the arts, they brought Italian-trained architects to the city, and they offered the most prestigious commissions. The types of buildings they requested were, however, quite traditional. Every high-ranking noble family (Harrach, Schwarzenberg, Kaunitz, Althan, Liechtenstein) possessed a representational palace within the walled city (a city palace) and a suburban *maison de plaisance,* or *Lust-Gebäude* (a garden palace), used in the summertime.[9] Both building types were far from being novelties around 1700; their uses had been established during the seventeenth century. The new ideas promoted by the architectural patrons who commissioned them were matters of style, not of typology or function.

My discussion of this topic is restricted to two examples: palaces for Prince Johann Adam von Liechtenstein and Prince Eugene of Savoy. The building activities of the princes will acquaint us with all the major architects active in Vienna around 1700, including Enrico Zuccalli, Domenico Martinelli, Domenico Egidio Rossi, Johann Bernhard Fischer von Erlach, and Johann Lucas von Hildebrandt, as well as with some of the most renowned artists working on the decoration of interiors.[10]

The building of the Kaunitz-Liechtenstein city palace (fig. 5) began around 1690 for Count Dominik Andreas Kaunitz, following an initial concept by Enrico Zuccalli, at this time court architect of the elector Max Emanuel of Bavaria in Munich and well informed about Roman architecture.[11] From 1692 the building was continued and finished—from 1694 for the new owner, Prince Liechtenstein—by the Italian architect

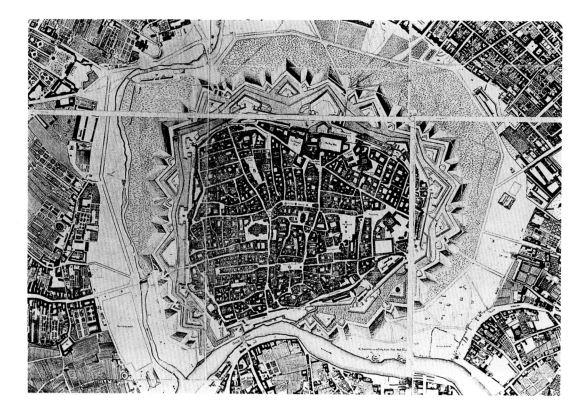

4. Joseph Nagel, *City Map of Vienna in 1770*
From Max Eisler, *Historischer Atlas des Wiener Stadtbildes* (Vienna, 1919), plate 35; Historisches Museum der Stadt Wien

5. Johann Adam Delsenbach, *Kaunitz-Liechtenstein City Palace, Vienna* (begun 1689/1690 by Enrico Zuccalli and Domenico Martinelli), engraving, 1719
Private collection, Vienna

6. Liechtenstein Garden
Palace, Vienna, begun c. 1690
by Domenico Egidio Rossi
and Domenico Martinelli
Photograph Kunsthistorisches
Institut der Universität, Vienna,
archive

Domenico Martinelli. Three Viennese noblemen—Count Harrach, Count Kaunitz, and Prince Liechtenstein—had brought Martinelli to Vienna from his chair as professor of architecture at the renowned Accademia di San Luca in Rome. The Roman training of both architects explains the siting of the palace as a Roman *isola*—a feature hitherto uncommon in Vienna—as well as the relationship of the facade to Gian Lorenzo Bernini's Palazzo Chigi-Odescalchi. This type of facade, accentuated by a central projection, soon set new standards for representational city palaces and was followed by numerous later examples.

At nearly the same time, starting as early as 1687, Prince Johann Adam von Liechtenstein had begun to build his garden palace outside the city walls, in the suburb of Rossau. Soon after 1690 the first concept, by Domenico Egidio Rossi, was transformed by Martinelli, who was hired again in this case because of his Roman experience. Prince Liechtenstein trusted only Italian artists—a result of his *Kavalierstour*, the grand tour

that every young noblemen had to experience, culminating in the study of art and architecture in Italy. Usually such a tour led first to the Netherlands (to study the art of fortification as well as collections of Far Eastern porcelain), then to Paris (to learn manners and court etiquette), then to Spain (where the best horses were to be bought), and finally to Italy, where the best paintings and the most splendid buildings of the world were to be seen and studied ("Welschland, alwo die schönsten Gebäu der Welt zu ersehen").[12]

Guided by the lasting influence of his study tour, Prince Liechtenstein gave all commissions for his highly representational garden palace (fig. 6) to Italians.[13] He engaged not only Rossi and Martinelli as architects, but also Santino Bussi for the stucco work and Giuseppe Mazza (Bologna) and Massimiliano Soldani (Florence) to design *bozzetti* for the garden sculptures and Giovanni Giuliani to execute them. Liechtenstein gave special attention to guiding and supervising the execution of the painted decoration of the

7. Marcantonio Chiarini (quadratura painting) and Lodovico Dorigny (figural painting), *Wedding of Hercules and Hebe,* ceiling fresco, Chambre de Parade, city palace of Prince Eugene of Savoy, begun 1697
Photograph Bundesdenkmalamt, Vienna

palace by his favorite, Marcantonio Franceschini from Bologna. The lengthy correspondence between the prince and the painter provides insights into the mentality and the motivation of the patron, who proudly defined himself as a passionate lover of the arts ("gran amatore di quelle trè virtù, cio'è della pittura, architettura, e scultura").[14] In another letter to the Bolognese sculptor Giuseppe Mazza, the prince explained his preference for Italian art with the remark that local artists would not be able to offer tasteful inventions to meet his demands ("in questo paese qui [Vienna] non si trova gente, che habbi buon gusto d'invenzione").[15] For patrons of his experience and knowledge, good taste in artistic invention, in architecture as well as in painting and sculpture, could be expected only of Italian artists, more specifically, of those from Bologna or Rome. Thus Liechtenstein was delighted by the presence of the virtuoso Andrea Pozzo in Vienna from 1702 on and immediately offered him a truly princely contract to paint the Great Hall in his garden palace (discussed later; see fig. 15).

The patronage of Prince Eugene of Savoy was characterized by a similar pattern and comparable aims. Born in France, the prince had come to Vienna in 1683 and soon attained the highest ranks in the imperial army. In his city palace, begun around 1696 by Johann Bernhard Fischer von Erlach, he did not leave the interior decoration to the architect, but took care of all important decisions himself. When abroad during his military campaigns, he was in continuing contact with agents in Genoa, Milan, and Bologna to hire artists from these cities or to acquire paintings by them for the state rooms in his palace.[16] He followed his personal taste as a princely collector when, in 1697, he gave the commission for the ceiling decorations to Marcantonio Chiarini, whose early examples of Bolognese *quadratura* painting (fig. 7) were to have lasting influence on the development of interior decoration in central Europe.[17] For oil paintings that were to be enframed in the wall paneling (fig. 8), he carefully selected pieces by leading painters from Bologna: Giuseppe Maria Crespi, Benedetto Gennari, Antonio Burrini, and Gian Gioseffo dal Sole.[18] Soon the palace became a museum-like treasure box, in which several facets of Italian baroque painting could be seen and studied. And when Prince Eugene started to build his magnificent garden palace, Belvedere, in 1714, Chiarini was once more

called to Vienna for its decoration. The fresco painter Carlo Innocenzo Carlone soon followed, and several other paintings by masters from Bologna and Naples (Giacomo de Pó and Francesco Solimena) contributed to the richly decorated ensemble.

Further examples of the importance of noble patrons in Vienna could be cited, among them the city palace of Count Wirich Philipp Daun, begun in 1713 by Johann Lucas von Hildebrandt.[19] They provide the best information about the status and development of the arts and architecture in Vienna around 1700, when new standards set by Italian baroque artists redefined traditional building types as well as interior decoration (sculpture, painting, plasterwork, and furniture). Only Italian artists—or artists who had the credential of study in Italy, as did Fischer von Erlach and Hildebrandt—had a chance at important commissions in this new cultural climate created by the nobility.

In this early phase of the development, which set the stage for the following decades, nothing comparable to these artistic ensembles could be credited to imperial artistic patronage. In 1693 Johann Bernhard Fischer von Erlach wrote to a patron in Brünn (Brno), expressing his regrets that he could not send his drawings in time because he was busy with fourteen major projects

that he had in hand ("14 Grose Werck under den hondten").[20] Today we can identify at least twelve of the fourteen, and of these buildings only one, the palace of Schönbrunn, was an imperial commission. The eleven others were for noble families, including Althan, Strattmann, Starhemberg, Liechtenstein, and Count Johann Ernst Thun, the archbishop of Salzburg. The predominance of the nobility is evident in quantity as well as in quality.

That the Hapsburg rulers did almost nothing in the years around 1700 to compete with the nobility in patronage of the latest trends in art and architecture is astonishing enough for the age of absolutism, in which Louis XIV set new standards for artistic policy for European sovereigns. During the long reign of Leopold I (1658–1705), who spent enormous sums on music and especially on opera, commissions for architecture were rare, and the situation did not change during the short reign of Joseph I (1705–1711), who had been educated in architecture by Fischer von Erlach. Only Charles VI (1711–1740) turned toward a more powerful demonstration of imperial magnificence. After some delay he started a building campaign around 1715/1720 with well-known monuments such as the church of Saint Charles Borromeo

9. Salomon Kleiner, *Church of Saint Charles Borromeo, Vienna* (begun 1715 by Johann Bernhard Fischer von Erlach), engraving, c. 1724
Private collection, Vienna

(fig. 9) and the Imperial Library, both late works of Fischer von Erlach.[21]

By this time, however, all the important issues of artistic development in the capital had been addressed by others, as we have seen. The so-called Caroline imperial style is a rather late flowering and should be considered more reaction than action. And many of the new efforts of Charles VI were rather short-lived, among them the project for the Michaelerfassade, or the principal elevation facing the city, of the imperial castle (fig. 10).[22] Joseph Emanuel Fischer von Erlach's brilliant idea of combining Bernini's first project for the Louvre with features of Claude Perrault's facade, developed in the late 1720s, was left unfinished after a few years (fig. 11) and could not be completed until more than a century and a half later (1889–1893).

Obviously there was no Sun King in Vienna, and none of the Hapsburg rulers would ever have invited Bernini (or even Carlo Fontana or Filippo Juvarra) to rebuild the imperial residence.[23] This rather modest, not to say poor, achievement of the emperors with respect to the promotion of art and architecture becomes even more evident when we compare the settings of two secondary residences: Louis XIV's Marly and the Hapsburgs' Laxenburg. Each accommodated the sovereign and the leading families at court. In Marly the position of the king of France and his relation to the nobility is clearly reflected in the architecture: the king's pavilion dominates the setting from its central position and is bigger and more sumptuously decorated than the uniform small pavilions for the nobles allowed to join the king during his sojourn (fig. 12). Just the contrary can be seen in Laxenburg (figs. 13 and 14), a residence near Vienna that the imperial court traditionally used during the spring: here it was the members of the nobility (Kaunitz, Dietrichstein, Schlick, Schwarzenberg, Schönborn) who possessed modern *maisons de plaisance*, while the residence of the emperor (labeled *Schloss* on the map in fig. 13) remained a medieval castle, surrounded by an old-fashioned moat.

More can be learned about Vienna's cultural climate and its focal points from the late career of Andrea Pozzo, which he spent in the Hapsburg capital.[24] Pozzo arrived in 1702 to serve the emperor: "per servizio della Maestà Cesarea del glorioso Imperatore Leopoldo," as we are told by his biographer Francesco Saverio Baldinucci.[25] But there was scarcely anything to do for the highest-ranking patron

10. Salomon Kleiner,
Hofburg, Michaelerfassade
(project by Joseph Emanuel
Fischer von Erlach, c. 1726),
engraving, c. 1733
Private collection, Vienna

Prospectus Propilei Principalis Palatij Cesarei, versus forum carboniorum.
secundum factam modellam perficiendi.

Prospect der Haupt Facciade von der Kays: Burg, wie solche gegen dem Kohl-
Marckt sollte zustehen können, nach dem daselbst befindenden Modell gezeichnet.

11. Johann Daniel Huber,
*Isometric Map of Vienna in
1770*, detail showing the
Hofburg
From Max Eisler, *Historischer Atlas
des Wiener Stadtbildes* (Vienna,
1919), plate 26; Historisches
Museum der Stadt Wien

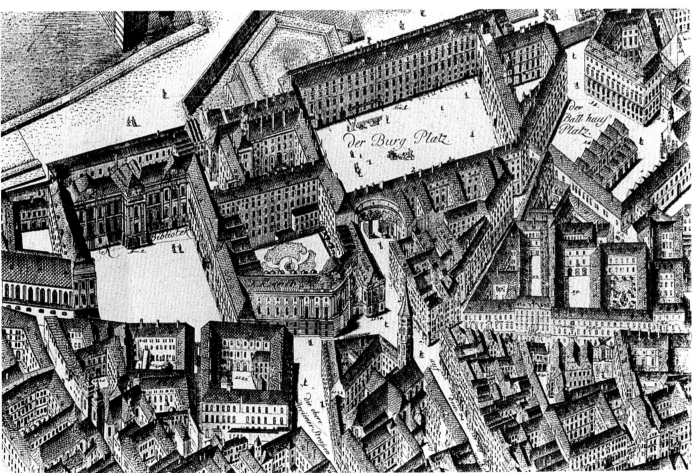

der Burg Platz

der Ball hauß Platz

Bibliotek

in town. Thus Pozzo worked for the religious order of which he himself was a member, transforming the interior of the Jesuits' University Church in accordance with Roman high baroque standards.[26] After the completion of the church in 1705, it was Prince Liechtenstein who commissioned the renowned artist to decorate the Great Hall of his garden palace (fig. 15). The artist had free choice of the subject (the admission of Hercules to Olympus), and when he insisted on having the entire ceiling at his disposal for his fresco, the prince gave an order to destroy existing stucco decoration (begun only a few years earlier) and allowed Pozzo to change the architectural articulation of the walls for continuity with the painted architecture of the ceiling. Obviously Prince Liechtenstein was extremely eager to incorporate a singular masterpiece of Roman painting into the Italianate ensemble of his palace and was well aware of the prestige of his new acquisition. Proudly, he reported that few foreign visitors failed to visit his palace during their sojourns in Vienna ("solo pochi forestieri passano, che non guardano questa fabrica").[27]

This constellation can be taken in a more general way as a paradigm of the promotion of the arts under the Hapsburg monarchy. While noble families dominated the artistic scene of Vienna around 1700, the emperor was still faithful to tradition. It is for good reason that the Vienna Gloriosa of the years around 1700 was never referred to as Vienna Gloriosa Hapsburgica.

This essay concludes with a brief look at the role of Vienna around 1700 in the broader context of the arts in the entire region of central Europe, which was also dominated by the patronage of the nobility. As all of the families who lived and built in Vienna also owned large properties in Hungary, Bohemia, or Moravia, they gave commissions in these places to the artists they employed in Vienna, in some cases earlier. Their predominance may therefore explain a strange phenomenon in central Europe, where major works of architecture from around 1700 were located not only in the capital, but also in places far away in the countryside.

The first monuments of the new style, dating from around 1680, were built outside Vienna.[28] One was the church of the Knights

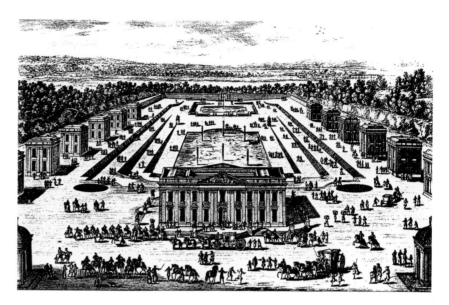

of the Cross in Prague, begun in 1679 by Jean Baptiste Mathey, who came from Rome, where he had worked in the circle of Bernini. It was commissioned by Count Johann Friedrich Waldstein, archbishop of Prague, who likewise had lived in Rome for a long time. This connection may explain why the church was one of the first monuments north of the Alps to reflect the new interest in Italian high baroque art, apparent in its oval interior as well as in its high cupola— the first truly "Roman" cupola in the cityscape of Prague.

Even more striking in its strictly Italianate character is the other primer of the

12. Pierre Perelle, *Marly*, engraving, 1680
From Jeanne and Alfred Marie, *Marly* (Paris, 1947), fig. 4; photograph Kunsthistorisches Institut der Universität, Vienna, archive

13. *Map of Laxenburg in 1716*, after a drawing by Johann Jacob Marinoni
From Quirin Leitner, *Monographie des Kaiserlichen Lustschlosses Laxenburg* (Vienna, 1878), 9; photograph Kunsthistorisches Institut der Universität, Vienna, archive

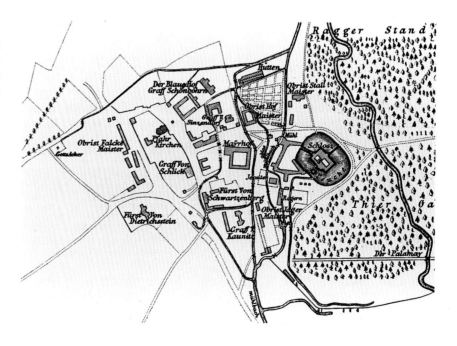

14. Salomon Kleiner,
Laxenburg, Imperial Castle,
engraving, 1725
Private collection, Vienna

new style in central Europe, the Chapel of Saint Elizabeth in the cathedral of Breslau (Wrocław) (fig. 16). It was commissioned in 1680 by Landgrave Karl Friedrich of Hesse-Darmstadt, at the time archbishop of Breslau, who had lived for several years in Rome before he moved to Silesia. For the building and decoration of the chapel, which was conceived also as his sepulchral monument, he imported a company of Roman artists (Giacomo Scianzi, Domenico Guidi, and Giovanni Simonetti) and ordered the sculptures for his tomb and the high altar directly from Ercole Ferrata.[29] The Roman-inspired articulation of the walls, the highly refined splendor of the materials, including different kinds of marble and gilded stucco work, combined with fresco painting—all these were completely new for the region north of the Alps. A description of the opening ceremony reports the reactions of surprise and admiration inspired by this creation of Italian art and craftsmanship.[30]

Thus the adoption of the new style in central Europe was decentralized from the beginning, and that pattern continued during the decades that followed. In 1688 the young Johann Bernhard Fischer von Erlach, who had just returned from his long study sojourn in Italy, received his first chance to demonstrate his Italian experience in commissions from two noblemen: Prince Liechtensein, who ordered the large stables at his country seat in Eisgrub (Lednice) and Count Johann Michael Althan, who commissioned the monumental oval-plan Ancestors Hall at his castle of Frain (Vranov nad Dyji). Both buildings were erected on sites in Moravia, rather distant from Vienna. On the other hand, in the same year the emperor rejected

15. Andrea Pozzo, *The Admission of Hercules to Olympus*, ceiling of the Great Hall of Liechtenstein Garden Palace, Vienna, 1705–1708
Photograph Bundesdenkmalamt, Vienna

Fischer's first project for the imperial hunting palace of Schönbrunn, in the capital.

Ten years later Johann Lucas von Hildebrandt, who had moved to Vienna in 1697, met with a comparable situation. He soon received three important commissions, only one of them to be built in Vienna: a garden palace for Count Heinrich Franz Mansfeld (today better known as the Schwarzenberg Palace). His first building for Prince Eugene of Savoy, a country seat to be used as a summer residence (fig. 17), was, however, situated far away from Vienna, at Ráckeve, a small village in Hungary. The monumental church of Saint Laurentius (fig. 18), commissioned in 1699 by Count Franz Anton von Berka, a member of the Viennese court, was built at a remote estate of the patron at Deutsch-Gabel (Jablonné v Podještědí) in northern Bohemia.[31] Its facade as well as its interior, inspired by Guarino Guarini's church of San Lorenzo in Turin, became an exemplar for the so-called radical group of the Bohemian baroque and was further developed in Hildebrandt's later works, for example, his church for the Piarist order in Vienna.[32]

All the buildings mentioned here have been considered, with good reason, to be true "primers" of the new style, and their

16. Wrocław (Breslau) Cathedral, Chapel of Saint Elizabeth, begun 1680
Photograph J. G. Herder Institut, Marburg

17. Summer palace for Prince Eugene of Savoy, Ráckeve (Hungary), begun c. 1701 by Johann Lucas von Hildebrandt
Author photograph

18. Church of Saint
Laurentius, Jablonné v
Podještědí (Deutsch-Gabel),
begun 1699 by Johann Lucas
von Hildebrandt
Photograph Kunsthistorisches
Institut der Universität, Vienna,
archive

importance for subsequent artistic development, not only in their locales (Bohemia, Moravia, Silesia, and Hungary), but also in Vienna cannot be doubted. The role of the capital of the Holy Roman Empire within the larger context of central Europe should, therefore, not be overstated. Vienna was an important site, but not the only and, often enough, not the earliest among those where the high baroque style began to flourish. As the leading families of the nobility were eager to promote the arts, not only in the capital, but also at their properties remote from Vienna, their patronage stimulated a decentralized artistic evolution that would be characteristic of the dispersed *Kunstlandschaft* of central Europe in the baroque period. This phenomenon is a striking contrast to France or the territories of the German electors, where the artistic policies of the ruler and the court were concentrated in the sovereign's place of residence and set the standards for artistic development in the entire region.

NOTES

1. Claude Mignot, "Paris 1700: A Green City" (paper presented at the symposium "Circa 1700: Architecture in Europe and the Americas," National Gallery of Art, Center for Advanced Study in the Visual Arts, Washington, D.C., 15–16 September 2000), and Claude Mignot, "Urban Transformations," in *The Triumph of the Baroque*, ed. Henry A. Millon [exh. cat., Palazzina di Caccia di Stupinigi] (Turin, 1999), 315–331.

2. Giovanna Curcio, "The Birth of the Modern Prison at the Ospizio di San Michele in Rome" (paper presented at the symposium "Circa 1700: Architecture in Europe and the Americas," National Gallery of Art, Center for Advanced Study in the Visual Arts, Washington, D.C., 15–16 September 2000).

3. Even the large complex of the poorhouse, begun around 1693 and later (from 1784) used as the central hospital (Allgemeines Krankenhaus), was initiated not by the government or an imperial foundation, but rather by a private donation of the physician Theobald Franckh.

4. The term was first used in a publication of this period: P. Ignatius Reiffenstuel, S.J., *Vienna Gloriosa* (Vienna, 1700).

5. Daniel Meisner, *Thesaurus Philo-Politicus, Das ist: Politisches Schatz Kästlein guter Herzen unnd bestendiger Freünd*, vol. 1 (Frankfurt am Main, 1628; reprint, Nördlingen, 1992).

6. The eighteenth-century development of Paris, Berlin, Munich, and Turin, among other cities, followed this course.

7. Salomon Kleiner, *Vera et accurata delineatio omnium templorum et coenobiorum quae tam in Caesarea Urbe et Sede Vienna Austriae . . . / Wahrhaffte und genaue Abbildung Aller Kirchen und Klöster welche sowohl in der Keysserl. Residenz-Stadt Wien . . . ,* 4 vols. (Vienna, 1724–1737), and Peter Prange, *Meisterwerke der Architekturvedute: Salomon Kleiner (1700–1761) zum 300. Geburtstag* [exh. cat., Österreichische Nationalbibliothek] (Salzburg, 2000).

8. Bruno Grimschitz, *Johann Lucas von Hildebrandt* (Vienna, 1959), 47–51, and Friedrich Polleross, "Geistliches Zelt- und Kriegslager: Die Wiener Peterskirche als barockes Gesamtkunstwerk," in *Jahrbuch des Vereins für Geschichte der Stadt Wien* 39 (1983): 142–208.

9. A still indispensable work on the baroque palaces of Vienna is Bruno Grimschitz, *Wiener Barockpaläste* (Vienna, 1944).

10. See the following monographs: Sabine Heym, *Henrico Zuccalli, 1624–1724: Der kurbayerische Hofbaumeister* (Munich, 1984); Hellmut Lorenz, *Domenico Martinelli und die österreichische Barockarchitektur* (Vienna, 1991); Günter Passavant, *Studien über Domenico Egidio Rossi und seine baukünstlerische Tätigkeit innerhalb des süd-deutschen und österreichischen Barock* (Karlsruhe, 1967); Hans Sedlmayr, *Johann Bernhard Fischer von Erlach* (Vienna, 1976); Grimschitz 1959.

11. Heym 1984, 71–75; Lorenz 1991, 34–39 and 227–235.

12. Quotations from the program of Prince Liechtenstein's grand tour are from Gernot Heiss, "'Ihro keiserlichen Mayestät zu Diensten . . . unserer ganzen fürstlichen Familie aber zur Glori': Erziehung und Unterricht der Fürsten von Liechtenstein im Zeitalter des Absolutismus," in *Der ganzen Welt ein Lob und Spiegel: Das Fürstenhaus Liechtenstein in der frühen Neuzeit*, ed. Evelin Oberhammer (Munich, 1990), 155–181.

13. Hellmut Lorenz, "Ein 'exemplum' fürstlichen Mäzenatentums der Barockzeit: Bau und Ausstattung des Gartenpalastes Liechtenstein in Wien," *Zeitschrift des Deutschen Vereins für Kunstwissenschaft* 43 (1989): 7–24.

14. Johann Adam von Liechtenstein to Marcantonio Franceschini, 13 February 1694, in Dwight C. Miller, *Marcantonio Franceschini and the Liechtensteins: Prince Johann Adam Andreas and the Decoration of the Garden Palace at Rossau-Vienna* (Cambridge, 1991), 218, doc. 45.

15. Johann Adam von Liechtenstein to Giuseppe Mazza, 26 December 1693; Bologna, Biblioteca Comunale dell'Archiginnasio, MS B 153, c. 152.

16. Hellmut Lorenz, "Unbekannte Ansichten Salomon Kleiners aus dem Stadtpalast des Prinzen Eugen in Wien," *Wiener Jahrbuch für Kunstgeschichte* 40 (1987): 223–233, and Richard Kurdiovsky, *Das Winterpalais des Prinzen Eugen: Von der Residenz des Feldherrn zum Finanzministerium der Republik* (Vienna, 2001).

17. Another example of this type of painting from nearly the same date—around 1698—can be found in the *sala dipinta* of the city palace of Count Enea Silvio Caprara in Vienna, painted by the Bolognese Antonio Beduzzi.

18. The paintings are now in the Kunsthistorisches Museum, Vienna.

19. The palace was restored in 1998–2000. See the full documentation in Amisola AG, ed., *Palais Daun-Kinsky, Wien, Freyung: Beiträge zum barocken Palast* (Vienna, 2001), with contributions on the baroque palace and its decoration by Hellmut Lorenz, Wolfgang Prohaska, Wilhelm G. Rizzi, and Luigi Ronzoni.

20. Julius Leisching, "Johann Bernhard Fischer von Erlach in Brünn," *Studien des Deutschen Vereins für die Geschichte Mährens und Schlesiens* 17 (1913): 277; Sedlmayr 1976, 338, doc. 37.

21. For full documentation see Franz Matsche, *Die Kunst im Dienst der Staatsidee Kaiser Karls VI: Ikonographie, Ikonologie und Programmatik des "Kaiserstils,"* 2 vols. (Berlin and New York, 1981).

22. John P. Spielman, *The City and the Crown: Vienna and the Imperial Court, 1600–1740* (West Lafayette, Ind., 1993); Hellmut Lorenz, "The Imperial Hofburg: Theory and Practice of Architectural Representation in Baroque Vienna," in *State and Society in Early Modern Austria*, ed. Charles W. Ingrao (West Lafayette, Ind., 1994), 93–109.

23. It should be noted, however, that both architects had received commissions from noble patrons. Carlo Fontana designed projects for Prince Liechtenstein (a castle at Landskron in Bohemia) and Counts Sternberg and Martinitz (palaces in Prague); see Allan Braham and Hellmut Hager, *Carlo Fontana* (London, 1977), 125–135. Several drawings (present whereabouts unknown) for a project by Filippo Juvarra for a princely palace sent from Rome to Count Hatzfeldt in Breslau (Wrocław) in 1708 are mentioned in the archive of the Hatzfeldt family (archive survey of 1782). I am grateful to Edmund Hatzfeldt, Cologne, for this information.

24. Richard Bösel, "Le opere viennesi e il loro riflessi nell'Europa centro-orientale," in *Andrea Pozzo*, ed. Vittorio de Feo and Vittorio [Valentino] Martinelli (Milan, 1996), 204–229.

25. Francesco Saverio Baldinucci, *Vite di artisti dei secoli XVII–XVIII*, ed. Anna Matteoli (Rome, 1975), 330.

26. Herbert Karner and Werner Telesko, eds., *Die Jesuiten in Wien: Zur Kunst- und Kulturgeschichte der österreichischen Ordensprovinz der "Gesellschaft Jesu" im 17. und 18. Jahrhundert* (Vienna, 2003).

27. Johann Adam von Liechtenstein to Marcantonio Franceschini, 8 October 1706, in Miller 1991, 265, doc. 129.

28. Hellmut Lorenz, "Italien und die Anfänge des Hochbarock in Mitteleuropa," in *L'Europa e l'arte italiana*, ed. Max Seidel (Venice, 2000), 418–433.

29. Konstanty Kalinowsky, "Roman Artistic Import to Wrocław: Sculptures of St. Elisabeth Chapel," *Artium Quaestiones* 6 (1993): 5–17.

30. " . . . rare und derorthen niemahls gesehene Kunst-Stücke, hat jedermann unter großem Zulauf des Volckes sich sehr verwundert, inmassen auch der ganze Bau von unten biß an den obersten Gesims von blau und weißem Marbel auffgerichtet ist, im Gewölbe aber die himmlische Glory aller Heiligen, welche von dem berühmten Architekten al Fresco verfertiget. . . . " See Lorenz 2000, 422.

31. For both buildings see Grimschitz 1959, 37–40 and 51–55.

32. Henry A. Millon, ed., *The Triumph of the Baroque* [exh. cat., Palazzina di Caccia di Stupinigi] (Turin, 1999), 580–581.

MÅRTEN SNICKARE
Nationalmuseum, Stockholm

The Construction of Autocracy: Nicodemus Tessin the Younger and the Architecture of Stockholm

O n the evening of 5 February 1701, a remarkable sight was visible all over Stockholm. A shining pyramid, twenty-five meters high, was erected on Brunkeberg, one of the highest points of the city. Hidden inside the pyramid were 2,500 lamps, which shone through large letters cut out of the black cardboard that covered the exterior. The glowing letters, each about one meter tall, spelled out a text in Latin describing the battle at Narva a couple of months earlier, in which the forces of Charles XII had defeated a much larger Russian army. The illuminated pyramid was part of the festivities celebrating the great victory.[1]

No visual documentation of the pyramid has been preserved, but its architect, Nicodemus Tessin the Younger, wrote a detailed description of it, published the same year by the Swedish Royal Printing Office.[2] The text includes a technical description of the pyramid's construction and a translation of its Latin inscriptions, as well as an account of the measures taken to prevent fire. It first sets forth the reasons and the historical precedent for celebrating and commemorating such a victory with a monument:

In old and ancient days, great Kings, Lords, and heroes were honored in the most splendid manner for their great deeds and exploits, and in their praise monuments and memorials were erected. Particularly the Senatus Populusque Romanus, that is, the mayor, the council, and the citizens of Rome, after successful deeds or great victories publicly declared their reverence to their brave and victorious commanders and emperors, by costly monuments and remarkable inscriptions, many of which still today can be seen and read. Likewise, the citizens of this [the Swedish] capital have, in the past as well as in our own time, declared their reverence and veneration for their great Kings, in such a way that both foreign and domestic visitors everywhere find proofs of their deep devotion. An example of this reverence and devotion is the tall pyramid, erected by the citizens of Stockholm, clearly visible in the public space of the town.[3]

The paragraph sheds light on the author's conception of the purpose and meaning of public art and architecture. First, Tessin shows an awareness of the significance of public space in a political and ideological context. He understands the importance of shaping public space as a visualization of ideological values—in this case, affirmation of the victorious absolute monarch. Furthermore, he upholds the importance of public art and architecture by referring to history or, more exactly, to classical Rome. Ancient Rome serves as prototype and pattern; it provides the reason for erecting a monument, and it fills the monument with meaning. Thus, the author establishes a parallel between ancient Rome, its citizens, and its emperors, and contemporary Stockholm, its citizens, and its king. My article is an attempt to show how this demanding parallel—and

Elias Martin, *View of Stockholm from the Royal Palace,* undated, gouache (detail)
Nationalmuseum, Stockholm

its ideological implications—constitutes a determining motive in the architecture and planning of the Swedish capital around 1700.

In Sweden, as in many other countries in Europe, the seventeenth century was a period of consolidation and strong concentration of military, economic, and political power. A loosely united country on the northern periphery of Europe, with a history of continual conflict between the king and members of the aristocracy, Sweden had gradually developed into a strong, centralized monarchy and a great military power involved in European politics at the highest level. The intervention of Gustavus Adolphus in the Thirty Years' War (1618–1648) played a crucial part in this development. Internally, the war accelerated the centralization of government and the militarization of the state. In a European context, Sweden emerged after the Peace of Westphalia in 1648 as one of the continent's great military powers.

Sweden's growing importance on the European scene, together with the centralization of government, spurred the rapid growth of the capital. At the beginning of the seventeenth century, Stockholm was a commercial city of medieval character, with about 10,000 inhabitants. Gradually, the government and administration became more and more concentrated there, and every nobleman with political ambitions had to build his own palace in town. By the end of the century, Stockholm's population was 60,000. This growth placed great demands on architecture and city planning, practically as well as symbolically: streets and squares had to be adapted to much greater numbers of people, administrative and military authorities required continually larger buildings, and those in power felt a growing need to demonstrate the new grandeur of the kingdom and its capital.

In the search for architectural models, Sweden, like other European monarchies of the time, turned to ancient Rome. As the only really strong and lasting state in European history, Rome stood out as the foremost historical example. Furthermore, the Roman Empire had manifested its greatness through great buildings. Thus, from around 1650 architects and artists working in Sweden began as a matter of course to travel to Italy and Rome to study ancient remains as well as modern architecture.

One of the first to make the journey was Jean de La Vallée (1624–1696), an architect of French origin who had worked in Sweden all of his career. After a two-year stay in Rome, La Vallée was called back to Sweden to prepare for the coronation of Queen Christina in the autumn of 1650. The triumphal arch that he designed for the queen's solemn entry into Stockholm preceding the coronation is obviously modeled on the Arch of Constantine in Rome (fig. 1).[4] The arch, a wooden structure covered with canvas that had been painted to look like ashlar masonry and sculptural decoration, marked the introduction of a Roman architectural idiom into the cityscape of Stockholm. Through its formal allusion to Roman antiquity, the arch emphasized the conceptual origin of the royal entry in the Roman triumph: the Swedish queen, in passing through the arch, was proclaimed the equal of a triumphant Roman conqueror and her kingdom a worthy heir to Rome.

La Vallée was followed by architects, including Nicodemus Tessin the Elder (1615–1681) and Erik Dahlbergh (1625–1703), and by painters such as David Klöcker Ehrenstrahl (1628–1698), who, after sojourns in Rome in the 1650s, put their Roman experience into practice in the service of the Swedish royal family and the nobility. Thus a rapid assimilation of Roman classical tradition into the art and architecture of Stockholm is apparent from the middle of the seventeenth century onward. Lorenzo Magalotti, an Italian diplomat who visited Stockholm in 1674, provides evidence of this development in his travel notes:

The visitor to Stockholm will find buildings with parallels not only in Germany but also—I dare to say—in France and, except for Italy, in no other nation of Europe. I say it not with respect to the number of buildings, and not regarding their size, but regarding the regularity of the buildings, through which they approach Italian architecture and, in consequence, Antiquity.[5]

It is noteworthy that Magalotti perceived a direct connection between the Italian architecture of his own time and that of ancient Rome, a viewpoint he seems to have shared

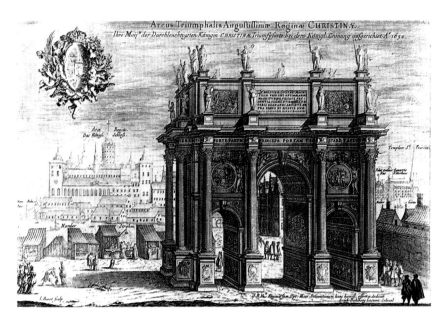

1. Jean Marot, *Triumphal Arch Designed by Jean de La Vallée for the Solemn Entry of Queen Christina into Stockholm in 1650,* undated, engraving
Nationalmuseum, Stockholm

with contemporary Swedish architects. It is impossible to find a dividing line between modern and classical architecture in the sketches and travel notes of La Vallée, Tessin the Elder, or Dahlbergh; all seem to regard the classicism of antiquity, the Renaissance, and the baroque as part of one continuous Roman tradition.

At the time Magalotti was visiting Stockholm and recording his impressions of its buildings in the Italian tradition, Nicodemus Tessin the Younger was in Rome, studying that tradition more eagerly and profoundly than any Swedish architect before or after him.[6] Born in 1654, the son of architect Nicodemus Tessin the Elder, he advanced rapidly in a remarkable career as architect and courtier. In 1673 a royal grant enabled him to make a long study tour. He spent six years abroad, five of them in Rome. In 1676, while still in Rome, he was appointed court architect. Five years later he succeeded his father as architect of the Royal Palace; in 1687 he became chamberlain to the Dowager Queen Hedvig Eleonora; and in 1697 he was appointed superintendent, a new office in Sweden, which gave him almost full control of all royal and public art and architecture. Later he also became marshal of the court, royal counselor, and count.

Tessin's career reflects and expresses an essential change in the Swedish power structure during the seventeenth century. In the first half of the century the king had to rely on a strong hereditary aristocracy, its power based on noble lineage and the possession of large estates. At the Riksdag (the Swedish parliament) in 1680 Charles XI proclaimed his autocracy and initiated a far-reaching confiscation of estates and fortunes.[7] The government in the last decades of the seventeenth century was truly an autocracy, with an absolute king surrounded by ambitious, capable men from different social backgrounds. Tessin was one of these, and his task was to visualize this absolute power, to build it in stone.

Tessin's most important commission was a new royal palace in the center of Stockholm.[8] The old palace (fig. 2), an irregular complex of medieval and Renaissance elements, did not conform to the architectural ideals Tessin had acquired in Rome.[9] At the beginning of the 1690s Tessin presented plans for a remodeling of the north wing, giving it an austere and regular baroque facade. The work, begun in 1692, was almost finished when, in May 1697, a fire destroyed almost all of the old palace, leaving only the new wing fairly intact. Suddenly, Tessin had been given the opportunity to realize his vision of a palace befitting the modern monarchy. Six weeks after the fire, the government approved his plans, and the work was begun.

An engraving from 1752 shows the result: four wings forming a forceful, closed square with lower wings projecting east and west (fig. 3).[10] The flat roof and the crowning balustrade create a sense of repose and horizontality. In comparison with the old palace, Tessin's building could be characterized in terms such as uniformity, order, and regularity. Two engravings, of the old and new courtyards, further emphasize the differences (figs. 4 and 5).[11] The first shows a structure that bespeaks a long building process, shifting architectural ideals, and accommodation of a variety of functions. The other shows a perfectly square courtyard surrounded by uniform facades, with doorways and windows placed with mathematical precision. Even the human figures in the courtyards move differently: in the first image coaches are driven and pairs and groups of people stroll in different directions; in the second soldiers march in perfect formation. It is as

ARX REGIA HOLMENSIS
versus Orientem

A . *Arx Regia* . B . *Porta et Pons Subvrbij septentr:* C . *Officina monetaria* . D . *Domus Thalassiarchi Flemingij* . E . *Palatium Com: Petri Brahe R. S. Drotzeti* . F . *Arcus triumphalis Reginæ Christinæ* .

2. Adam Perelle, *"Tre Kronor," the Old Royal Palace in Stockholm*, undated, engraving
Nationalmuseum, Stockholm

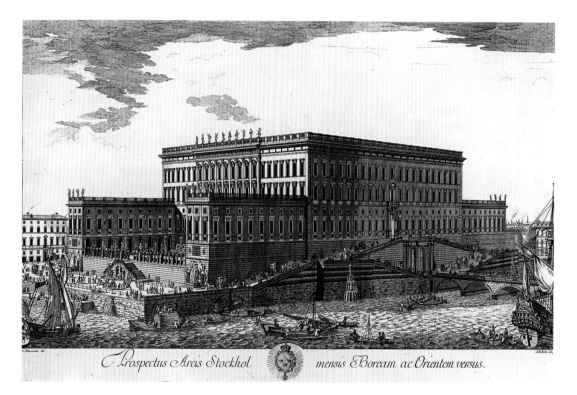

Prospectus Arcis Stockhol mensis Boream ac Orientem versus.

3. Jean Eric Rehn, *The Royal Palace in Stockholm*, 1752, engraving
Nationalmuseum, Stockholm

4. Jean Marot, *The Courtyard of the Old Royal Palace in Stockholm*, undated, engraving
Nationalmuseum, Stockholm

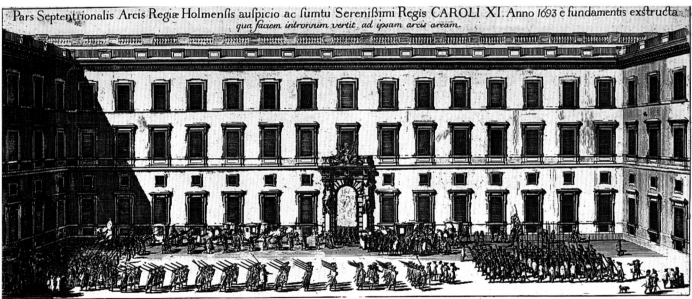

5. Sebastien le Clerc, *The Courtyard of the Royal Palace in Stockholm*, undated, engraving
Nationalmuseum, Stockholm

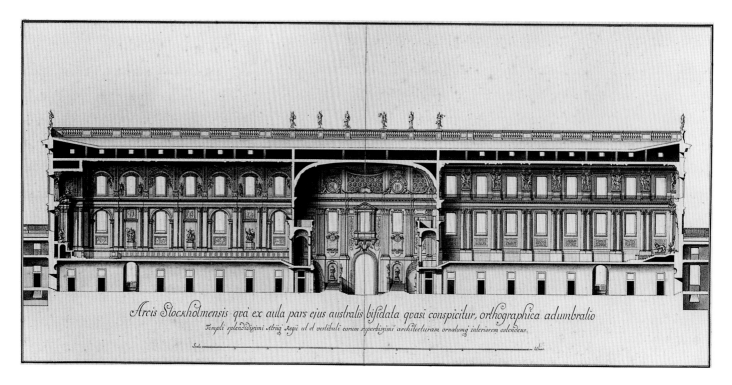

Arcis Stockholmensis qva ex aula pars ejus australis bifidata qvasi conspicitur, orthographica adumbratio
Templi splendidissimi Atrisq́ Regii ut et vestibuli eorum svperbissimi architecturam ornatvmq́ interiorem ostendens.

if these details illustrate a shift from an aristocratic society, with the power spread among many equals, to an absolute monarchy and a military state under perfect discipline.

In almost every detail, the new Royal Palace follows Roman models: the severe north facade (to the right in fig. 3) is reminiscent of the Palazzo Farnese and the Palazzo Barberini, while the more open and inviting eastern facade, with its colossal order, bears a resemblance to Bernini's Palazzo Chigi-Odescalchi. The ramps leading to the north gate are derived from the Palazzo Farnese in Caprarola, and the gate itself is almost a copy of the gate of the Palazzo Sciarra. Not without reason has the Royal Palace been called the most Roman baroque palace outside Rome.

Through all these references to Roman Renaissance and baroque architecture, Tessin incorporated the palace into what he understood as a Roman tradition unbroken from the classical period onward. But this indirect link to ancient Rome was not enough: Tessin sought sources for a return to a truer picture of antiquity. One example of this is his conception of the Hall of State, one of the largest and most important rooms in the palace, intended for ceremonies and, particularly, for sessions of the Riksdag. A longitudinal section of the south wing shows the palace

chapel and the Hall of State on either side of a monumental vestibule (fig. 6).[12] The Hall of State, to the right, is a spacious, rectangular hall with a flat ceiling. The walls are articulated as two stories, the lower with coupled half columns in the Composite order and the upper with atlantes on pedestals. The shorter wall to the right, where the royal throne is placed, is accentuated by freestanding columns.

It is easy to find contemporary models for the design of the hall. One example is Inigo Jones' Banqueting House, whose earnest Palladian classicism must have appealed to Tessin. However, as Björn Kommer has pointed out in his monograph on the Royal Palace, Tessin's study of Vitruvius, and, particularly, of Alberti seems to have been decisive for the conception of the hall.[13] In *De re aedificatoria*, Alberti attempts to reconstruct the Curia, or senate house, of ancient Rome. Tessin's comprehensive library included two editions of Alberti's treatise.[14] One, an Italian edition published in 1550, contains illustrations, among them a plan and an elevation of the Curia (fig. 7).[15] Many connections to these images, together with Alberti's written description, are evident in Tessin's Hall of State: the proportions are similar, as are the wall division, the articulation of the walls with columns, and the

6. Studio of Nicodemus Tessin the Younger, *South Wing of the Royal Palace, Longitudinal Section*, undated, pen and ink
Royal Collections, Stockholm

7. After Leon Battista Alberti,
*Reconstruction of the Curia
in Rome*
From Leon Battista Alberti,
L'Architettura (Florence, 1550),
engraving Royal Library, Stockholm

placement of the rectangular windows. Another similarity is the flat ceilings; the other monumental halls in Tessin's palace have vaulted ceilings.

Thus, Tessin seems to have modeled the Hall of State on the Roman Curia or, to be precise, on Alberti's reconstruction. For the architect, this was not only a formal model, but a model pregnant with meaning: the hall to be used for the sessions of the Swedish Riksdag was given a form corresponding to the hall where the Roman Senate gathered. To take the parallel further, the Swedish Riksdag stands out as a worthy heir to the ancient Roman institution.

As the new Royal Palace began to take shape, the need to order its surroundings seemed more and more urgent. This was no easy task: immediately north of the palace was the irregularly shaped islet of Helgeandsholmen, and the area to the south and west was occupied by medieval buildings of various sizes and styles. Architects had been tackling the problem since the middle of the century. A plan drawn around 1660 by Tessin the Elder after Jean de La Vallée shows an effort to accentuate an axis through the palace, from the central tower through the north entrance and continuing with a bridge connecting the palace with the northern parts of the town (fig. 8).[16] Of special interest are some additions in graphite on the plan. Made by

Tessin the Younger in the 1680s, they show an attempt to add an east-west axis to La Vallée's and Tessin the Elder's south-north axis, thus connecting the palace with Riddarholm church, which was used for royal funerals. Tessin has tentatively placed two curved wings west of the palace and steps breaking through a block farther west. The perspective that would have been created by the steps bears witness to a careful study of Bernini's Scala Regia and Borromini's perspective in the Palazzo Spada.[17]

The fire of 1697 opened new possibilities for the planning of the area. With the new palace as center and point of departure, Tessin tried increasingly bold solutions, until in 1713 he presented the grandest and most radical plan ever for central Stockholm; a plan that, had it been realized, would have obliterated considerable parts of the medieval town and replaced them with a modern imperial capital (fig. 9).[18] The plan is characterized by uniformity, axiality, rectilinearity, and order: broad bridges and straight streets connect the palace with monumental squares and buildings. Important official and public buildings are gathered around the palace: to the west, a new building for the royal courts of justice and government offices; to the north, on Helgeandsholmen, the royal stables with an indoor tiltyard; and, farther toward the northeast, an enormous armory intended for permanent display of trophies and war booty.

Perhaps the most spectacular aspect of Tessin's plan is the square north of the palace. Following the main idea from La Vallée and Tessin the Elder, he conceived a bridge leading at a right angle from the north entrance of the palace. To that he added his own early conception of an axis connecting the palace with the royal burial church. Now, however, he simply abandoned the old Riddarholm church west of the palace and located a new royal church opposite the north palace facade, thus constructing a ceremonial axis between palace and church, the two most important buildings in the capital. The church, in the form of a Latin cross crowned by a dome, faced a rectangular square with the proportions of two to three, flanked by uniform palaces meant to house prominent court officials (figs. 10, 11, and 12).[19] In the written explanation, which he presented

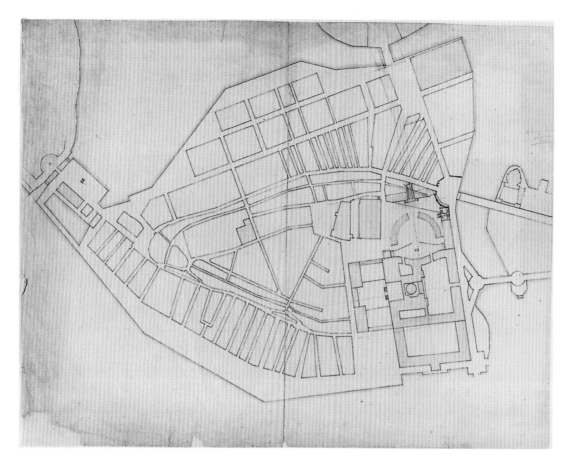

8. Nicodemus Tessin the Elder, with additions in graphite by Nicodemus Tessin the Younger, *Plan of the Old Royal Palace in Stockholm and Its Surroundings*, undated, pen and ink with graphite
Nationalmuseum, Stockholm

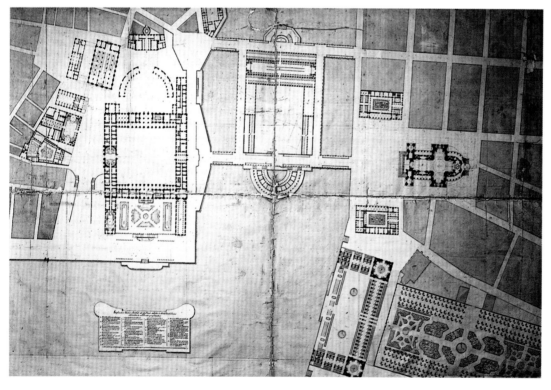

9. Studio of Nicodemus Tessin the Younger, *Plan for Central Stockholm*, 1713, pen and ink
State Archives, Stockholm

10. Nicodemus Tessin the Younger, *Project for a Royal Funeral Church in Stockholm, View from the Royal Palace*, 1713, pen and ink
Nationalmuseum, Stockholm

to the king together with the drawings, Tessin pointed out several contemporary models for the church: Saint Peter's, Sant'Ignazio, Sant'Agnese, and other Roman baroque churches; Val-de-Grâce in Paris; and Saint Paul's in London.[20] But he also leveled criticism at these modern churches:

The ancient architects much loved to place porticoes before their temples, which gave magnificence and grandeur [to the buildings], and furthermore provided shelter from the rain. . . . As a portico, and the shadows it casts, distinguish and ennoble a facade more than anything else, I cannot understand why the architects in Rome in the last centuries descended to the use of flat facades, which, seen from a distance, do not distinguish themselves, but merely appear as a bunch of half columns and pilasters with ornaments around niches, windows etc. . . . The facade of Saint Peter's (the part of the building least esteemed by all competent judges) would have had a much nobler character, had there been a large portico before it. For these reasons I have found it proper to place a portico before the facade. . . .[21]

The drawing of the church facade shows a Pantheon-like portico. Of course there were contemporary churches with porticoes. What is interesting here, however, is that Tessin explicitly refers to antiquity.

The plan of the church shows another, even more interesting departure from contemporary models: in an explicit attempt to approach ancient ideals, the architect placed columns not only in front of the facade but all around the building. Tessin wrote:

The ancient [architects] also used to place columns alongside their temples. . . . In modern church architecture nothing similar is to be seen, no doubt because of the chapels required on both sides of Catholic churches. As we have no need for such chapels alongside our churches, I have found it suitable to imitate the beauty of the ancient buildings in this case.[22]

These examples show that Tessin looked to Rome and Roman architecture for more than one purpose. In the search for concrete models and patterns he often turned to contemporary Roman architecture, which he understood as a continuation of a classical tradition. But when he needed a theoretical foundation, he turned directly to ancient Rome, as it was known from the architectural remains themselves, as well as from treatises and later reconstructions.

The title of this article is intended to emphasize that Tessin's foremost task was to give constructed form and visual shape to an ideology—the ideology of the absolute monarch, ruling in the name of God. The concepts of absolutism and autocracy have been questioned in recent decades. The historian Nicholas Henshall, for example, maintains that, in the true sense of the words, they never existed.[23] Of course it goes without saying that there has never been a society in which all power was in the hands of one person. Under the Swedish autocracy, Charles XI and Charles XII relied on many individuals: their generals, their bishops, and their experts in different fields—among them their court architect and superintendent Nicodemus Tessin the Younger.

Thus the architecture of Tessin did not mirror an existing society, with all its weaknesses and imperfections. Rather it should be interpreted as a representation of a vision—the vision of an ideal state, a utopia. Neither did it reflect an actual form of government; it expressed and illustrated an ideal one. And Tessin found the model for this vision in the architecture of ancient Rome. Its character of austerity and order, of something immovable and enduring, was consistent

11. Studio of Nicodemus Tessin the Younger, *Project for a Royal Funeral Church in Stockholm, Elevation,* 1713, pen and ink
Nationalmuseum, Stockholm

gate with a monumental square was realized around 1800. The square was flanked on the west by a palace, and on the east by the opera house, both in neoclassical style. In the center of the square, an equestrian statue of Gustavus Adolphus was installed. Another century later, the parliament building was inaugurated on the island site of Helgeandsholmen, where Tessin had planned the royal stables. The architecture of the parliament building clearly refers to the Royal Palace, as does the architecture of the opera house that, at the end of the nineteenth century, replaced the neoclassical opera house. Today, therefore, the area north of the Royal Palace resembles Tessin's plan in scale and regularity as well as in the concentration of official and public buildings. An architectural vision intended to glorify the absolute monarch of a great military power was finally realized by a modern democracy on the northern periphery of Europe.

with the vision of an eternal, absolute monarchy established by God.

For posterity a dramatic contrast appears between, on the one hand, a fragile government that suddenly collapsed in 1718 after the death of Charles XII and, on the other hand, Tessin's architectural vision of an absolute, eternal monarchy—an architecture expressing something powerful and lasting. A similar contrast can be perceived between Tessin's vision of Stockholm and the existing city of his time. Almost a century after Tessin presented his plan, the Swedish artist Elias Martin painted the view north from the Royal Palace (fig. 13).[24] Instead of uniformity, order, and monumentality, the painting shows a disordered townscape with ramshackle houses next to grand palaces, a wooden bridge at an oblique angle to the Royal Palace, and, on the stream just outside the palace, an unsightly mill.

From a longer perspective, though, Tessin's vision turned out to be fruitful. His idea of a stone bridge connecting the northern palace

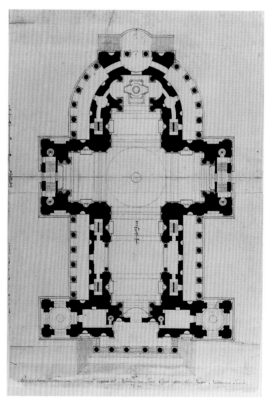

12. Studio of Nicodemus Tessin the Younger, *Project for a Royal Funeral Church in Stockholm, Plan,* 1713, pen and ink
Nationalmuseum, Stockholm

13. Elias Martin, *View of Stockholm from the Royal Palace*, undated, gouache
Nationalmuseum, Stockholm

14. The Royal Palace in Stockholm and its surroundings
Photograph Svenska Aero-Bilder AB

NOTES

1. Mårten Snickare, *Enväldets riter: Kungliga fester och ceremonier i gestaltning av Nicodemus Tessin d.y.* [with a summary in English] (Stockholm, 1999), 157–159.

2. Nicodemus Tessin the Younger, *Den förträflige Heders-Pyramid och Illumination, som Hans Kongl. May:t til ähra på stora Tacksägelse Dagen för den oförlijkelig erhållna Segren emot de Trolösa Ryssar Denna Konglige Hufwud Staden upsättia och lysa låtet uppå Brunkebärg* (Stockholm, 1701).

3. "Såsom uti gamla och forna tider store Konungar Herrar och Hieltar för sina dråpeliga gerningar och bedrifter altid på det herligaste äro behedrade och til deras priss allehanda minnes- och äretecken upsatte wordne / och i synnerhet Senatus Popolusque Romanus Borgmästare och Råd / samt menigeheten i Rom wid alla besynnerlig lyckeliga och / stora handlingar eller segerwinningar med kåsteliga wärk och märkeliga skrifter offenteligen fröklarat all wyrdnad emot sina tappra och segersälla män / Höfwidsmän / Fäldtherrar och Keysare / så / at man ännu idag här och där många heders märken skåda och läsa kan / som S. P. Q. R. upsättia låtet: Altså hafwer jämwäl så i forna som i wåra tider så märkerligen förklarat sin allerunderdånigsta wyrdnad emot sina stora Konungar denna Kongl. Residentz Staden at både inländske som utländske dess devotion altid åskådat med hugnad. Exempel för alla andra hafwer oss denna gången för ögonen stält den på tacksägelse dagen store och högt upreste Pyramiden."

4. Jean Marot, *Arcus Triumphalis Augustissimae Reginae Christinae*, engraving, 24.8 × 37.5 centimeters, in Erik Dahlbergh, *Suecia Antiqua et Hodierna* (Paris and Stockholm, 1715). On the arch, see Sten Karling, "L'Arc de triomphe de la Reine Christine à Stockholm," in *Queen Christina of Sweden: Documents and Studies*, ed. Magnus von Platen (Stockholm, 1966), 159–186.

5. " . . . [C]hi arriva a Stockholm vi trova delle fabbriche che non solo hanno le compagne in Alemagna, ma, mi sia permesso il dire, anche in Francia e, salvo che in Italia, in nessun'altra parte d'Europa; non dico né per la moltitudine né per la grandezza, dico per la regolarità dell'architettura, nella quale s'accostano più che altrove all'italiane, e per conseguenza all'antico." Lorenzo Magalotti, *Relazioni di viaggio in Inghilterra, Francia e Svezia*, ed. Walter Moretti (Bari, 1968), 231.

6. On Nicodemus Tessin the Younger, see Mårten Snickare, ed., *Nicodemus Tessin the Younger: Royal Architect and Visionary* (Stockholm, 2002).

7. On the Swedish autocracy, see Anthony F. Upton, *Charles XI and Swedish Absolutism* (Cambridge and New York, 1998).

8. On the Royal Palace, see Björn R. Kommer, *Nicodemus Tessin der Jüngere und das Stockholmer Schloss* (Heidelberg, 1974).

9. Adam Perelle, *Arx Regia Holmensis versus Orientem*, engraving, 24.6 × 37.4 cm, in Dahlbergh 1715.

10. Jean Eric Rehn, *Prospectus Arcis Stockholmensis Boream ac Orientem versus*, engraving, 54.7 × 89.8 centimeters, Nationalmuseum, Stockholm, NMG 16a/1896.

11. Jean Marot, *Arcis Holmensis area interior versus Occidentem*, engraving, 25.5 × 32.7 cm; Sebastien le Clerc, *Pars Septentrionalis Arcis Regiae Holmensis*; both in Dahlbergh 1715.

12. Studio of Nicodemus Tessin the Younger, *South Wing of the Royal Palace, Longitudinal Section*, pen and ink, 37.7 × 80.2 centimeters, Royal Palace, Stockholm, SAK 3, p. 330.

13. Kommer 1974, 51–54.

14. Per Bjurström and Mårten Snickare, eds., *Nicodemus Tessin the Younger: Catalogue des livres, estampes & desseins du cabinet des beaux arts, & des sciences appartenent au Baron Tessin, Stockholm 1712* (Stockholm, 2000), 1–2.

15. Leon Battista Alberti, *L'Architettura: Tradotta in lingua fiorentina da Cosimo Bartoli* (Florence, 1550), 314–318.

16. Nicodemus Tessin the Elder, with additions in graphite by Nicodemus Tessin the Younger, *Plan of the Royal Palace in Stockholm and Its Surroundings*, pen and ink with graphite, 43.3 × 56.5 centimeters, Nationalmuseum, Stockholm, NMH CC 797.

17. In the Nationalmuseum are drawings of the Scala Regia by Tessin (NMH THC 2172, NMH THC 2173, and NMH CC 268) and of the perspective in the Palazzo Spada (NMH Cels. 155).

18. Studio of Nicodemus Tessin the Younger, *Plan for Central Stockholm*, 1713, pen and ink, 140 × 94 centimeters, State Archives, Stockholm, P S189/1. On the plan, see Ragnar Josephson, *Tessins slottssomgivning* (Stockholm 1925).

19. Nicodemus Tessin the Younger, *Project for a Royal Funeral Church in Stockholm, View from the Royal Palace*, pen and ink, 19.5 × 34 centimeters, Nationalmuseum, NMH CC 777; studio of Nicodemus Tessin the Younger, *Project for a Royal Funeral Church in Stockholm, Elevation*, pen and ink, Nationalmuseum, THC 5324; studio of Nicodemus Tessin the Younger, *Project for a Royal Funeral Church in Stockholm, Plan*, pen and ink, 63.5 × 42.5 centimeters, Nationalmuseum, THC 5326.

20. Manuscript in the archives of the Nationalmuseum, Stockholm: Nicodemus Tessin, H II A, A 315.

21. "De gambla hafwa mycket ällskat Portiquer fram för deras kyrckior som gåfwo een stor Magnificence och grandeur, och derjemte uti rägnwäder tiente till retraite; Will man då hafwa en Vestibule fram för en Sale, huru mycket mehra fram för Gudz huuss, och är intet i en facciat som så distingerar den samma som den starcke skuggan uti en stor Portique, så att iag intet kan begrijpa huru Architecterne i Rom nu i några Siecler äro förfallne till de platte Facciaterne, som långt bort intet distinguera sig, utan bestå af en hoper halfwe Colonner och pilatser med sina Ornamenter kring Nicher, Fönster etc. Hwilket de gamble aldeles hafwa undflyt, och emellan stoorleken och rijkheten af sielfwa Ordren hafwa lämbnat en hwilo åt Ornamenterne. Facciaten af S:te Peters kyrckia, (som hoss alle förståndige minst af hela dess Structure skattas) skulle hafwa helt ett annat anseende, i fall där hade warit en stoor Portique förre. Desse skiähl hafwa warit orsak att iag har funnit en Portique anständig fram för dess Facciat. . . . "

22. "De gamble hafwa och mycket brukat Colonner ändalångz deras Templer somde hafwa kallat peripteros och Italiennerne alato intorno, af hwilket nu intet exempel finnes wid de Moderne kyrckior, twifwels utan för Capeller som å begge sijdor i de Catholske kyrckiorne requireras, men som wij intet hafwa dem behof, ty har iag intet kunnat underlåta någorlunda att imitera de Antiques skiönhet i detta fallet."

23. Nicholas Henshall, *The Myth of Absolutism: Change and Continuity in Early Modern European Monarchy* (London and New York, 1992).

24. Elias Martin, *View of Stockholm from the Royal Palace,* gouache, 51 × 59 centimeters, Nationalmuseum, NMB 484.

DMITRY SHVIDKOVSKY

State Academy of the Fine Arts of Russia; Moscow Architectural Institute

The Founding of Saint Petersburg and the History of Russian Architecture

The idea that, at the moment of Saint Petersburg's founding, Peter the Great envisioned the city in precisely the form it took a century afterward remains one of the most durable and widespread myths surrounding the first emperor of Russia. It first appeared in the 1740s during the reign of Peter's daughter, Elizabeth I, who wished to underline the significance of her father and his dynasty in opposition to another branch of Romanovs descended from Peter's elder brother, Ivan V. Elizabeth's predecessors, Anna I and the child emperor Ivan VI, came from this other Romanov line.

In the middle of the eighteenth century the Russian court created an imperial cult that would take various forms during the subsequent history of the Russian Empire. The story of the foundation of the new capital, the symbol of the new, Western character of the state, remained its keystone. In the Age of Enlightenment, Catherine the Great based her claim to legitimacy as the Russian sovereign on continuing the achievements of the first emperor. It is not an accident that, for the famous equestrian statue of Peter the Great by Etienne Falconet, she chose the inscription, "To Peter the *First* from Catherine the *Second.*"

In the early nineteenth century, for Aleksander Pushkin and other writers of the time, the foundation of Saint Petersburg was the creation of Russia's "window on Europe." In Pushkin's famous words, at the time of Peter the Great, Moscow became "the porphyry-clad widow," pushed aside by the "new tsarina," the capital on the Neva. Pushkin's contemporary Vladimir Odoevsky wrote in one of his romantic fairy tales: "The tsar started to lift one rock after another and lay them one on top of another in the air. And in this way he built the entire city in the air and set it down on the earth."[1] Through both official ideology and literature, the myth that Peter the Great had conceived the image of Saint Petersburg whole became part of Russian tradition.

Unfortunately the myth and the reality of Saint Petersburg's founding do not look alike. In the chorus of historical personages of the eighteenth, nineteenth, and twentieth centuries, it is necessary to listen to the voice of the most important witness: Peter himself. Numerous decrees and letters and his own drawings provide the evidence, which differs from the official version. They reveal the complicated, contradictory, and sometimes irrational process by which the new city was established.

There is no doubt that 27 May 1703, the day Saint Petersburg was founded, was a turning point in the development of Russian architecture. Art historians, both in Russia and abroad, have published voluminously on this subject, from Igor Grabar, who, in the early twentieth century, summarized the knowledge of previous periods in his *Istoriia russkogo iskusstva* (History of Russian art)

Peter and Paul Fortress, Saint Petersburg
Photograph by William Brumfield; National Gallery of Art Photographic Archives

79

(in my opinion still unrivaled), to James Cracraft, in his fundamental work *The Petrine Revolution in Russian Architecture*, published in 1988.[2] Nevertheless, the early history of Saint Petersburg presents a number of unresolved problems that could change the traditional view of its foundation.

First is the relationship of the building of Saint Petersburg to the previous history of Russian architecture. Peter the Great's distinct Europeanism overshadowed the realization that the architecture of his time was the outcome of a long transformation of Russian art by Western influences. Once, before the creation of Saint Petersburg, Russia had realized a kind of "European" capital: Renaissance Moscow around 1500. In this period the cathedrals, palaces, and walls of the Kremlin, as well as a number of parish churches, were built by Italian masters from Bologna, Milan, Venice, and Florence.

Because of the political and religious context, from the mid-sixteenth through the seventeenth century, architectural relations between Russia and the West received only episodic endorsement, which was not enough to reinforce the development of architecture in a European manner. Buildings by Renaissance Italian architects, together with their decoration, remained the main source for an architectural language that symbolically expressed the tsar's power. New Western elements always came into Russian architecture as a reflection of state ideology.

For Peter the Great, the meaning of architecture was, again, linked to a new idea of order in the state. His buildings were to create the ideal image of a new empire that looked toward the future—a utopia to be realized through architecture. Similar attempts resided in the Muscovite mentality and artistic tradition. This idea was central to an understanding of Russia as the heir of Byzantium and of its capital as the Second Constantinople, the Third Rome, and the New Jerusalem, all in one. During the sixteenth and seventeenth centuries it existed mainly as a theocratic conception. Peter the Great strengthened its secular and pragmatic realities, but he reserved a utopian spirit for the architectural image of an ideal Russian tsardom. He wished to promulgate the vision of his political inheritance to the whole of Europe. His political ambitions are revealed

in the title of emperor, appropriated from imperial Rome,[3] as well as in the buildings he had constructed in Moscow (fig. 1) and later in Saint Petersburg.

After a victory over Turkey in 1696 (seven years before the foundation of Saint Petersburg), Peter ordered preparations for a triumphal return to Moscow following ancient Roman examples.[4] This event was the first direct appeal to antiquity in the history of Russian architecture. Wooden triumphal arches were built "in the image of ancient Roman triumphal gates" (fig. 2). Paintings and inscriptions on the arches compared the tsar with the Emperor Constantine, who had defeated Maxentius, and especially with Julius Caesar.[5] The library of Peter the Great includes a manuscript translation of a book by Giovanni Jacomo de Rubeis on triumphal arches, published in Rome in 1690. It probably served as the source for the designs of the arches erected for Peter.[6] For centuries Russians had commemorated victories by building churches. For the first time, secular structures, derived from a Western tradition, were erected for that purpose. It is impossible to relate the arches to any of the European architectural styles of the seventeenth century; they had no features that may be identified with the baroque or with classicism. The character of Russian architecture at the beginning of Peter the Great's reign is clear in this regard: references to antiquity appear in advance of the imitation of any classical style. At the turn of the seventeenth century, architects continued to combine motifs of different stylistic origins in a free mannerist style, producing strange structures in which allegorical paintings and inscriptions played the main role. These were set in architectural frameworks that have no easily recognizable classical models. The wooden triumphal arches built in Moscow were very different from structures of the same type from the mid-eighteenth century, the time of the flowering of the Russian imperial baroque, such as those built for the coronation of Elizabeth I in 1740.

At the same time, the constructions for the triumphal entrance of Peter the Great were different from anything designed for the tsar's relatives and courtiers. The buildings he commissioned answered to his tastes and

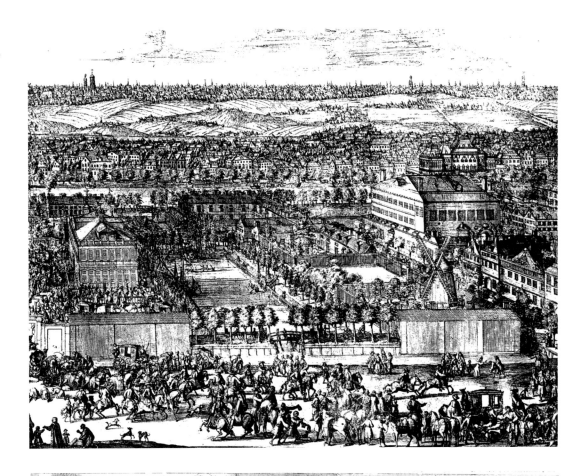

1. Henryk de Witte, *View of
the Golovin Palace and Its
Surroundings in the Lefortvo
District, Moscow*, before
1706, engraving
Library of Moscow Architectural
Institute

2. Henryk de Witte (?),
*Triumphal Arches Erected
in Moscow to Honor the
Victories of Peter the Great*,
c. 1710, etching
Library of Moscow Architectural
Institute

had a special architectural character. But his was not the only architectural manner that existed; moreover, it did not dominate. There were other sources for works that reflected private architectural tastes.

The ancient and new capitals of Russia presented completely different conditions for architectural practice. In Saint Petersburg everything was decided by one patron, the emperor himself, who invited foreign masters of his choice. In Moscow, on the other hand, during the childhood of Peter the Great there appeared several architectural manners associated with certain aristocratic families, related not only to the tastes of a family but also to the manner of an architect or a group of builders used by a particular circle of patrons.

A most eccentric manner characterized the buildings commissioned by the Golitsyn family throughout the dramatic changes in the fortunes of some representatives of this aristocratic clan. Prince Basil Golitsyn, the ruler of Russia during Peter's childhood and the favorite of Peter's older sister Sophia, was known for his "Westernism," reflected, most notably, in the design of his palace "in Polish taste."[7] After the disgrace and exile of the famous courtier, his second cousin Prince Boris Golitsyn became one of the closest followers of Peter the Great, who by that time had seized power. Boris Golitsyn commissioned the famous church in Dubrovitsy near Moscow (1690–1704).[8] A central-plan structure on a heavy, rusticated socle, finished with a cupola surrounded by a crown, it is adorned by numerous statues and rich sculptural decoration, including heraldic images. It is one of the most distinctive mannerist buildings of the age of Peter the Great.

Peter's mother's family, the Naryshkins, also created their own architectural manner. Typical of Naryshkin buildings was a tall, centralized church composed of a number of geometrically clear volumes, placed on a high socle and surrounded with an open gallery. Also typical was the use of interpretations of Ukrainian baroque motifs in the decoration of these churches. In the early twentieth century the style became known as Naryshkin baroque. Examples include churches in Fili, Z'uzino, and Troitske-Golenischevo, among others.[9]

Here the use of the term *baroque* seems to me unwarranted. The massing of Naryshkin baroque churches is more evidently connected with the central-plan buildings of the Renaissance. This type of composition passed through a number of versions, from Italian architectural treatises, which appeared in central Europe in the sixteenth and seventeenth centuries, to various attempts at implementation in Ukraine and Belorussia (Belarus). At the time of Peter the Great these countries were part of Poland. The majority of their inhabitants adhered to the Orthodox Church and preserved their connections with Russia. The presence in Moscow of Ukrainian architects, masons, and carvers is documented. And although some of their works are close to the decorative motifs of the baroque, at that stage of the development of Russian architecture it is more likely that they were searching for an artistic language in a context of post-Byzantine mannerism than for a baroque style in the European sense. It is easy to find elements reminiscent of baroque buildings of various European countries in the architecture of Peter the Great's time. But very rarely, only in a few buildings, is it possible to discern the systematic use of the artistic principles and forms of this style.

The buildings commissioned in Moscow by Prince Alexander Menshikov, one of the beloved favorites of Peter the Great, illustrate another special architectural manner. The construction history of his residences is very complicated, but it is reasonable to conclude that the church of Saint Gabriel the Archangel (better known as the Menshikov Tower), built on his city estate in Moscow, has the elements of a distinctly European baroque.[10] Again, these elements are not used in the context of a stylistic system; on the contrary, they are torn out of one. The volutes of the church are an example. In baroque buildings they are typically used in the decoration of portals, windows, or attics, but in this case they are placed at ground level and transformed into gigantic buttresses. Here the baroque has been dissected into characteristic details and applied in a mannerist way.

The architectural tastes of the epoch of Peter the Great in Moscow were an aspect of the turn to the West. Johann Gottfried Shädel of Hamburg[11] and the Italian Giovanni Mario Fontana[12] worked for Menshikov, architects from Saxony[13] for Boris Golitsyn. Many aristocrats, including the Naryshkins and the Menshikovs, commissioned work from the Ukrainian architect Ivan Zarudny,[14] who studied in Poland. But there is no basis for identifying a single Muscovite architectural style in this period. Its appearance would have required an authoritative will capable of melding into a single tendency the disparate attempts to emulate European achievements. That will existed in Saint Petersburg, in imperial power and its ideology, which needed an artistic expression that could speak for the reformed state.

After the foundation of Saint Petersburg, Peter the Great's building activity assumed new features. The emperor started to implement his utopia, to give visual form to the new state. It is important to underline that, along with new laws and state institutions, he undertook the creation of a new environment, through means that were not symbolic, but realistic. Earlier in Russia, the expression of ideology through architecture relied on the symbolism of discrete forms and decorative elements while preserving traditional spatial structures. Now ideology was expressed through the creation of new types of space, in both architecture and city planning. In the imagination of Peter the Great, the city and the life within it came together. He believed that a new form created according to his will and taste would change ways of life.

The most astonishing document in this connection is the plan for a new capital on the Baltic Sea, thought to be from the emperor's own hand (fig. 3).[15] He proposed to situate the city far from the present site of Saint Petersburg, on the long and narrow island of Kotlin, more then ten kilometers from the mouth of the Neva, in open sea in the Gulf of Finland. The emperor issued an entire series of decrees for building a capital city on Kotlin Island after construction had begun on the Peter and Paul Fortress and the Admiralty on the site of the future Saint Petersburg.

The fortress was erected according to European models, with regularly planned *Vorstädte* (settlements), as was a fortified dockyard with housing for workers, all types that were well known to Peter, who had built more than twenty fortified settlements of this sort during the war fought with

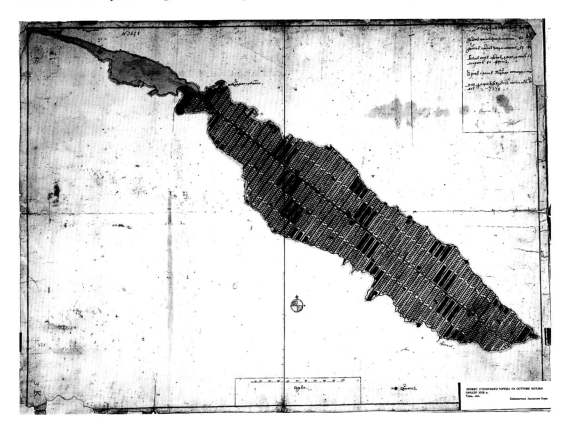

3. Peter the Great, *Plan for a Capital City on Kotlin Island*, c. 1709, pen and ink
Department of Architectural History, Library of Moscow Architectural Institute, collection of photographs and negatives

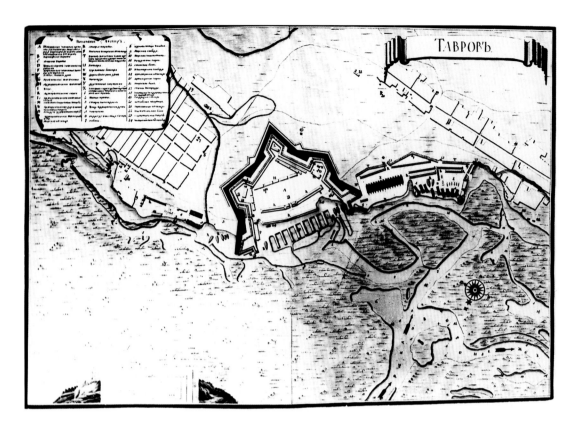

4. Unknown draftsman, *Plan of the New Town of Tavrov with Fortified Dockyards*, 1690–1700, pen and ink with watercolor
Library of Moscow Architectural Institute

Turkey over access to the Black Sea at the end of the seventeenth century, well before Saint Petersburg (fig. 4).

All were military or naval establishments. By contrast, the conception of a city that reflected the emperor's vision of ordinary civilian life was totally new. By examining his plan for the city on Kotlin Island, we can picture this existence, which, it must be said, seems truly frightful.

The whole island, according to Peter's sketch, was to be transformed into a city. The plan was strung along the axis of a long central avenue, as if impaled on a sharp sword, with parallel canals along both of its banks. The main avenue was crossed by shorter perpendicular streets and canals forming equal-sized blocks. The impression of a mechanical order is strengthened by the plots for private owners, which are of uniform size despite an edict that representatives of different social groups should build dwellings on Kotlin: gentry, merchants, and workers, each group to consist of 3,000 inhabitants. The highly regular spatial scheme clearly reflected the notion that all subjects were equal before the absolute power of the emperor.

The project was unsuccessful. No one was willing to live on an island in the middle of the sea, and severe decrees were to no avail. Nevertheless, Peter forced the architect Domenico Trezzini to use these ideas in a plan for Saint Petersburg designed in 1714. By then it had been decided to situate the capital city on another island—Vasilyevsky.[16] Here spaces of the same character—a main axis crossed by perpendicular streets with parallel canals from one bank of the island to the other—were not only planned but realized, expressing Peter's conception of the order of life in the empire (figs. 5 and 6).

But the social structure of the city on Vasilyevsky Island was realized spatially in a more sophisticated manner. By this time, copying the Prussian system, Peter the Great had introduced into the Russian Empire a division of all the servants of the state according to official categories, or "ranks." The army, the navy, civil and court servants, and, to some extent, the clergy were divided into seventeen classes following a "table of ranks." For merchants, tax rates substituted for ranks. In the new capital on Vasilyevsky Island, a representative of every rank was to

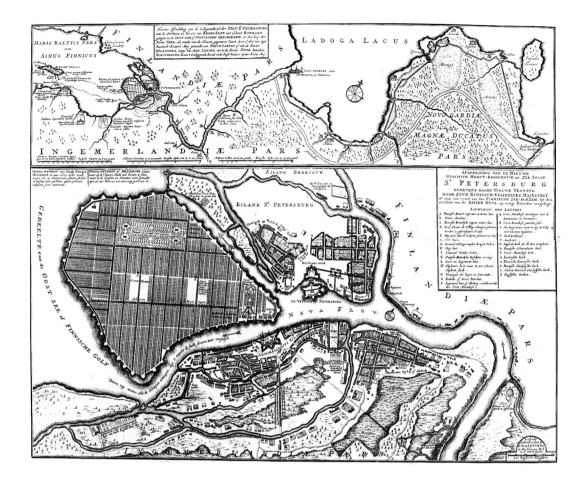

receive a certain spatial "cell." The higher the rank of a person in the imperial hierarchy, the larger the plot of land.[17]

It is known that Domenico Trezzini designed prototype town housing estates for every category of citizen.[18] These were different in size but organized in the same way. Both the individual houses and the estates were regularly planned. The flat decoration of the facades calls to mind an ascetic northern baroque (figs. 7 and 8).

The planning regulations for Vasilyevsky Island, which was announced as the "city" itself, were followed precisely. In the parts of Saint Petersburg that were designated as suburbs, for instance, in the Admiralty district, control over construction was not as complete. But there as well, the specifications for a regular network of streets were mandatory. And the siting of buildings and construction materials for private developments were regulated by imperial orders.

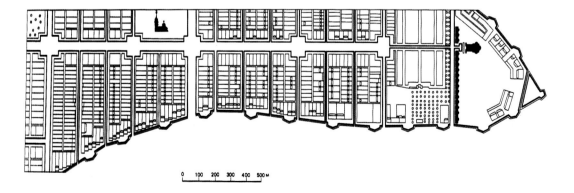

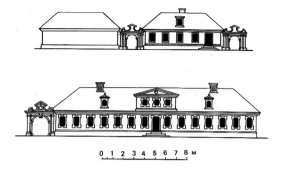

7. Designs for model dwellings for Saint Petersburg citizens of different social ranks, by Domenico Trezzini, 1714–1716 (?), reconstruction by Andrei Bounin, 1953
Library of Moscow Architectural Institute

0 1 2 3 4 5 6 7 8 м

It is surprising that the real image of Saint Petersburg, as fixed in the site plans of the last years of Peter the Great's reign and the first years after his death in 1725, appear irregular and even chaotic, despite all attempts to create a regular structure. Saint Petersburg consisted of many separate parts: the fortress and settlement on the island behind it; the Admiralty with the streets around it; the imperial residence and the suburb of the Summer Palace with its gardens; various small suburban settlements separated from each other by marshes or wasteland; and,

finally, the "city center" of Vasilyevsky Island. The suburbs were inhabited by artisans or laborers of different trades; were owned by institutions like the Alexander Nevsky Monastery; or were the property of various state organizations (for instance, the Admiralty developed the area near the sail factories, ropeworks, and tar works, where the Smolny (tar) Palace was later built (fig. 9).

All this seems very far from the early-eighteenth-century ideal of a European city. In fact, Peter commissioned such a plan from the French architect Jean-Baptiste-Alexandre Le Blond.[19] Le Blond's plan (1717) was a classic example of a regularly planned European city of that time, with all of the typical features: compactness; siting inside a circle of fortifications following the system designed by the French military engineer Sébastien Le Prestre de Vauban; the complicated, orderly hierarchy of state, civic, and dwelling spaces. The character of its structure derived from the importance of public zones, avenues, and squares, not from model estates such as those planned by Peter the

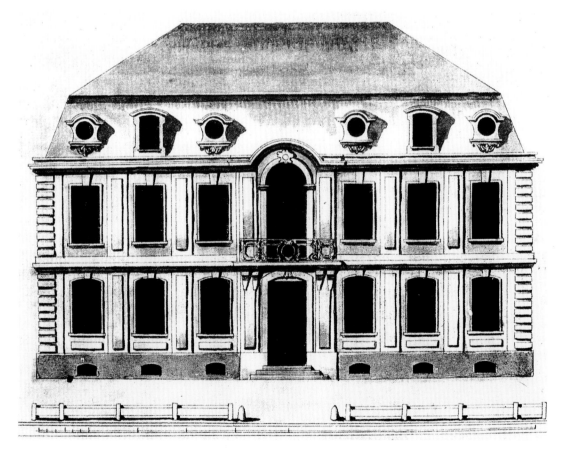

8. Jean-Baptiste-Alexandre Le Blond, after a prototype by Domenico Trezzini, *Design for a Model Dwelling for Saint Petersburg Citizens of the Highest Social Ranks,* engraving, second decade of the eighteenth century
Library of Moscow Architectural Institute

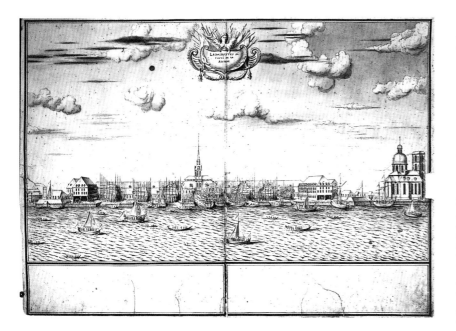

9. *View of the Admiralty, Saint Petersburg,* engraving, c. 1730
Library of Moscow Architectural Institute

Great and Domenico Trezzini. In Le Blond's plan, the role of the monarch is underlined by central placement of the emperor's palace. But the plan did not express the most important features of the new state power: strict control over every individual and the system of social ranks. It was probably for that reason that the emperor rejected Le Blond's design.

At the time of Peter's death in 1725, the image of Saint Petersburg was far from the image of a new Amsterdam or Berlin, but it had some features in common with them. At the same time Saint Petersburg's spare appearance, its division into districts according to professional or social rank, the tendency to regularize every part, and the state's regulation of private ownership—all present an unexpected parallel with the attempts of Peter the Great to rebuild Moscow.

Saint Petersburg looked like an ideal "New Moscow." Of course it was not the Moscow of the sixteenth and seventeenth centuries, or the Moscow of the later period, after its regular reconstruction in the classical era. The new capital recalled an ideal, utopian Moscow, as it existed in the imagination of the first emperor.[20] The idea that Peter the Great founded Saint Petersburg because he hated Moscow, or that, in creating the new capital, he disregarded the old, is incorrect. We have the whole corpus of his decrees on the reconstruction of Moscow, dating from the very beginning to the end of his reign. The

final orders about the rebuilding and improvement of the ancient Russian capital, including every detail, were included in a document titled "Instruction of the Moscow Police Chancery" (1722), which reveals the complete image of Moscow as imagined by Peter the Great.[21]

It is important to say that this document and the earlier decrees were devoted to domestic and commercial buildings, not to the architecture or property of churches and monasteries. The main feature of the Petrine city planning method was an emphasis on housing estates, as in Saint Petersburg. The planning principles that changed the residential context of the city were formulated at the beginning of the Instruction. First was the principle of "linear" construction: "All dwelling houses, whether someone should build something or rebuild an old [house], . . . according to the order should [be sited] along lines, and no building should go beyond the line."[22] Streets were to be straightened and made a uniform width, "so as in time to make all the streets and byways equal."[23]

The second paragraph of the Instruction ordered the "siting of masonry buildings [directly] on streets and byways, not in yards as was the custom in the old times."[24] The Instruction was not merely a compilation of earlier orders. A new and important regulation stated that, as part of construction, house owners had to "connect [their buildings] with the neighboring ones sharing a common wall."[25] Thus the houses would create an uninterrupted street front. Later in the eighteenth century this principle was expressed as the requirement of building "a continuous facade." As the summation of all the decrees and the Instruction, it is possible to imagine an ideal Moscow street of consistently designed residential buildings as the main element of a reconstructed city.[26]

The Instruction of 1722 laid down many other regulations devoted to civic life and not directly related to architecture. For instance, it directed bread sellers to wear robes of "white linen with white bands" and "all shelves and benches to be covered with pure canvas, and if someone disobeys, then he should be beaten with sticks."[27] Hundreds of orders of this kind are connected with Peter's reign. Through them it becomes obvious that, according to the ideas of the emperor, changing the image of the ancient capital in its architecture and modes of life would necessarily lead to a new structure of life in the city, and that the visual expression of the changes had a special role in this process.

In Saint Petersburg, Peter's determined approach to urban form influenced the stylistic features of buildings of the period. Architects invited from nearly every country of Europe—Switzerland, Italy, France, and many German states, but primarily Saxony and Prussia—had to follow the spatial schemes and building regulations endorsed by the emperor, as well as his tastes or direct orders. Professional concerns of architectural style and experience acquired at home were to be put aside. Architects of different origins often worked on a building in succession, and each brought one of the "tints" of European architecture at the turn of the seventeenth century. Thus in the first quarter of the eighteenth century a mixture of European architectural tastes appeared in the new capital.

It is difficult to see a permanent preference for the masters of one country in the architecture of the new capital in Peter the Great's time. But they were chosen according to something like a system of selection. The main principle was to invite architects who had gained the highest professional stature in their home countries. For some projects, architects who could best carry out the task of the moment would be chosen. Peter's tastes changed as he learned about new developments from books and travel. Sometimes the emperor set out to surpass European monarchs. In 1720 he requested an architect from China for the construction of pavilions in his gardens.[28] Unfortunately the Russian embassy failed in this assignment.

In the beginning the Swiss architect Domenico Trezzini (1670[?]–1734), together with his assistants, played a leading role. He came to Russia in 1703, soon after Saint Petersburg's founding. He was from Astano (near Lugano), had probably studied in northern Italy,[29] and from 1699 had worked in Copenhagen.[30] His manner can be connected with the northern Italian, especially Lombard, baroque of the late seventeenth century.[31] The strict graphic character of his decoration is probably due to the four years spent in Denmark.

There is, however, no general opinion about the characterization of his style. He was seen as belonging to the "Dutch-Danish" line in Saint Petersburg's architecture.[32] Some researchers insist on the Dutch features of his manner,[33] while others underline the parallels of his work with Danish architecture.[34] Recently it has been suggested that his work shows the influence of Sir Christopher Wren.[35]

There is no doubt that Domenico Trezzini knew the buildings of Copenhagen well. But there is no serious evidence of a specialized knowledge of Dutch or British architecture. Influence there may be, but it came rather through the tastes of Peter the Great himself. Indeed, the emperor showed his preference for Dutch ships, harbor buildings, sluice gates, and gardens.[36] But there is insufficient evidence that he preferred the Dutch architectural style of the late seventeenth century as the most suitable for the new capital. Britain attracted the monarch as well, mainly as a great naval empire rather than an architectural one. But the work of Christopher Wren so impressed him during his visit to Saint Paul's Cathedral in London that he is said to have made a sketch of its facade.[37]

It is impossible to argue, however, that Trezzini's design for the main cathedral of Saint Petersburg—the Cathedral of Saints Peter and Paul, in the fortress of that name—resembles Christopher Wren's work (fig. 10). The plan structure and the composition of the principal facade, with a single bell tower, are quite different from the corresponding features of Saint Paul's. But the most important difference lies in Wren's spatial sense, which was so natural for him as a great geometrician. The facade of the Cathedral of Saints Peter and Paul, on the contrary, appears to be a flat surface, a kind of a screen. It is probably possible to find sources common to the two architects, and Dutch churches and books on the architectural orders published in Amsterdam may be among them. But the differences in personal taste are obvious: Wren admired Gian Lorenzo Bernini, while for Trezzini it is difficult to think of someone more antithetical

10. Peter and Paul Fortress,
Saint Petersburg
Photograph by William Brumfield;
National Gallery of Art Photographic
Archives

They are both long structures, but different in spatial arrangement, reflecting their different functions. Both have decoratively treated gables in a regular rhythm, but of very different forms.

The Twelve Colleges building is made up of twelve pavilions, each for one of the twelve government bodies housed within, while the composition of the facade of the Copenhagen Exchange suggests a single volume, the great meeting hall. The two buildings display opposite attitudes toward the classical orders. On the facade of the Copenhagen Exchange, the orders are treated as decorative mannerist sculpture, with caryatids in place of columns. In the building by Trezzini, Corinthian pilasters are placed on rusticated piers framing arched windows, suggesting an arcade. In one case we see Danish mannerism of the early seventeenth century; in another, the early style of Saint Petersburg, which tried to overcome mannerist features in favor of the baroque.

In this connection it is important to remember that the main administrative building in Moscow from the time before Peter the Great—the so-called Prikazy, in the Kremlin—had the same form, a long body rhythmically divided.[40] In the Twelve Colleges we encounter a typical practice of foreign architects working in Russia: the building is organized in a familiar Russian way but is more regular than the Russian prototype and is clothed in a decorative order.

One of the most recent of the dozens of terms Russian art historians have used for Trezzini's architectural style is "Dutch-Danish-Russian-Italian."[41] Leaving aside his city planning works, the Italian element of this compound should be underlined. Until the age of twenty-nine, Trezzini lived and worked in an Italian cultural context in Ticino and Lombardy. There he spent about fifteen years of his apprenticeship, practically all of the period of his transformation into a professional architect. Having no notable success at home, he moved to Denmark, where his engagement at the Danish court was undoubtedly the result of a high evaluation of the skills he had gained in the Italian artistic sphere.

It is obvious that Trezzini was attracted to Russia by the opportunity to make his

than that famous Italian architect, despite Trezzini's Italo-Swiss origin.

Another of Trezzini's works for the new Russian capital is the Twelve Colleges, the principal government building, designed to house twelve bodies corresponding to ministries. Scholars have found similarities between the Twelve Colleges and the Copenhagen Exchange, although examination reveals no evidence of a connection. The two were built a hundred years apart, the Exchange in 1619–1624 and the Twelve Colleges in 1720–1742 under the supervision of several architects.[38] It is surprising that these buildings have so often been compared.[39]

fortune and the prospect of many commissions in which he could use his talents. And it is obvious that he found it extremely difficult to live and work in the unusual circumstances. But it seems that at the same time he tried to keep his individual style. Having absorbed the manner of the epoch of Peter the Great, he managed to preserve the elements of the northern Italian baroque, which we can recognize in the flat decoration of the facades of Milanese palazzi of his time. He continued to play an important role throughout the reign of Peter the Great, even though many other foreign architects were invited to the new capital of Russia. He even became the founder of a kind of architectural clan; Carlo Giuseppe Trezzini[42] and Pietro Antonio Trezzini[43] collaborated on many of his works. Both of them continued to work in Saint Petersburg until 1768[44] and thus were active throughout the baroque period in Russia (the style disappeared from Saint Petersburg soon after Catherine the Great came to power in 1762). This fact is important for understanding the historical role of Trezzini and his collaborators: throughout the age of the baroque in Saint Petersburg, architects from northern Italy—to be more precise, representatives of the Lombard artistic tradition—were present.

After 1712, when Saint Petersburg was officially designated the capital of the empire, the speed and scale of its construction changed. In 1713 the Prussian architect Andreas Schlüter was invited to Saint Petersburg. At home, he had served as *Oberbaudirektor* at the Prussian court until the death of Frederick I and had built the Arsenal on Unter den Linden in Berlin.[45] Frederick I was an ally of Peter the Great, and the Russian sovereign paid careful attention to what was happening in Berlin. The importance of Prussian town planning models in the creation of Saint Petersburg's plan and spatial configuration has been insufficiently recognized. In this connection it is important to look at the relationship between the famous "three axes" formed by the main avenues in the Admiralty district of Saint Petersburg and the same planning concept in the Friedrichsvorstadt in Berlin in the first years of the eighteenth century.[46]

With Schlüter's arrival the architecture of Saint Petersburg became more exuberant.

Baroque features, not only in sculptural decoration, but also in the more elaborate spatial compositions of the buildings, became more pronounced. It is difficult to speak of a special Schlüter style in Saint Petersburg because the master died only a year after his arrival. But it was on Schlüter's initiative that the very simple facades of the emperor's Summer Palace were decorated with bas-reliefs (fig. 11).[47] The decoration of the palace is more restrained than that of Schlüter's Arsenal in Berlin and has a more allegorical character. Some researchers cite the influence on the master of a Dutch manner,[48] but too few of his buildings exist to provide strong evidence for the assertion. After the famous Prussian architect's death, his pupil Johann Braunstein, who came to Russia with Schlüter and worked there for the rest of his life, continued and developed his manner. Johann Gottfried Schädel came from Hamburg to work with Schlüter as well; he stayed in Russia until 1752, but it is difficult to assess his role in the creation of Saint Petersburg's architectural style. The many documents he left provide evidence that he was a master mason rather than an architect. His activity was connected primarily with the construction or finishing of buildings designed by other architects.[49]

The German line in the architecture of Saint Petersburg was not interrupted after Schlüter's death. Georg Johann Mattarnovy was invited to Russia from Dresden on Schlüter's recommendation. They had worked together at the court of elector of Saxony and later king of Poland August the Strong, another ally of Peter the Great. Mattarnovy built both the church of Saint Isaac of Dalmatia (on the site of the later Saint Isaac Cathedral) and the second Winter Palace. The best-known project in which he participated was the building considered the first Russian museum, the Kunstkammer, on Vasilyevsky Island.[50] He designed the building in 1718 but died only months later. Construction, under the supervision of another German master, Nikolaus-Friedrich Herbel, the Italian Gaetano Chiaveri, and the Russian Mikhail Zemtsov, lasted until 1734. After a fire in the mid-eighteenth century, the Kunstkammer was rebuilt by the Russian architect Savva Chevakinsky. A central five-story tower connects two similar volumes

11. Summer Palace, Saint Petersburg, bas-relief by Andreas Schlüter

Photograph by William Brumfield; National Gallery of Art Photographic Archives

century, came to Saint Petersburg around 1714, at almost the same time as Schlüter and Mattarnovy. He worked in Russia until 1738, initially for Prince Menshikov. In 1720 he was appointed architect of the Alexander Nevsky Monastery, the most important religious center of the new Russian capital. The cathedral Schwertfeger built there is known from a model that survived (it was totally rebuilt by Ivan Starov in the time of Catherine the Great).[51] Schwertfeger's building incorporated numerous quotations from various Renaissance and baroque churches, including the main portal of the Gesù, by Giacomo della Porta, and even a cupola of the same type as that of Saint Peter's in Rome. But the general character of the building is closer to the southern German or Austrian than to the Roman branch of the baroque.

Schwertfeger's work in Saint Petersburg is unique not only in the reign of Peter the Great, but also in the baroque period in Russia.[52] A monastery of this kind would be quite at home in the suburbs of Vienna or Würzburg. During the Soviet period scholars identified Russian features in its architecture, probably because of the ideological bent of scholarship of that time. But it is difficult to find a more European building among the baroque buildings of Russia. Thirty years later, Francesco Bartolomeo Rastrelli, in his first variant of the Smolny Monastery, tried to approach this style.[53] Peter the Great's daughter, Elizabeth I, made him return to the more usual Petersburg manner. She also, but much later, ordered the introduction of features found in a typical Orthodox church. In the early years of Saint Petersburg, when its style was developing, direct quotations from European architecture were possible. Despite Schwertfeger's departure from Russia in 1719, construction of the Alexander Nevsky Cathedral was completed by Pietro Antonio Trezzini without significant changes to the initial design.

After Peter the Great's visit to France in 1716, Jean-Baptiste-Alexandre Le Blond was invited to Saint Petersburg as general architect for the capital.[54] He had probably attracted the emperor's attention with his book on gardens, *La Théorie et la pratique du jardinage*.[55] Peter the Great wrote of him, "This master is among the best and is truly a wonder."[56] At that time, the founder

(fig. 12). The relative complexity of the spatial composition and the richness of the decoration make the Kunstkammer the most "baroque" building of the age of Peter the Great. Some art historians see in the building features of Schlüter's manner, as if Mattarnovy had followed his drawings.

Theodor Schwertfeger, another prominent Prussian architect of the early eighteenth

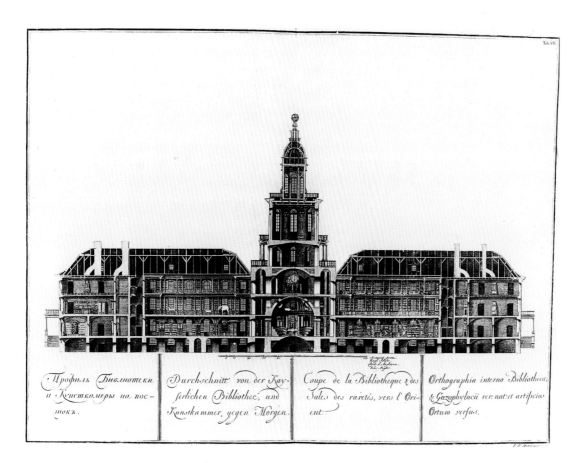

12. Gerasim Kachalov, *Section of the Imperial Library and the Kunstkammer*, constructed 1718–1734; engraving, 1741
Library of Moscow Architectural Institute

of Saint Petersburg wanted to improve the gardens of the Summer Palace in the capital and to plan the building and gardens of his residence outside the city in Peterhof. As mentioned earlier, Le Blond also designed the ill-fated general plan for Saint Petersburg, which, despite its aesthetic merit, the emperor would not adopt because it did not conform to his vision of the relationship between the plan of the city and the organization of the empire. In this case, a design in a European manner was less successful than was Schwertfeger's for the cathedral of the Alexander Nevsky Monastery.

Most of Le Blond's other designs for the imperial country residences were likewise unexecuted. Nevertheless, they made a strong impression on the emperor and the court. It is interesting to note that several of Le Blond's unrealized projects, which remained in the imperial drawings collection, did influence the development of the seaside residences in Strelna and Peterhof.[57] For France at the beginning of the rococo, Le Blond's ideas may have seemed too strict, but in the Russia of Peter the Great, with its passion for

regularity, their triumphal grandeur and geometric clarity seemed proper. In Peterhof the intersection of two compositions of radial axes still constitutes the most original feature of the park. One of the axes starts from the large cascade near the foot of the Great Palace. Another runs from the Marly Palace, situated on the west side of it. In designing the gardens of the Summer Palace, Le Blond had to follow Peter's wish for an orchard, recalling Versailles, even though the land was not suitable.

Le Blond died of smallpox in 1718. Despite the brevity of his time in Russia, his works proved important. He was the first to bring to the architecture of Russia features of French classicism in the manner of Jean François Blondel. Moreover, he introduced a new level of refinement to regular ensembles that changed the character of the Russian baroque. It is important not to overlook Le Blond's attempt to organize the entire building industry to meet the demands of the Saint Petersburg court. He organized nineteen workshops devoted to all types of building construction and interior decoration.[58] The architect brought a group of artisans from France, including the outstanding carver Nicolas Pineau.[59]

But the French influence in early Saint Petersburg was not as dominant as it might have been. While Le Blond was still alive, the Russian ambassador to Rome, Juriy Kologrivov, received an order from the emperor to find an Italian architect for the new capital.[60] Nicola Michetti was invited. At that time he worked for the papal court and was finishing the hospital of San Michele in Rome as assistant to the elderly Carlo Fontana. His work in Saint Petersburg incorporates motifs that could be linked to Fontana. But they are evident mainly in interiors.[61] Michetti was famous for sculptural decoration that seemed "ready to come out of the walls."[62] It is preserved today in his interiors for the Kadriorg Palace, near Tallinn. He proposed the same kind of decoration for other buildings, including the palace in Strelna.[63] In the exterior elevations of his Russian buildings, Michetti showed a strange northern reticence. Only rarely did the Italian master create dramatic baroque spaces, as in the arcade that runs through the central section of the Strelna palace. He is most famous in the history of Russian art as the engineer who played an important role in the making of the cascades and fountains of Peterhof during Peter's reign.[64]

Gaetano Chiaveri, another Roman architect who was in Saint Petersburg at the same time as Michetti, has already been mentioned. He would become famous for his buildings in Warsaw and Dresden.[65] Neither stayed in Russia for long. Michetti was in Saint Petersburg for four years, but he spent part of that time in Italy buying sculptures for the gardens at the Summer Palace. Chiaveri lived in Saint Petersburg until 1727 without receiving an important commission.[66]

Nevertheless, Italian tendencies in the architecture of Peter the Great were supported by the presence and activity of these architects, as well as by the Italian strain in the work of Trezzini and his followers. Also to be mentioned is Giovanni Mario Fontana, who rebuilt the Menshikov Palace (fig. 13).[67] In addition, the year 1716 saw the arrival of Carlo Bartolomeo Rastrelli, a sculptor with

13. Aleksei Zoubov, *View of the Menshikov Palace on Vasilyevsky Island*, 1714, engraving
Library of Moscow Architectural Institute

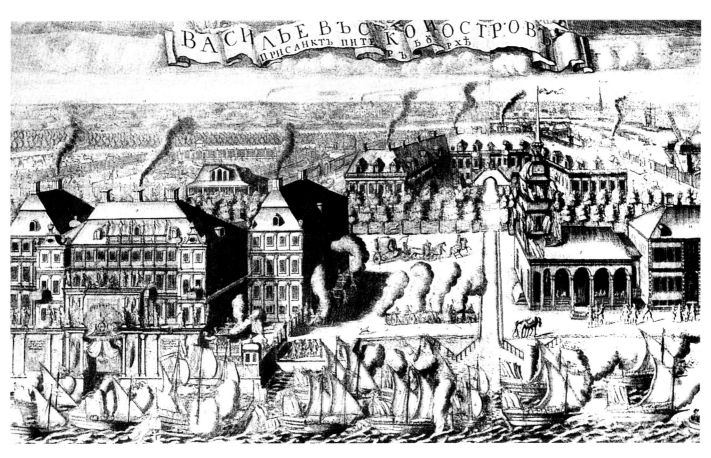

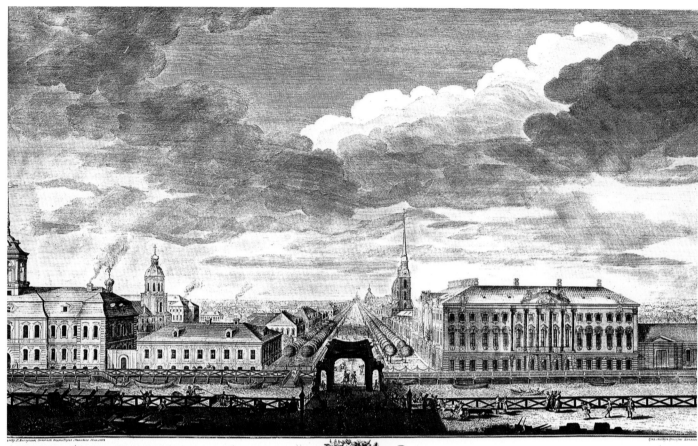

Проспектъ Невской Перспективой дороги *Vûe d'une partie de la Ville de S.t Petersbourg*
отъ Адмиралтейскихъ триумфальныхъ воротъ ко востоку. *en regardant de la Porte Triomphale de l'Amirauté vers l'orien.*

an international reputation and the father of Francesco Bartolomeo Rastrelli, who created the Russian imperial baroque in the 1730s–1750s.[68] The elements of this lavish style were certainly introduced by the Italian predecessors of Rastrelli.

The appearance of spatial three-dimensional decoration, sculptural and architectural—first of all, of the use of orders with fully round columns—would signal that the baroque in Russian architecture was approaching its mature form. The plain, geometric compositions of the time of Peter the Great only indicated the direction which Russian architecture had to take in order to become European. Throughout the reign of the first emperor, stylistic polyphony remained the characteristic feature of Russian architecture. The creative output of foreign masters in Saint Petersburg underwent a strange

transformation: The work of the Italians became more geometric, while that of the Germans assumed an Italianate character. The Swiss showed an inclination for the northern variants of baroque. And they all had to accommodate the emperor's admiration for Dutch interiors and gardens.

Overall, the work of architects of different nationalities assumed the features characteristic of early Saint Petersburg, among which the regularity that dominated everything should be underlined: the rational tendencies in town planning, the rectangular outlines and simple plans of buildings, a similar rhythm in division of elevations. Exterior decoration during the first quarter century of the new capital's existence developed rapidly from the framework of the earliest buildings to the sophisticated baroque of Chiaveri. And most important was the

14. Mihail Mahaev, *View of the Nevsky Prospect from the Admiralty, Saint Petersburg,* engraving, 1753
Library of Moscow Architectural Institute

determination of the imperial power that the architectural image of the city should achieve a European quality.

The post-Byzantine mannerism of the sixteenth and seventeenth centuries came to an end, leaving its last traces in Petrine Moscow. It was replaced by the unique style of architecture of the new empire. Perhaps Peter the Great imagined that his architecture was developing toward an image of ancient Rome. He never rejected the old vision of Russia as the new empire or the Third Rome, as Moscow was called from the sixteenth century onward. Among the expressions of this dream was Saint Petersburg's revival of antiquity in the mentality of the northern baroque at the turn of the seventeenth century.

But it was only a dream. Peter the Great did not realize the building of a new capital. His grandson, Peter II, moved back to Moscow. Another quarter of a century would pass before the planning of Saint Petersburg would impart the full glory of the Russian imperial baroque style to all the elements of the capital founded by Peter the Great (fig. 14). This achievement occurred during the reigns of two empresses, Anna I and Elizabeth I, mostly through the work of two men who were brought up in the spirit of Peter the Great's time, with his personal involvement in their education: Petr Eropkin in the planning of Saint Petersburg and Bartolomeo Francesco Rastrelli in its architecture.[69]

NOTES

1. Vladimir F. Odoevsky, *Sochineniya,* 2 vols. (Moscow, 1981), 2:146.

2. Igor E. Grabar, ed., *Istoriia russkogo iskusstva,* 6 vols. (Moscow, 1912), vol. 3; James Cracraft, *The Petrine Revolution in Russian Architecture* (Chicago, 1988).

3. Ivan Ivanovich Golikov, *Sravenie svoistv i del Konstantina Velikogo, pervogo iz rimskih hristianskih imperatorov, so svoistvami i delami Petra Velikogo . . .* (Moscow, 1810).

4. *Pis'ma i bumagi imperatora Petra Velikogo,* 13 vols. (Saint Petersburg, 1887), 1:109.

5. Ivan Ivanovich Golikov, *Dopolneniya k deyaniyam Petra Velikogo,* 7 vols. (Moscow, 1790), 4:192–193.

6. Elizaveta Ivanovana Bobrova, *Biblioteka Petra Pervogo* (Leningrad, 1978), 41; Natal'ia A. Evsina, *Arkhitekturnaia teoriia v Rossii vtoroi poloviny 18 veka* (Moscow, 1975), 59. The manuscript was a translation of Giovanni Pietro Bellori, *Veteres arcus Augustorum triumphis insignes ex reliquiis quae Romae adhuc supersunt cum imaginibus triumphalibus restituti, antiquis nummis notisquae Io: Petri Bellori illustrati, nunc primùm per Io: Iacobum de Rubeis aeneis typis vulgati* (Rome, 1690).

7. Petr P. Golitzin, *Rod kniazey Golitzinyh,* 2 vols. (Saint Petersburg, 1892), 1:383; Georgii K. Vagner, "O proishojdenii tsentricheskih kompozitsiy v russkom zodchestve kontsa 17 veka," *Pamiatniki kulturi* 3 (1961): 123–133; Andrei I. Nekrasov, *Ocherki po istorii drevnerusskogo zodtchestva 11–17 vecov* (Moscow, 1936), 384.

8. Andrei Grech, "Dubrovitzy," *Podmoskovnie muzei* 4 (1925): 70–87; Mihail V. Krassovsky, "Tserkov sela Dubrovitzy," in *Izvestia Imperatorskoy arheologitcheskoy komissii* 34 (1910): 55–71.

9. Feodor F. Gornostaev, "Barokko Moskvy," in Grabar 1911, 2:417–468; Vladimir V. Zgura, "Problema vozniknoveniya barokko v Rossii," in *Barokko v Rossii* (Moscow, 1926), 13–42; Nikolai I. Brunov, "K voprosu o tak nazyvaemom russkom barokko," in *Barokko v Rossii* (Moscow, 1926), 43–55; Andrei I. Nekrasov, "O nachale barokko v russkoi arhitekture 18 veka," in *Barokko v Rossii* (Moscow, 1926), 56–78; Irina L. Buseva-Davydova, "Kategoria prostrantsva v russkom iskusstve 17 veka," in *Barokko v Rossii* (Moscow, 1994), 16–26.

10. Elizabeta Kunitskaya, "Menschikova bashnia," *Arkhitekturnoe nasledstvo,* no. 9 (1959): 157–168.

11. Viktor G. Vlasov, *Arkhitektura petrovskogo barokko: Epokha, stil', mastera* (Saint Petersburg, 1996), 70–71.

12. Anna A. Kiparisova, "Lefortovskiy dvorets v Moskve," *Soobstcheniya instituta istorii i teorii arhitectury* 9 (1948): 45–54; Roman Podolsky, "Petrovsky dvorets na Yauze," *Arkhitekturnoe*

nasledstvo, no. 1 (1951): 14–55; Tatiana A. Gatova, "Giovanni Mario Fontana," in *Zodchie Moskvy*, 2 vols. (Moscow, 1981), 1:106–113.

13. Gerald I. Vzdornov, "Zametki o pamiatnikah russkoi arhitectury kontza 17–nachala 18 veka," in *Russkoye iskusstvo 18 veka* (Moscow, 1973), 21–25.

14. Vsevolod P. Vygolov, "Novoe o tvorchestve I. P. Zarudnogo," *Arhitekturnoe nasledstvo*, no. 9 (1964), 157–168; Igor E. Grabar, "Moskovskaya arhitektura nachala 18 veka," in Grabar 1960, 5:40–62.

15. Sergei P. Luppov, "Neosustchestvlenniy proekt petrovskogo vremeni stroitelstva novoi stolitzy Rossii," in *Trudy biblioteki Akademii nauk SSSR*, vol. 3 (Leningrad, 1957), 97–121; Sergei P. Luppov, *Istoriia stroitel'stva Peterburga* (Moscow, 1957), 54–55.

16. Marina V. Iogansen, "Raboty Domeniko Trezini po planirovke i Zastroike Strelki Vasilevskogo ostrova v Peterburg," in *Russkoye iskusstvo 18 veka* (Moscow, 1973), 45–56; *Polnoye sobranie zakonov Rossiyskoy imperii*, vol. 5 (Saint Petersburg, 1848), nos. 3016, 3188, 3399; Luppov 1957, 35–45.

17. *Polnoye sobranie zakonov*, vol. 5, no. 3305.

18. Luppov 1957, 10; Sergei S. Ogegov, *Tipovoe i povtornoe stroitelstvo v Rossii 18–nachala 19 vekov* (Moscow, 1984), 16–26.

19. Natalia Kaliazina, "Arhitektor Le Blond v Rossii" in *Ot Srednevekoviya k Novomy vremeny* (Moscow, 1984), 94–124; Tatiana F. Savarenskaya, Feodor A. Petrov, and Dmitry O. Shvidkovsky, *Istoria gradostroitelnogo iskusstva*, vol. 2 (Moscow, 1989), 107–109.

20. Aleksei A. Mousatov and Dmitry O. Shvidkovsky, "Predstavlenie o reguliarnosti v arhitekture i gizni russkogo goroda v pervoi tchetverti 18 veka," in *Gorodskoye upravlenie* 7 (1999), 21–25; Tatiana F. Savarenskaia, Alexei A. Mousatov, and Dmitry O. Shvidkovsky, "Moskva pervoi poloviny 18 veka," in *Arhitekturnye ansambli Moskvy XV–nachala XX vekov* (Moscow, 1997), 176–201.

21. Pavel V. Sytin, *Istoriia planirovki i zastroiki Moskvy*, 2 vols. (Moscow, 1950), 2:240.

22. Sytin 1950, 2:240.

23. Sytin 1950, 2:241.

24. Savarenskaia 1997, 399.

25. Savarenskaia 1997, 400.

26. Savarenskaia, Petrov, and Shvidkovsky 1989, 2:125–126.

27. Savarenskaia 1997, 402.

28. Rossiyskiy Gosudarstvenniy Arhiv Drevnih Aktov (Russian State Archive of Ancient Documents), fond 9, opis 2, edinitza hranenia 45, list 200; Dmitry O. Shvidkovsky, *The Empress and the Architect: British Architecture and Gardens at the Court of Catherine the Great* (New Haven, 1996), 167–169.

29. Mihail Korolkov, "Arhitektory Trezzini," in *Starye Gody*, April 1911, 17–36; Vladimir F. Shilkov, "Arhitektory-inostrantzy pri Petre I," in Grabar 1960, 5:85–87; Boris R. Vipper, *Arhitektura russkogo barokko* (Moscow, 1978), 43–46; Youtiy M. Ovsiannikov, *Domenico Trezzini* (Leningrad, 1987); Boris M. Kirikov, "Proobrazy kompozitzii Petropavlovskogo sobora," in *Kraevedcheskie zametiki*, vol. 2 (Saint Petersburg, 1994), 13–17.

30. Rossiiskii Gosudarstvenniy Arhiv Drevnih Aktov, Dela o viezdah, delo 12, listy 1–8.

31. Luciano Roncai, "The Construction of Great Building Complexes and Private Palaces in Milan during the Seventeenth and Early Eighteenth Centuries," in *Milan*, ed. Giuliana Ricci (Turin, 1999), 71–81.

32. Vipper 1978, 46.

33. Vipper 1978, 47.

34. Vlasov 1996, 56.

35. Kirikov 1994, 15–16.

36. Vladimir I. Piliavskii, "Ivan Kouzmitch Korobov," *Arhitekturnoe nasledstvo*, no. 4 (1953), 42; Vipper 1978, 43.

37. Andrei L. Pounin, "Petr I i Christopher Wren: k voprosu o stylevih istokah petrovskogo barokko," in *Iskusstvo arkhitektury: sbornik nauchnykh trudov* (Saint Petersburg, 1995), 34–42.

38. Vipper 1978, 168–169.

39. Vlasov 1996, 56.

40. Iogansen 1973, 45–56.

41. Vlasov 1996, 60.

42. Korolkov 1911, 30–36.

43. Gerold I. Vzdornov, "Arhitektor Pietro Antonio Trezzini," in *Rousskoye iskusstvo 18 veka* (Moscow, 1968), 20–30.

44. Vlasov 1996, 61–62.

45. Vasiliy S. Voinov, "Andreas Schlüter—arhitektor Petra Velikogo: K voprosu o formirovanii stylia 'Petrovskoye barokko,'" in *Sovetskoye iskusstvoznanie iskusstvo*, 2 vols. (Moscow, 1976), 1:45–67.

46. Savarenskaia, Petrov, and Shvidkovsky 1989, 78–79.

47. Rossiysky Gosudarstvenny Arhiv Drevnih Aktov, Kabinet Petra I, edinitza hranenia 57, listy 38–39.

48. Vipper 1978, 47.

49. Shilkov 1960, 93.

50. Alexandre Lipman, *Petrovskaya kunstkamera* (Moscow, 1945); *Palaty Sankt-Peterbourgskoy Akademii Nauk, Biblioteki i Kunstkamery* (Saint Petersburg, 1741).

51. Museum of the Russian Academy of Fine Arts in Saint Petersburg, model of Alexander Nevsky Cathedral.

52. Antonin A. V. Sviatyni, *Sankt-Peterburga* (Saint Petersburg, 1994), 1:32–34.

53. *Triumph of the Baroque: Architecture in Europe, 1600–1700*, ed. Henry A. Millon [exh. cat., Palazzina di Caccia di Stupinigi] (Turin, 1999), 582–584.

54. Kaliazina 1984; Boris Lossky, *Le Blond* (Prague, 1936), 193; Boris Lossky, "L'Hôtel de Vendôme," *Gazette des beaux-arts* 2 (1934), 30.

55. Jean-Baptiste-Alexandre Le Blond, *La Théorie et la pratique du jardinage: ou l'on traite a fond des beaux jardins apelles communement les jardins de proprete, comme sont les parterres, les bosquets, les boulingrins, &c . . .* (Paris, 1709).

56. Shilkov 1960, 14.

57. Tatiana B. Doubiago, *Russkie reguliarnie sady i parki* (Leningrad, 1963), 63–101; Elena A. Borisova, Arkadiy F. Krasheninnikov, and Anatoliy N. Petrov, *Arhitekturnie pamiatniki okrestnostei Leningrada* (Leningrad, 1983), 322–334, 580–582; and Anna N. Voronikhina, ed., *Arkhitekturnaia grafika Rossii: Pervaya polovina 18 veka* [exh. cat., Hermitage State Museum] (Leningrad, 1981), 52–57.

58. Vipper 1978, 49.

59. David Rosh, "Risunki Nikolaia Pino, prednaznachennie dlia Rossii," *Starie Gody* (May 1913), 3–21; Leningrad 1981, 120–125.

60. Grabar 1911, 3:141; Vipper 1978, 53.

61. German G. Grimm, "Proetky arhitektora N. Miketti dlia Peterburga i okrestnostei v sobranii Ermitazha," in *Soobshcheniia Gosudarstvennogo Ermitazha* 13 (1957), 21–24.

62. Vipper 1978, 52.

63. Anna N. Voronikhina, *Peterburg i ego okrestnosti v chertegah i risunkah russkih arhitektorov pervoi chetverti 18 veka* (Leningrad, 1972), 33–41.

64. Shilkov 1960, 97.

65. Eberhard Hempel, *Gaetano Chiaveri, der Architekt der katholischen Hofkirche zu Dresden* (Dresden, 1956); Eberhard Hempel, "Gaetano Chiaveri: Supplementi alle opere dell'architetto romano," *Palladio* 7 (1957), 172–178; Vladimir F. Shilkov, "Dve raboty arhitektora Kiaveri v Rossii," in *Arkhitekturnoe nasledstvo*, no. 9 (1964), 61–64.

66. Shilkov 1960, 113.

67. Ninel V. Kaliazina, *Dvorets Menshikova: Khudozhestvennaia kul'tura epokhi* (Moscow, 1986).

68. Petr N. Petrov, "Materialy dlia biografii grafa Rastrelli," *Zodchiy* 5 (1876): 55; Boris R. Vipper, "B. B. Rastrelli," in Grabar 1960, 5:175.

69. Bobrova, *Biblioteka*, 1978, 41.

GILES WORSLEY

Institute of Historical Research, University of London

Wren, Vanbrugh, Hawksmoor, and Archer: The Search for an English Baroque

To illustrate the entrance hall at Castle Howard, Yorkshire (fig. 1), designed by Sir John Vanbrugh with Nicholas Hawksmoor in about 1699, and then express doubts about the existence of an English baroque may seem perverse. Here, surely, emerging fully formed, *is* the English baroque, a domed interior of astonishing spatial complexity that would hardly look out of place if dropped into a contemporary Italian church.

The entrance hall at Castle Howard is proof that the English were quite capable of designing recognizably baroque buildings that fit comfortably within the Continental baroque tradition. What is astonishing is how rare an example it is. Cast around for other truly baroque buildings in England and the list is soon exhausted: Sir Christopher Wren's Saint Paul's Cathedral in London, perhaps, or certainly its west towers, and some of the spires of the City churches; Wren, Vanbrugh, and Hawksmoor's Greenwich Hospital, London; Vanbrugh and Hawksmoor's Blenheim Palace, Oxfordshire; Hawkmoor's Easton Neston, Northamptonshire; a handful of churches, country houses, and garden buildings by Thomas Archer. And then what?

The English baroque was a stuttering phenomenon, a handful of works that bear comparison with anything on the Continent, but little more. Reasons for the scarcity of examples are not hard to find. For a start, classical architecture was a late-developing phenomenon in England. The complexity of baroque designs called for a mastery of the classical language that was lacking in England in the middle years of the seventeenth century, despite the earlier efforts of Inigo Jones. Sir Roger Pratt noted at the time: "Architecture here has not as yet received those advantages which it has in other parts, it continuing here almost as rude as it was at the very first."[1] It was not until the end of the century that a sufficient level of skill had developed, thanks largely to the rigorous exertions of Sir Christopher Wren, above all in Saint Paul's Cathedral and the City churches.

Then there was the limited nature of the English monarchy. The baroque as a style tended most to flourish where it was the expression of absolute monarchy, whether the papacy in Rome, the court of Louis XIV at Versailles, or a petty German principality. England, by contrast, was a parliamentary democracy, or, perhaps it would be fairer to say, a parliamentary oligarchy. The struggle between Crown and Parliament, which had led to civil war in 1642, was finally resolved in Parliament's favor with the Bill of Rights in 1689. Power now rested not with the king but with the landowning classes in general.

One side effect of this struggle was that the English were not prepared to tolerate a monarch who sought to express personal power through architecture, least of all in the capital. The only seventeenth-century monarch to try, Charles I, who longed to

Saint Paul's Cathedral, London, by Sir Christopher Wren, 1704
Photograph by A. F. Kersting

rebuild Whitehall as a great classical palace, lost his head in 1649. Charles II, who returned as monarch in 1660 after eleven years in penniless exile, began a great palace at Greenwich to celebrate his new power. He soon realized the folly of his scheme. The Restoration did not mark the return to absolute monarchical rule, and, as Charles II was anxious not to share the fate of his father, work at Greenwich was abandoned. The third of the building that was completed was never decorated. Instead, Charles II devoted his architectural energies to remodeling the ancient castle of Windsor, outside London. Here Hugh May created a fine, and expensive, sequence of baroque interiors. But instead of boldly announcing these with an impressive baroque exterior, as at Versailles, May masked them with gaunt, castle-like elevations. In doing so he emphasized the quintessential Englishness of Windsor Castle, consciously linking the monarch with medieval ancestors who had lived there before him. Windsor Castle, which could have been a great baroque statement of power, instead became a statement about the monarch's self-conscious identification with his country.

In London English monarchs were forced to put up with rambling Tudor Whitehall Palace until it burned down in 1698. Despite regular calls, it was never rebuilt. Instead, the court moved to the even more decrepit Saint James' Palace, the monarchs, William and Mary, preferring to live at Kensington Palace, no more than a large suburban house, and at Hampton Court, Middlesex, another Tudor palace only partially rebuilt. The Hanoverian kings followed their example.

Thus those who might have wanted to develop a baroque manner could not rely on its usual exponent, the monarch. Nor was there much opportunity for the large public works encouraged by absolute monarchies, such as new city plans, barracks, hospitals, orphanages, or state-funded industries. Royal revenues were too small and the state's power was too circumscribed for such activities.

Only very occasionally were the English prepared to fund major architectural statements, and when they did, it was not the monarch who was celebrated but the English nation, and in particular the feats of English arms. Thus Charles II's abortive Green-

1. Entrance hall, Castle Howard, Yorkshire, by Sir John Vanbrugh and Nicholas Hawksmoor, c. 1699
Photograph *Country Life* Picture Library

wich Palace, abandoned in 1669, was completed and greatly extended beginning in 1696 as a hospital for seamen. Prominently sited on the Thames at the entrance to London, it was a proud statement of English naval power. Similarly, after the crushing series of victories that humbled Louis XIV in the War of the Austrian Succession, a great palace, begun in 1705, was built at public expense for the victorious general who had come to symbolize the English army's triumphs, the duke of Marlborough. The linkage was made explicit by naming the palace after his greatest victory, Blenheim. As Vanbrugh made clear to the duchess of Marlborough, "This Building, tho' ordered to be a Dwelling house for the Duke of Marlborough, and his posterity, is at the same time by all the World esteemed or looked on as a Publick Edifice, raised for a Monument of the Queen's Glory through his great Services."[2]

With power largely in the hands of the landowning classes, the principal outlet for architectural endeavor in the late seventeenth and early eighteenth centuries was the country house. Here again the baroque never took firm hold. As already suggested, English architects lacked the skills necessary for ambitious baroque designs before the end of the seventeenth century. The most commonly followed model for substantial country houses was the tripartite, astylar, pedimented design introduced by Sir Roger Pratt at Kingston Lacy in Dorset in 1663. The one major exception was Chatsworth House, Derbyshire, where the south front was rebuilt by John Talman for the duke of Devonshire in 1687. Here the model was not baroque, but Palladian: the range at Greenwich Palace designed by Inigo Jones' pupil John Webb in the 1660s.

The first two decades of the eighteenth century are not much more rewarding. If one looks beyond the work of Hawksmoor, Vanbrugh, and Archer, the scarcity of houses that could be considered baroque only emphasizes their value.[3] When country house building surged after 1715, it was the new, neo-Palladian manner that landowners espoused, not the baroque.

If proponents of the baroque could not rely on the monarch or the true power brokers, the landed classes, neither could they turn to the other principal patron of the baroque, the Roman Catholic church. England was a Protestant country, so there was no role for the baroque as a Counter-Reformation style. As it was, few new churches were built in England in the seventeenth century, the exception being the fifty-one in the City of London rebuilt under Wren's direction following the Great Fire of 1666. Except for a handful of steeples built in the 1690s, these owe little to the baroque.

The Fifty New Churches Act of 1711 brought England closer to developing a baroque ecclesiastical tradition. The churches (only about a dozen were actually built) symbolized the high Anglican, Tory ascendancy during the reign of Queen Anne. From the beginning the intention was that they should make powerful architectural statements, in contrast to the rational restraint of Wren's churches, epitomized by Saint James, Piccadilly. For churches on this scale and with this degree of architectural ambition, the baroque was an obvious model, and Saint Paul, Deptford, and Saint John, Smith Square (fig. 2), both designed by Thomas Archer and begun in 1713, can fairly be described as baroque. The same could be said of James Gibbs' Saint Mary-le-Strand, begun the following year. But these churches, which were criticized at the time for being too directly inspired by contemporary Roman architecture, had no stylistic progeny. Most of the other churches commissioned under the act were designed by Hawksmoor and are far removed from conventional baroque, as will be explained later.

Despite these institutional disadvantages, there was a moment at the turn of the seventeenth century when an English baroque comparable to that of the Continent seems to have emerged. The stimulus was a building boom that followed the signing of the Treaty of Ryswick in 1697, ending a war with France that had raged since 1688. It was in the context of this peace that Charles II's incomplete palace at Greenwich was transformed into Greenwich Hospital and abortive plans were drawn up to rebuild Whitehall Palace with giant colonnades similar to those at Greenwich. These years also saw the building of the west towers of Saint Paul's Cathedral (fig. 3), together with the more baroque of the spires for the City churches, such as Saint Vedast, Foster Lane, and Saint Bride, Fleet Street. They were also the years in which Easton Neston was built and work began at Castle Howard.

All of these buildings were overtly baroque in manner. The giant colonnades built at Greenwich and proposed for Whitehall, the sophisticated play of curves and solids and voids of the west towers of Saint Paul's and the spires of the City churches, the manipulation of light and space in the interiors of Easton Neston, Castle Howard, and the Painted Hall at Greenwich, all would have been recognized as sophisticated essays in the baroque by Continental architects. But this brief burst did not last.

War is partly to blame. Hostilities with France broke out again in 1702, lasting until

1713. Although some building work continued, most famously at Blenheim Palace, begun in 1705 to mark the previous year's victory over the French, the decade from 1702 to 1713 was not a period of great architectural activity. Hawksmoor, for instance, had no new commissions between 1704 and 1711 and Vanbrugh had only limited work. This situation changed after the Peace of Utrecht in 1713. A new building boom, particularly in churches and country houses, made the second half of that decade particularly frenetic. But by then the architectural climate, which had been so favorable to the baroque in the late 1690s, had changed. Of the leading architects of the day only Thomas Archer now wholeheartedly subscribed to the style.

Archer had spent four years on the Continent, visiting Padua in 1691 and therefore, presumably, Rome.[4] Saint Paul, Deptford, together with its geometrically complex rectory, and Archer's other principal works, particularly Saint John, Smith Square; Heythrop House, Oxfordshire (1707); Chettle House, Dorset (c. 1715); and the garden pavilions at Chatsworth House, Derbyshire (1702), and Wrest Park, Bedfordshire (1709), are clearly baroque in their fascination with complex forms and curves. But they stand out as exceptions. Despite their quality Archer, who was essentially an amateur architect and, unlike Wren, Hawksmoor, or Vanbrugh, held no post in the Office of Works, remained a marginal figure in English architecture. After setting up as a landed gentleman in 1715, he withdrew from architectural involvement.

The architect who might have taken up where Archer left off was James Gibbs, who literally built on Archer's foundations when he took over the task of designing Saint Mary-le-Strand for the Fifty New Church Commissioners in 1714. Uniquely among British architects of his day, Gibbs had received a professional training at the fountainhead of the baroque, under Carlo Fontana in Rome. But when he tried to develop his own English baroque at Saint Mary-le-Strand in 1714 he was savagely criticized by Colen Campbell in the introduction to the first volume of *Vitruvius Britannicus* in 1715. A subtle baroque scheme for designing Saint Martin-in-the-Fields around a circular nave

2. Saint John, Smith Square, London, by Thomas Archer, 1713
Photograph by A. F. Kersting

was subsequently abandoned in favor of a more overtly classical scheme. As Gibbs discovered to his cost, Campbell's diatribe was evidence of changing public taste that was to lead to the rise of neo-Palladianism. Gibbs was forced to swim with the tide, abandoning his baroque aspirations in favor of a watered-down Palladian manner.

With Archer a marginal figure and Sir Christopher Wren growing old, it was Hawksmoor and Vanbrugh who dominated British architecture between 1700 and 1720 and who determined the fate of the English baroque. Their official preeminence in these years was clear. Vanbrugh held the post of comptroller of the Office of Works (the second senior official under the aging Wren) from 1702 until his death in 1726. Hawksmoor occupied a host of influential posts, includ-

3. Northwest tower of Saint
Paul's Cathedral, London, by
Sir Christopher Wren, 1704
Photograph by A. F. Kersting

tant on the west towers of Saint Paul's Cathedral, on the spires of the City churches, and on the abortive baroque scheme for Whitehall Palace. At Greenwich Wren may have been surveyor, but Hawksmoor was clerk of works and Vanbrugh a member of the board of directors. Above all, in the entrance hall at Castle Howard the two architects had shown that they could compete with anything that Continental baroque architects could design. But despite this they turned away from the baroque to create a series of extraordinary buildings that remain some of the most remarkable, little-understood masterpieces in Western architecture.

Hawksmoor, who had trained under Sir Christopher Wren, was certainly capable of baroque design on his own, as Easton Neston (1702; fig. 4), his first major independent commission, shows, both in the massing of the elevations and the complex spatial planning of the interior. But, freed from the rational constraints of his master, Hawksmoor soon developed in his own direction. What fascinated him was ancient Rome.

As he had never traveled to Italy to examine classical remains firsthand, Hawksmoor's interest in the antique was not based on the careful study of archaeological remains, as was the case with Andrea Palladio and Antoine Desgodetz. Nor was it rooted in reverence for Vitruvius, as their work was. It belongs instead to a long tradition of bold reconstructions of antiquity seen in the work of men such as Jacques Androuet du Cerceau, Pirro Ligorio, Jacopo Lauro, and Giambattista Montano in the sixteenth century and Johann Bernhard Fischer von Erlach in the eighteenth century. Fired by Hawksmoor's study of his extensive collection of books and engravings, it is perhaps best described as a neoclassicism of the imagination. As he explained when discussing "Authors and Antiquity" in a letter to Lord Carlisle, "I don't mean that one needs to Coppy them, but to be upon the same principalls."[5]

Though Hawksmoor never visited Italy—indeed, never left England—his obsession with antiquity comes out repeatedly in letters and drawings. One can see it in his design for a garden building at Castle Howard, inscribed "The Belvidera after Ye Antique Vid. Herodatus, Pliny, and M. Varo" and in his explanation of the antique precedents

ing key clerkships in the Office of Works and at Greenwich Hospital, as well as the office of surveyor to the Fifty New Church Commissioners. From 1715 to 1718 he was secretary to the Board of Works. Nor did he or Vanbrugh lack well-funded commissions with clients prepared to allow their architectural imaginations full rein, mainly private in the case of Vanbrugh, principally the Fifty New Churches Commissioners in the case of Hawksmoor.

No one was better placed with the skills, the authority, and the clients to inaugurate an English baroque. The two architects had, after all, been instrumental in the design of key baroque works that followed the Treaty of Ryswick. Hawksmoor was Wren's assis-

4. Easton Neston,
Northamptonshire, by
Nicholas Hawksmoor, 1702
Photograph *Country Life* Picture
Library

5. Triumphal Arch, Blenheim
Palace, Oxford, by Nicholas
Hawksmoor, 1722
Photograph *Country Life* Picture
Library

6. Jacques Androuet du Cerceau, *Reconstruction of the Arch of Titus*
From *Quoniam apud veteres alio structurae genere templa fuerunt aedificata* (Orléans, 1550); photograph The British Architectural Library

behind the mausoleum at Castle Howard.[6] His triumphal arch at Blenheim Palace (1722; fig. 5) was based on du Cerceau's unusual reconstruction of the Arch of Titus in Rome (fig. 6) in his selection of reconstructions of classical buildings, *Quoniam apud veteres alio structurae genere templa fuerunt aedificata*.[7] One of Hawksmoor's designs of 1720 for All Souls College in Oxford suggested a giant colonnade facing Radcliffe Square "after the Greek." This is almost certainly a reference to a colonnaded building in Greece illustrated by Serlio.[8] Given the chance, he would have rebuilt the universities of Oxford and Cambridge as Roman cities. One scheme for Oxford, inscribed in

Latin "Regio Prima Accademia Oxoniensis amplificata et exornata," includes such Roman features as a chapel in the form of a great columned temple, labeled "Capella Universitatis," a "Forum Universitatis," a new east gate in the form of a triumphal arch, and a colonnaded "Forum Civitatis" with a central column modeled on that of Trajan in Rome.[9]

Hawksmoor's obsession with the antique emerges at its most intriguing in his work for the Fifty New Church Commissioners.[10] With their soaring towers and bold masonry, these churches are unlike any other group of buildings of their time and owe little if anything to Continental baroque precedents. In some the antique roots of Hawksmoor's designs are obvious. He based the portico of Saint George, Bloomsbury, begun in 1716 and the only one of the six great churches that has a conventional Roman portico, on his reconstruction of the Temple of Jupiter at Baalbek, which he had made to illustrate the 1714 edition of Henry Maundrell's *Journey from Aleppo to Jerusalem*—a reference picked up at the time by William Stukeley, who noted that the portico was designed "in imitation, and of the size, of that at Balbek."[11] Hawksmoor then used a reconstruction of the Mausoleum at Halicarnassus—a subject that had interested Wren—as the model for the spire.

These two references are well known. What has not been appreciated is the way in which Hawksmoor derives the forms of the inside of his churches largely from antique models. Kerry Downes noted that Hawksmoor used Vitruvius' Egyptian Hall, either in Palladio's or Perrault's reconstruction, as a model for an earlier idea for Saint Mary Woolnoth.[12] Similar sources can be found for the interiors of most of the other new churches.

Saint Alfege, Greenwich (fig. 7), designed in 1712, was the earliest of Hawksmoor's City churches. At first sight it is the most conventionally classical of his designs. With its temple front and single-gabled roof, it is the closest of them all to a standard Roman temple, appropriately, in the engraving made of it, Hawksmoor referred to the "Templum Sti Alphagi" and reinforced the point by setting four emphatically Roman altars in front of the church. What makes Saint Alfege unusual are the projecting bays, with entrance and stairs, along the side elevations. The source for this is probably Vitruvius' Basilica at Fano, which, in both Daniel Barbaro's and Claude Perrault's reconstructions, also has a protruding bay housing entrance and stairs on one of the long elevations.[13] In both reconstructions the stairs lead to galleries, as at Saint Alfege. For the altar Hawksmoor did not follow the model of the sanctuary of the Basilica at Fano, which projects in the middle of the other long elevation. Instead he incorporated elements from Vitruvius' description of another basilica in which the sanctuary is more conventionally placed at the short end wall and terminated by a broad, shallow apse, as in Saint Alfege. This detail appears in Barbaro's reconstruction, but not Perrault's, suggesting that Barbaro was Hawksmoor's source.[14] As at Greenwich, neither Barbaro's nor Perrault's reconstructions has an external colonnade.

Hawksmoor chose a different model for Saint Anne and Saint George-in-the-East, both designed in 1714. In both cases the nave of the church is a large, square room with a column projecting in at each corner, marking the line of the galleries. The model would appear to be Andrea Palladio's reconstruction of Vitruvius' Corinthian atrium.[15] In Saint Anne the altar is set back, parallel with the east wall, behind what appears to be a proscenium arch. At Saint George-in-the-East it is another wide, shallow apse, presumably, as at Saint Alfege, based on the Vitruvian basilica.

The grandest of the new churches was Christ Church, Spitalfields, on the very edge of the City, which was also designed in 1714. It is unusual among Hawksmoor's new churches in having not a large, undivided nave, but a central nave and aisles divided by Corinthian columns. These originally supported galleries. The source again is probably Vitruvius, this time Perrault's reconstruction, which shows giant Corinthian columns supporting a gallery.[16] A particularly close link is provided by the pair of Corinthian columns that Hawksmoor used as a screen to separate the altar from the nave.

A similar pair of columns can be found in Perrault's basilica.

Hawksmoor did not follow Perrault exactly—but then it is a feature of Hawksmoor's use of Vitruvian models that he adapted them rather than following them literally. In particular, he used a flat roof rather than the French-influenced barrel vault preferred by Perrault. He also ran an arch in each space between columns, marking a series of barrel vaults over the aisles running at right angles to the nave. The form of these side aisles and the use of hexagonal coffer vaulting suggest that the idea may have been taken from the Basilica of Maxentius as illustrated by Palladio.[17]

Thus Hawksmoor turned to Vitruvius, as interpreted by Barbaro, Palladio, and Perrault, for ideas for the interiors of his churches. Vitruvius was less helpful with their exteriors, for he provided no model for the tower or spire Hawksmoor was required to include by the wording of the act that called for the churches: "fifty new churches of stone and other proper Materials, with Towers or Steeples to each of them." At both Saint George, Bloomsbury, and Saint Alfege the towers stand somewhat uncomfortably detached, to one side of the church. At Christ Church, Spitalfields; Saint Anne; and Saint George-in-the-East, Hawksmoor succeeded in incorporating the tower into the body of the church (fig. 8).

These three churches seem at first sight the antithesis of the Roman temple. Certainly, their bold towers, round extrusions, and unconventional porticoes owe little to the ordered rationality of Palladio's reconstructions. But Hawksmoor had access to sources that would have allowed him to explain his buildings as homages to ancient Rome; the temples in Giovanni Battista Montano's *Scielta di varii tempietti antichi* and, above all, the reconstructions of Roman temples in du Cerceau's *Quoniam apud veteres*. Tellingly, du Cerceau included among the reconstructions in his work a number of his own designs for churches in the same manner.

One of du Cerceau's temples allowed Hawksmoor to reconcile the commissioners' requirement for steeples with his own interest in antiquity, by integrating the tower into the body of the church, to dramatic effect (fig. 9). Du Cerceau also gave Hawksmoor license to include the curiously proportioned giant porticoes, boldly cut round-headed windows, projecting turrets, and bowed apses that are such a feature of these three churches (fig. 10).

Hawksmoor was also influenced by studies by contemporary theologians of the Church of England on the rituals and buildings of the early Christian church, as one of his drawings makes clear through its inscription: "The Basilica after the Primitive Christians." This movement, which Pierre du Prey has clearly documented, sought to provide Anglicanism with a doctrinal foundation rooted in the early church as a response to Counter-Reformation Rome.[18] Its research concentrated on liturgy but inevitably also shed light on church design and thus provided arguments against contemporary baroque church design. Although Hawksmoor was profoundly influenced by this thinking, knowledge of actual early Christian churches was scarce, and they afforded few practical models for Hawksmoor to follow. Thus, though his churches may have been underpinned by early Christian theology, their forms are the products of Hawksmoor's imagined Rome. As du Prey puts it, "while remaining true to his personal vision of classical architecture, [Hawksmoor] fulfilled the call for Anglican churches renewed through emulation of early Christian models."[19]

Hawksmoor's personal vision of antiquity may have been legitimized by the earlier reconstructions of architects such as Montano and du Cerceau, but to veer so far from the conventional path of classical architecture, where the accepted rules were tight and considered authoritative, was extraordinary. One explanation may be Hawksmoor's interest in the Hobbesian concept of fancy. David Cast, in his article "Seeing Vanbrugh and Hawksmoor,"[20] picked out this key phrase in Hawksmoor's description of Vanbrugh's designs for a belvedere at Castle Howard: "What Sir John proposes is well and founded upon ye Rules of ye Ancients. I mean by that upon Strong Reason and Good Fancy, joyn'd with Experience and Tryalls."[21] Cast goes on to discuss the use of the word *fancy*. "Fancy, as understood in England, was something close to Imagination, the part of the mind that envisages Ideas and Images, elements that come more from the mind itself than from nature, that is to say, less from mimesis, the imitation of the natural world, than from the separate world of intelligence."[22]

Cast argues that Hawksmoor was alluding to Thomas Hobbes: "If we come across phrases like 'the quickening pulse' or 'unexpected curiosity,' or see an idea like Hawksmoor's 'Good Fancy' we are entirely justified in tracing these back to the writings of Hobbes." As he explains, "Hobbes knew of Judgement, but his essential materialism, which directed him to politics, made him in time think of art not as ideal imitation but as mere resemblance and, as such, based on Fancy."[23]

Was it this Hobbesian concept of fancy that allowed Hawksmoor to break with the classical conventions—which from his studies with Wren he would have known presented a limited view of the past—and freed his imagination to create a new vision of antiquity? Fancy also helps explain the violent swing away from Hawksmoor's vision of antiquity to the ordered, conventional view of antiquity of the neo-Palladians. For Lord Shaftesbury, after all, all true architecture was made "independent of Fancy."[24]

If Hawksmoor is right in asserting the importance of "Strong Reason and Good Fancy, joyn'd with Experience and Tryalls" in Vanbrugh's work then the same reasoning may lie behind Vanbrugh's equally unprecedented designs, although the results of his thinking were very different.

Having, like Hawksmoor, demonstrated his ability to design conventional baroque buildings, Vanbrugh also soon moved away from that style. He shared with Hawksmoor an interest in antiquity that emerges in his garden designs and buildings. There is a strong sense of *Romanitas* in the bastioned garden he created at Blenheim, described by Stephen Switzer as being "after the ancient Roman Manner,"[25] and in the bridge there, built on the scale of a Roman aqueduct.[26] The temple at Praeneste as reconstructed by Pietro da Cortona and Andrea Palladio seems to have had a particular attraction, forming the model for the garden at Eastbury Park, Dorset; the amphitheater at Claremont, Surrey; and, through one of Palladio's drawings, perhaps even the Temple of the Winds at Castle Howard.[27]

8. Saint George-in-the-East, London, by Nicholas Hawksmoor, 1714
Photograph by Julian Nieman

The landscape at Castle Howard, where he worked alongside Hawksmoor, is perhaps the key example of Vanbrugh's interest in antiquity. It is possible to read the entire design as an attempt to re-create in England the landscape of the ancient Roman Campagna. Hawksmoor's Mausoleum and Vanbrugh's Temple of the Winds have already been mentioned. Among numerous other features that are best explained as Roman are the walls and pyramid, which are most plausibly seen as evocations of the walls of Rome and the Mausoleum of Caius Cestius; the straight Roman road that forms the approach to the house; and the meandering paths of Raywood.

This interest in physically re-creating ancient Rome in England, which was to be a particular feature of English neo-Palladianism, can be linked with the way in which, after the Revolution of 1688 and the establishment of a parliamentary oligarchy, the English ruling classes wrapped themselves in the

9. Jacques Androuet du Cerceau, *Reconstruction of a Roman Temple*
From *Quoniam apud veteres alio structurae genere templa fuerunt aedificata* (Orléans, 1550); photograph The British Architectural Library

10. Jacques Androuet du Cerceau, *Reconstruction of a Roman Temple*
From *Quoniam apud veteres alio structurae genere templa fuerunt aedificata* (Orléans, 1550); photograph The British Architectural Library

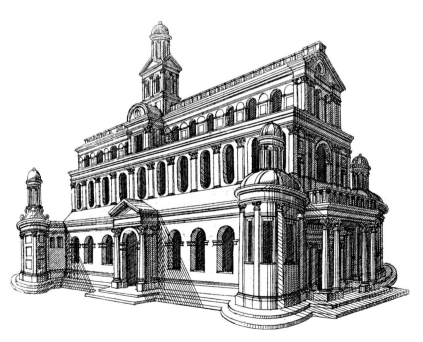

rhetoric and arts of antiquity, self-consciously identifying themselves with the Roman ideals of "liberty" and "civic virtue."[28] The rhetorical language of the remarkable landscape at Castle Howard emphasizes just those points. It may be that this conception of liberty, in which England was seen in contrast to Continental, and particularly French, absolutism, also helps explain why the baroque never established itself firmly in England. It may also help explain why neo-Palladianism, with its evocations of ancient Rome and of Venice, considered as a model for the English oligarchic state, established itself so swiftly in the years around 1720.

But antiquity was never the dominating passion for Vanbrugh that it was for Hawksmoor, and it does not explain the idiosyncratic designs of his country houses, his greatest works. Here what drove Vanbrugh was the search for an architecture that drew its inspiration from Elizabethan, Jacobean, and, to a lesser extent, medieval, buildings.[29] Unlike most English architects of the seventeenth and eighteenth centuries, for whom it was the detail, particularly the imitation of windows, battlements, and vaulting, that mattered in designing buildings that drew on England's past, Vanbrugh was not concerned with the detail of medieval and Tudor architecture. The direct imitation of specific antiquarian detail is rare in his work, and he was happy to use a strongly classical language in his buildings. What interested him instead was their form and massing.

Vanbrugh's use of Elizabethan models is clearest in his skylines. Most of his contemporaries preferred orderly skylines, broken up perhaps by a cupola or a calm run of classical statues or urns. For Vanbrugh, as for Elizabethan architects, an energetic skyline was essential.

Even more distinctive is the way Vanbrugh masses his buildings to create powerful silhouettes that, from a distance, appear like towers. The silhouette of the square pavilions rising dramatically above the roofline of Hardwick Hall (1590) finds strong echoes in Vanbrugh's first design for Eastbury Park (1718–1738; demolished 1775), in which the chimney stacks are grouped to give the appearance of a tower (figs. 11 and 12). Again, it is Hardwick that springs to mind when seeing the towers of the Kitchen Court at Castle Howard from across the lake. By contrast, at Vanbrugh House in Greenwich a pair of circular drums rises above the house, one at each end. An appropriate model could have been Robert Smythson's Worksop House, Nottinghamshire (1585).

The final design for Eastbury Park closely follows the massing of Wollaton Hall, Nottinghamshire (1580), another foursquare house with towerlike corner pavilions and a clerestory rising over the center of the house (figs. 13 and 14). The clerestory at Eastbury would have lit a great rooftop hall,

11. Hardwick Hall,
Derbyshire, by Robert
Smythson, 1590
Photograph *Country Life* Picture
Library

an extraordinary conceit unparalleled in the work of any other architect of the day. The only apparent precedent is Wollaton, which is presumably what Vanbrugh had in mind. In the event, the clerestory at Eastbury was never completed, but a comparable rooftop hall lit by clerestory windows was built at Seaton Delaval, a house that is in many ways a reduced version of Eastbury (fig. 15). At Wollaton a second row of clerestory windows lights the great hall in the center of the building. The hall at Blenheim is lit by similar clerestory windows, again an unprecedented feature for the age, although one that Vanbrugh also used for the great hall at Claremont.

One of the most characteristic features of Elizabethan and Jacobean houses is the long gallery. It was a fashion that had fallen out of favor by the early eighteenth century. Nevertheless, at Blenheim Vanbrugh included a "great gallery," a double-height room 180 feet long and twenty to thirty feet wide, along the west side of the house.[30] In scale and impressiveness the only fair comparison is with the long gallery at Hardwick, which stretches 166 feet and is twenty-two to forty-four feet wide.

Other features characteristic of Elizabethan houses to be found in Vanbrugh's work include walled courtyards with corner pavilions, seen at Eastbury, Seaton Delaval,

and, above all, Grimsthorpe Castle. Montacute House, Somerset (1599), and Syon House, Middlesex, are good comparisons. Similarly, Vanbrugh's interest in towers, as at Claremont, Surrey, Swinstead, Lincolnshire, and the Water Tower at Kensington Palace, probably owes something to Elizabethan hunting towers.

Vanbrugh's fascination with Elizabethan and Jacobean architecture was explored most fully in his own houses, where he had no clients to worry about. Here Vanbrugh exper-

12. Sir John Vanbrugh,
*First Design for Eastbury
Park, Dorset* (1718–1738;
demolished 1775)
From Colen Campbell, *Vitruvius
Britannicus*, vol. 1 (London, 1717)

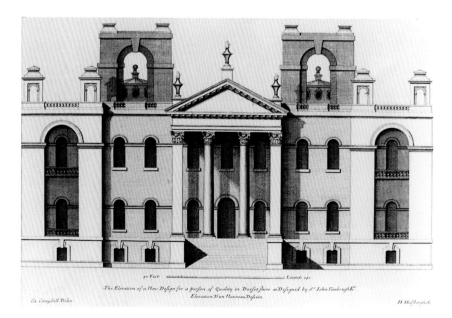

The Elevation of a New Design for a person of Quality in Dorsetshire as Designed by Sᵗ John Vanbrugh Kᵗ
Elevation D'un Nouveau Dessein

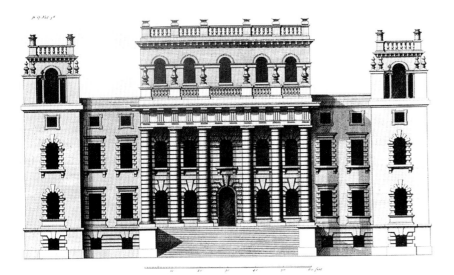

imented more directly with Elizabethan and Jacobean plan forms. The plan of Vanbrugh's villa at Chargate (renamed Claremont when it was sold to the duke of Newcastle), with its central hall and wings, is clearly modeled on an Elizabethan H-plan house.[31] Vanbrugh House at Greenwich, built at Vanbrugh's expense for his brother Charles, followed Elizabethan tradition by having an off-center hall and screens passage. Vanbrugh Castle, also at Greenwich, a mock fort with towers and castellated fore-buildings, and its now-demolished constellation of smaller buildings, of which Vanbrugh House was one, is a remarkable conception (fig. 16). Again it is hard to think of a contemporary comparison, but one obvious model is the Little Castle at Bolsover, built for Sir Charles Cavendish beginning in 1612 (fig. 17).

Though most of Vanbrugh's references are Elizabethan or Jacobean, some have medieval overtones. The great square corner towers rising massive and dominant over Grimsthorpe Castle, Lincolnshire, seem to echo the late medieval quadrilateral castles or fortified homes of the North of England, such as Bolton Castle and Wressle Castle in Yorkshire, and particularly Lumley Castle, County Durham, where Vanbrugh worked (figs. 18 and 19). Similarly the East Gate at Blenheim Palace, with its massive, round-headed archway, is perhaps best seen as Vanbrugh's reinterpretation of Norman city or castle gates such as Micklegate Bar at York. There is also something almost Romanesque about the arcading that lines the Kitchen Court, a

13. Sir John Vanbrugh, *Final Design for Eastbury Park, Dorset* (1718–1738; demolished 1775)
From Colen Campbell, *Vitruvius Britannicus,* vol. 3 (London, 1725)

14. Wollaton Hall, Nottinghamshire, by Robert Smythson, 1580
Photograph *Country Life* Picture Library

15. Seaton Delaval, Northumberland, by Sir John Vanbrugh, 1720
Photograph *Country Life* Picture Library

16. William Stukeley,
Vanbrugh Castle, Greenwich,
1721, pen and ink
Photograph Society of Antiquaries

17. The Little Castle,
Bolsover, by John Smythson,
1612
Photograph *Country Life* Picture
Library

feeling that is picked up in the double arcading of the hall at Blenheim. In the hall at Blenheim—and indeed the halls at Seaton Delaval and Grimsthorpe—the impression is almost that of sitting within the double-height hall of a great Norman keep (fig. 20).

Such a wealth of references to Elizabethan, Jacobean, and medieval buildings is exceptional in English architecture of this date, or indeed of any date in the second half of the seventeenth or the eighteenth century.

Nor is there any reason to believe that the architecture-obsessed Vanbrugh would not have known these earlier houses. They were, after all, among the greatest buildings of an age that clearly fascinated him, owned by leading aristocrats, many of them his friends or clients, and all easily accessible.

So what was Vanbrugh trying to achieve in this self-conscious and highly original series of references to an earlier English architecture? Understanding Vanbrugh's

aesthetic motivation is not easy, as he left few clues to his thinking and no record of his library. One well-known letter of 1707 that does survive is to the earl of Manchester, for whom Vanbrugh remodeled Kimbolton Castle: "As to the Outside, I thought 'twas absolutely best, to give it Something of Castle Air, tho' at the Same time to make it regular. . . . This method was practic'd at Windsor in King Charles's time, And has been universally Approv'd . . . to have built a Front with Pillasters, and what the Orders require cou'd never have been born with the Rest of the Castle: I'm sure this will make a very Noble and Masculine Shew; and is of as Warrantable a kind of building as Any."[32]

It is easy to assume that this letter provides the key to explaining what Vanbrugh was about: easy but dangerous. Vanbrugh was writing to Lord Manchester not about the design of a new house but about an ancient house that was to be remodeled. Hence his concern about what could "be born with the Rest of the Castle." This search for a "Castle Air," of worrying about designing in sympathy with existing fabric, was an essentially antiquarian idea that was not uncommon at the time. Vanbrugh cited Hugh May's work at Windsor in the 1670s as a precedent. Other examples he might have included would be Skipton Castle, Yorkshire; Chirk Castle, Clwyd; Drayton House, Northamptonshire; Hoghton Tower, Lancashire; and Hampton Court, Herefordshire.[33]

This antiquarian approach was the forerunner of the Gothic Revival of the latter eighteenth century, and it was into this strong tradition that Vanbrugh's work at Kimbolton and Lumley castles fits. In both cases Vanbrugh was essentially concerned not with form and necessity, but with decorative features; hence his consequent use of crenellations at both Kimbolton and Lumley, features that he otherwise used only at Vanbrugh Castle.

Nor was the idea of building in sympathy with existing fabric restricted to old houses and castles. It was a long-established tradition at the universities. Vanbrugh would have known Tom Tower at Christ Church, Oxford, of 1681, which Wren had argued "ought to be Gothick to agree with the Founders worke."[34] These were words Hawksmoor

20. Hall, Grimsthorpe Castle, Lincolnshire, by Sir John Vanbrugh, 1722
Photograph *Country Life* Picture Library

was to echo when working on All Souls' College, Oxford, in 1715, where he cited "your Revd founder" as a reason preserving the existing fabric.[35] Vanbrugh's celebrated defense of Woodstock Manor, "rais'd by One of the Bravest and most Warlike of English Kings," argues along the same lines.[36]

But all these examples concern alterations to existing buildings. Both Wren and Hawksmoor, and, later, Kent had no doubts that when it came to designing new buildings, the classical language was the only appropriate one to use. Vanbrugh was exceptional in using historical models for new buildings. This preference cannot be explained away by an antiquarian interest in the "Castle Air."

Vanbrugh's approach to his new buildings was very different from that at Kimbolton and Lumley castles. Here he was concerned not with the careful use of the symbols of antiquity (principally, crenellations), but with abstracting the essence of Elizabethan and Jacobean buildings. At Kimbolton and Lumley his motivation was the essentially negative desire to remain in keeping with an existing structure. With his new buildings he was using the past to invigorate architectural design. More specifically, it would seem that Vanbrugh was making a deliberate attempt to create a national style, a new, self-consciously English architecture, and not an architecture mired in the past, but a modern architecture. This ambition was to be achieved by marrying the forms of the last great period of English architecture, the prodigy houses of the Elizabethans and the Jacobeans, with their overtones of Elizabethan greatness, with up-to-date classical detail.

If David Cast is right, then the Hobbesian concept of fancy, discussed above, may have helped Vanbrugh break with the classical conventions and create a new architecture that combined earlier form with classical detail. A more directly architectural influence may have been the thinking of Claude Perrault, one of the most controversial architectural theorists of the time. Vanbrugh was certainly aware of Perrault's work. He subscribed in 1707 to John James' translation of Perrault, *A Treatise of the Five Orders in Architecture . . .* (1708), and it is likely that Perrault's edition of Vitruvius, published in 1684, was a source for some of Vanbrugh's garden buildings.[37] Lee Morrissey argues that Vanbrugh's position had parallels with Perrault's argument with French classicism. In particular, Perrault undermined the mathematical, universal understanding of Vitruvian architectural theory, pointing out that, if music is to be considered as an analogy for architecture, it is important to take into account the cultural differences in music. The way "harmonies" are applied "differs with different musicians and countries, just as the application of architectural proportions differs with different authors and buildings."[38] This parallel suggested that, instead of there being one universal classicism that all architects had to follow, it was valid for nationalities to develop their own forms of classicism, an argument that for Vanbrugh

could have been a justification for his attempt to form an English style.

The England of Vanbrugh's day was an increasingly self-confident nation. After the disastrous seventeenth century, in the course of which England had been torn apart by civil war, beaten repeatedly by the Dutch at sea, and finally invaded by a Dutch army that overthrew the English king, the years of the duke of Marlborough's triumphant campaigns were a liberation. With the signing of the Treaty of Utrecht in 1713, the English could again hold their heads high, confident that they were one of the most powerful nations in Europe.

It was natural that this confident mood should be represented in architecture and that an English architect casting around for a model on which to build should fasten on the country houses of the reigns of Queen Elizabeth and James I. These houses exuded confidence. Compared to anything built since, they stood out for scale and architectural ambition. What was more, the years of Elizabeth's reign in particular were implanted in the English consciousness as years of greatness. The Battle of Blenheim was a triumph on the scale of the defeat of the Spanish Armada. And as Downes suggests, as a playwright intimately involved in a theatrical world in which the works of Shakespeare and Fletcher were still regularly performed, Vanbrugh may have felt a particular affinity to Elizabethan architecture.[39]

But Vanbrugh's vision of a self-consciously English architecture was not to be. As with Hawksmoor, his challenge to the canons of classical architecture was too radical to be accepted. Instead, architecture in England went off in a totally different direction, toward an architecture that stressed respect for the classical conventions instead of seeing them as a starting point for new invention.

To call Hawksmoor and Vanbrugh baroque architects in any but the loosest manner is to misunderstand their buildings. That they understood contemporary Continental baroque examples and were capable of designing buildings that followed them is clear from their designs of the late 1690s and early 1700s. But they soon moved away from the Continental baroque to develop their own fascinations, in Hawksmoor's case antiquity, in Vanbrugh's case the search for an authentically English architecture.

They were able to do so because of a favorable conjunction of events. The absence of an absolute monarch meant that the state made no attempt to impose an official architecture. Hawksmoor and Vanbrugh were able to develop their own obsessions, at least to the degree that they could persuade their clients. In addition, English architecture was in a transitional state. Classicism arrived late, and despite the efforts of Inigo Jones, the level of skills required to develop a rich classical language emerged only toward the end of the seventeenth century. Thus by the time Hawksmoor and Vanbrugh reached maturity, English craftsmen were sophisticated and knowledgeable enough to cope with their demands, but classical architecture had not been established long enough to settle into fixed conventions. Finally, there was no academy of architecture in London to try to construct conventions into which architects should fit. Hawksmoor and Vanbrugh benefited not only from a skilled and knowledgeable workforce, but also from an intellectual freedom that allowed them to develop their own idiosyncrasies. Under the neo-Palladians who followed them, order and convention became far more important.

It is possible in all this that Hawksmoor and Vanbrugh owed something to the Continental baroque, even though they deliberately broke with it. The baroque age encouraged innovation and played down rules. It was a period of relative freedom, which perhaps allowed Hawksmoor and Vanbrugh to go their own way without appearing as eccentric as they would have in a time when the canonical rules were more strictly applied. Nevertheless, except for a brief period early in their careers, it would be wrong to label them as baroque architects.

NOTES

1. R. T. Gunther, *The Architecture of Sir Roger Pratt* (Oxford, 1928), 60.

2. Lawrence Whistler, *The Imagination of Vanbrugh and His Fellow Artists* (London, 1954), 237.

3. Possible examples would include Cound Hall, Shropshire (1704); Wentworth Castle, Yorkshire (1708); and Beningborough Hall, Yorkshire (1716).

4. Sir John Summerson argues that the plan of St. Paul, Deptford, owes much to Saint Agnese in Agone, in Rome. See John Summerson, *Architecture in Britain 1530–1830* (Harmondsworth, 1970), 234.

5. Kerry Downes, *Hawksmoor*, 2d ed. (London, 1979), 244.

6. Kerry Downes, *Hawksmoor* (London, 1970), 195; Goeffrey F. Webb, "The Letters and Drawings of Nicholas Hawksmoor Relating to the Building of the Mausouleum at Castle Howard," *Walpole Society* 19 (1930–1931).

7. Giles Worsley, *Classical Architecture in Britain: The Heroic Age* (New Haven and London, 1995), 59, and Jacques Androuet du Cerceau, *Quoniam apud veteres alio structurae genere templa fuerunt aedificata* (Orléans, 1550).

8. Worsley 1995, 61.

9. Roger White, *Nicholas Hawksmoor and the Replanning of Oxford* (London and Oxford, 1997), 86–87.

10. For a fuller account of Hawksmoor's use of Roman models for his churches, see Worsley 1995, 54–63.

11. "Family Memoirs of the Rev. William Stukeley: III," *Surtees Society* 80 (1887): 9.

12. Downes 1979, 192.

13. Daniel Barbaro, *I dieci libri dell'architettura di M. Vitruvio tradotti e commentati da Daniel Barbaro* (Venice, 1567), 219; Claude Perrault, *Les Dix Livres d'architecture de Vitruve* (Paris, 1684), 152.

14. Barbaro 1567, 211.

15. Andrea Palladio, *I quattro libri dell'architettura*, 4 vols. (Venice, 1570), 2:28.

16. Perrault 1684, 154.

17. Palladio 1570, 2:13.

18. Pierre de la Ruffinière du Prey, *Hawksmoor's London Churches: Architecture and Theology* (Chicago and London, 2000).

19. Du Prey 2000, xvii.

20. David Cast, "Seeing Vanbrugh and Hawksmoor," *Journal of the Society of Architectural Historians* 43 (December 1984): 310–327, quotation on 315.

21. Quoted in Cast 1984, 315.

22. Cast 1984, 315.

23. Cast 1984, 316.

24. Cast 1984, 315–316.

25. Stephen Switzer, *Ichnographia rustica,* 2 vols. (London, 1741–1742), 2:174–175. I owe this reference, which is not in the 1718 edition, to Robert Williams.

26. Howard Colvin, *Essays in English Architectural History* (New Haven and London, 1999), figs. 205 and 206.

27. Giles Worsley, "'After ye Antique': Vanbrugh, Hawksmoor and Kent," in *Sir John Vanbrugh and Landscape Architecture in Baroque England 1690–1730,* ed. Christopher Ridgway and Robert Williams (Stroud, 2000), 136–139.

28. For an analysis of the landscape at Castle Howard and the reasons for seeing it as a re-creation of the Roman Campagna, see Worsley 2000, 140–152.

29. A fuller account of Vanbrugh's interest in earlier English architecture can be found in Giles Worsley, "Sir John Vanbrugh and the Search for a National Style," in *Gothic Architecture and Its Meanings, 1530–1830,* ed. Michael Hall (Reading, 2002), 99–134.

30. The gallery at Blenheim was decorated by Hawksmoor after Vanbrugh's dismissal in 1716.

31. Downes suggests that the unusual H plan may have resulted from Vanbrugh's use of the foundations of an earlier Elizabethan farmhouse. This explanation seems unlikely. Houses built on earlier foundations normally adapted them to contemporary fashion. Kerry Downes, *Vanbrugh* (London, 1977), 51.

32. Kerry Downes, *Vanbrugh* (London, 1977), 48.

33. For a fuller account of late-seventeenth- and early-eighteenth-century antiquarian architecture in England, see Worsley 1995, 178–190.

34. *The Wren Society* 5 (1928): 17.

35. Nicholas Hawksmoor, *Explanation of Designs for All Souls, Oxford* (reprint, Oxford, 1960), 5.

36. Bonamy Dobrée and Geoffrey Webb, eds., *The Complete Works of Sir John Vanbrugh,* 4 vols. (London, 1927–1928), 27–30.

37. Worsley 2000, 137, 147; John James, *A Treatise of the Five Orders in Architecture . . .* (London, 1708), translation of Claude Perrault, *Ordonnance des cinq espèces de colonnes selon la méthode des anciens* (Paris, 1683).

38. Lees Morrissey, *From the Temple to the Castle* (Charlottesville, 1999), 59.

39. Downes 1977, 50–54.

AMSTELODAMI VETERIS ET NOVISSIMÆ VRBIS ACCVRATISSIMA DELINEATIO.

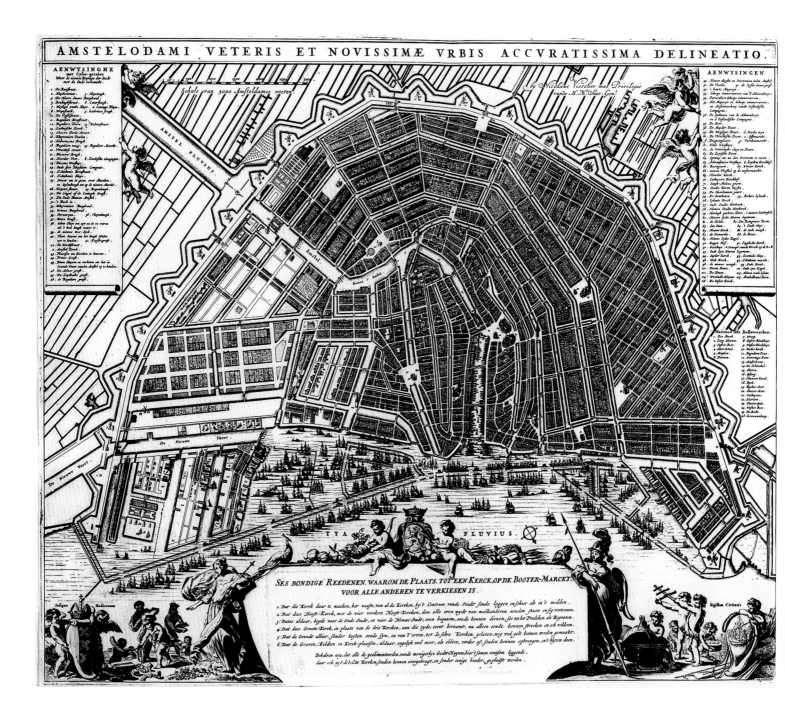

SES BONDIGE REEDENEN, WAAROM DE PLAATS, TOT EEN KERCK, OP DE BOOTER-MARCKT,
VOOR ALLE ANDEREN TE VERKIESEN IS.

KONRAD A. OTTENHEYM

University of Utrecht

Amsterdam 1700: Urban Space and Public Buildings

The Dutch Republic may be regarded as the most prosperous and advanced nation in seventeenth-century Europe, especially in the decades following the Peace of Westphalia (1648). Within the republic the province of Holland was the wealthiest and most influential region, and within Holland the city of Amsterdam was preeminent.[1] This paper concentrates on public building activity that responded to the tremendous physical growth caused by Amsterdam's economic prosperity and, in so doing, focuses on civic, as opposed to imperial, royal, or noble building projects. Here there was no king and almost no superior national government. The power of the States-General, the central authority of the republic, was restricted to war and foreign diplomacy. In all other regards Amsterdam was an almost independent city-state.

It is inaccurate to call this republican city-state a democracy. Although there was no nobility, for centuries Amsterdam was ruled by a rather closed group of about two hundred families whose members held the seats in the main bodies of the city administration.[2] In the seventeenth century the city was ruled by a class of wealthy merchants and bankers who had direct interests in shipping and trading companies and other commercial concerns. In their view the task of the city government was to create the best opportunities for commerce, from which not only they but the community as a whole

would profit. The seventeenth-century rise of Amsterdam as a center of world trade and commercial exchange caused an unprecedented expansion of its population and urban space. It was a task of the city government to maintain order in the growing urban structure as well as in political, economical, and social life.

The larger city needed new public buildings, not only those required by a center of world trade—mercantile infrastructure and its maritime defense—but also buildings for social control and betterment, such as churches, social institutions, and houses of correction. The city had no predetermined building program or master plan in place, but in apparently isolated initiatives we can discern a certain system in the planning of these kinds of buildings. They were commissioned and built by the city government and its dependent semipublic organizations to create a well-ordered mercantile society. This effort resulted in the development of several new building types.

The city authorities also closely regulated the aesthetic appearance of the city. In this period, when aesthetics were closely connected with ethics, the beauty of the city was regarded as an expression of good government as well as a symbol of prosperity. Order and beauty could first be achieved through a well-ordered plan for the city's extensions, one that would regulate not architecture in detail, but the character of the new urban

1. Nicolaas Visscher, *Map of Amsterdam*, c. 1695, engraving
From Nicolaas Listingh, *Niew Desseyn tot een Seer Groote, Stercke, en om te hooren, heel bequame Coupel-Kerck met een Hooren Tooren daer miden uyt rysende* (Amsterdam, 1695); Gemeente Archief Amsterdam

areas: scale of streets, squares, houses, and gardens. From the beginning it was established that space along three new semi-circular canals would become spacious and comfortable residential areas for the well-to-do. Noisy and polluting trades would be located in the outer parts of the new extensions. Although almost all houses along the canals were erected individually, building regulations ensured uniformity, regularity, and order in outward appearance, considered the first principles of beauty in seventeenth-century Holland. The city authorities also commissioned the planting of trees in public space alongside the canals and on squares as an expression of beauty, prosperity, and comfort.

The city government could enhance the beauty of the city through the quality of its own public buildings.[3] Of course the town hall and other representative city buildings should be designed in a more or less magnificent manner, appropriate to Amsterdam's position and power. But more utilitarian city buildings were also regarded as an expression of civil authority and civic pride. Therefore these too needed a certain imposing appearance. Architecture of high quality adorns the city and magnifies its fame, as Constantijn Huygens, secretary to the prince of Orange, explained in 1655 in a letter to the authorities of the city of Leiden. He argued that it was necessary to engage a highly qualified architect, not a mere craftsman, as the head of the city's building company "si decus et ornatum Urbis amatis" (if you love the grace and ornament of your city).[4]

The City's Building Company

As did any Dutch city, Amsterdam had its own building company. A member of the city council was appointed to oversee the company's finances. Design and construction were headed by a capable staff of master tradesmen: a stonemason, a carpenter, and a bricklayer.[5] Below them were dozens of employees and, when necessary, project workers. The master carpenter was responsible for all interior wooden construction. Although all facades were stone or brick, most of the structural components—floors, ceilings, staircases, and roofs—were wood. Thus the master carpenter was in effect the

technical engineer of the tripartite staff. The master bricklayer's responsibility included masonry not only of buildings and bridges but also of the miles and miles of quays in the new urban areas. More prominent in architecture was the contribution of the master stonemason. He and his fellows cut all stone elements such as portals, moldings, and sculptural decorations. Therefore the stonemason had to be a sculptor as well. During the first decades of the seventeenth century, when facade architecture was dominated by fancy and fantastic ornament, he was also responsible for the artistic part of the design. In the late sixteenth century and the first two decades of the seventeenth century, Hendrick de Keyser, as master stonemason of Amsterdam, was the preeminent Dutch architect. After his death in 1621 he was succeeded by his sons Pieter de Keyser (until 1647) and Willem de Keyser (from 1647 to 1651).[6] But their contribution to architecture was less prominent. After 1630, as architecture became more and more based on strict classical principles, there was no more demand for the artistic contributions of the stonemason. His work was now restricted to the production of classical details: capitals, bases, friezes, and so on, exactly following Italian treatises such as Vincenzo Scamozzi's *L'Idea della architettura universale*.[7] In 1651 Simon Bosboom was appointed master stonemason. He was not a sculptor but an expert in the classical orders. He published a small pocket edition of Scamozzi's orders, which was much used by his fellows and pupils.[8]

Although all three building masters were experts in construction, there was a certain lack of artistic capability in the city building troika after the death of Hendrick de Keyser. From the 1630s onward the city invited a famous architect from outside when a design was required for a new and prominent city building. Jacob van Campen, for example, designed the extension of the city orphanage in 1633 as well as a city gate and the municipal theater in 1637. He was also asked to design the new Town Hall in 1648, but he was never formally in city service. It was only when the construction of Van Campen's Town Hall had started that a city architect as such was appointed to work with the three masters. This was Daniel

Stalpaert, who assisted Van Campen in the realization of his project. Stalpaert was also engaged in the planning of the latest city extensions as well as the designs of several important public buildings commissioned by the city government.[9]

New Urban Space

During the seventeenth century the population of Amsterdam more than tripled, from 60,000 in 1600 to 200,000 in 1700. Many of the new inhabitants came from the southern Netherlands (present Belgium), and even more arrived from the east (especially from Germany). Of course all could not possibly find homes inside the confines of the former medieval city. The city was expanded in several increments from the end of the sixteenth century onward. It is amazing that this unprecedented population increase did not lead to rampant growth and uncontrolled development. Even though there was no comprehensive master plan for the city extensions, a series of interlinked decisions led to a clearly laid-out city plan, embodying a definite vision of economic and social organization of urban life (fig. 1).

As a result, in 1700 the city's area had more than tripled since the late sixteenth century, by expansion in four phases (fig. 2).[10] The first took place in 1578–1585 east of the old city, as well as on its west side, where the principal building project related to expansion was a new city wall with modern bastions. The second started in 1595, again on the east side, where several new islands were created in former swampland between the river Amstel and the harbor, forming an area called the Lastage. The famous canals that surround the old city center in three concentric semicircles—the Herengracht, the Keizersgracht, and the Prinsengracht—were constructed in the third and fourth phases. The third phase started in 1613 on the city's western boundary, and the work was continued southward. In 1662 the triple semicircle was continued on the south and east sides including new islands on the east side of the harbor. In the last decades of the seventeenth century, the enormous expansion slowed down, and the development of the new urban area on the east side was never completed. It was given over to private gardens and the botanical gardens of the university.

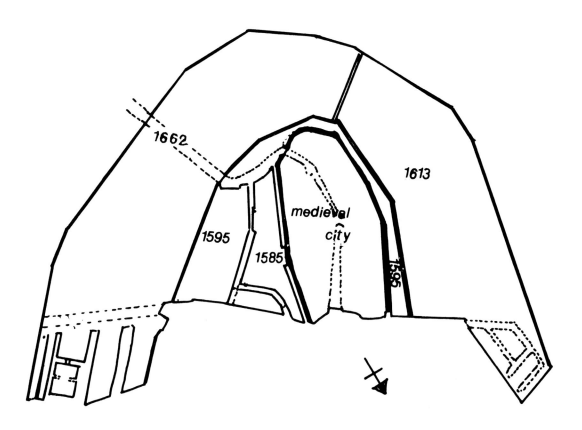

2. Schematic plan of Amsterdam's extensions in the sixteenth and seventeenth centuries
Author drawing

Socioeconomic zoning was established by the dimensions of building plots in the new urban areas. From the beginning of work in 1613, the new ring of canals was intended to become a fashionable residential area of expensive houses. The large, broad plots along the three new canals were thus planned to be affordable for the new wealthy mercantile class.[11] Industries that generated noise or smoke were excluded from this part of the city. The scale and the geometry of the layout of canals, quays, streets, and building plots provided a well-ordered living area. In contrast, the development of the wide leftover space between the ring of canals and the defensive ramparts was not governed by aesthetics or geometry. The original agricultural character of this land, drained by a rectangular grid of small ditches and canals, survived in the new urban context. Small independent craftsmen could buy plots in this modest area, called the Jordaan, which was reserved for crafts and industry.

Public Buildings

We find many new city buildings under construction during the seventeenth century.[12] Societal institutions such as orphanages and homes for the elderly had strong support from the municipal government because they served a semipublic function.[13] Most important in the support of the poor, orphans, and the elderly were three charities, the Huiszittenmeesters, the Diakonie, and the Aalmoezeniers. The Huiszittenmeesters, who took care of poor people still living in their own homes, were the oldest formal institution for poor relief, founded by the city authorities in the early fifteenth century. Their help was restricted to citizens, that is, to those who were born in Amsterdam or had acquired formal citizenship. The Diakonie (diaconate) was established shortly after the establishment of the Reformation in Amsterdam (1578). The deacons had direct links to the Calvinist church and ministered to their members only. The Aalmoezeniers (almoners) were founded in 1613 by the city government to prevent begging. They supported the poor of all religions by distributing private alms. All the poor relief societies had their own boards, but their activities and finances were under the control of the city government.

The city also supported these institutions financially by raising special taxes on behalf of charitable organizations. Several other private foundations for Lutherans, Baptists, and Catholics were not officially supported by the city government and so cannot be considered semipublic.

The old city remained the political and economic center, with the Dam as its hub. The Stock Exchange, the Weigh House, and the principal city church, the Nieuwe Kerk, stood there as well as the Town Hall. Since the new parts of the city were developed mainly as areas of private residences of various sizes for different income groups, until the middle of the seventeenth century public buildings were almost entirely lacking in the new neighborhoods. Most were in the medieval city, in former monasteries, all of them abandoned after the Reformation of 1578.[14] In the late sixteenth and early seventeenth centuries they were assigned to new public institutions such as orphanages, housing for the elderly, houses of correction, and the university. In the second part of the seventeenth century, when such institutions needed additional space to meet the needs of an expanding population, new homes for several of them were built in the expansion areas. Since there was no urban plan to indicate where these buildings should be erected, they rose on building sites offered by the city authorities that had been left vacant by default. Only the new Protestant city churches were given assigned places within the new urban areas.

Some of these buildings are discussed here in detail to give an overview of the range of building types erected by the city government. The building types themselves were not completely new in this period, but they exhibit far more rational planning than earlier examples in designs that strictly follow the rules of the various organizations.

Churches

Since Calvinist Protestantism was the only faith officially recognized by the state,[15] it was a responsibility of the city government to provide Protestant churches for the new residential areas.[16] A well-organized and socially regulated civic community had to support its churches to maintain morality

and the true religion. In the sixteenth-century extension on the east side of the medieval city, the Zuiderkerk was built in 1603–1614 by Hendrick de Keyser, master stonemason and sculptor of the city in the early seventeenth century. Six new churches were planned on the new ring of canals. They are shown on the city plan of 1695, even though only three were built. Two were designed by Hendrick de Keyser: the Noorderkerk (fig. 3) and the Westerkerk (fig. 4), both started in 1620.[17] Half a century later this series of churches was to be continued by another four on the second ring of canals. Only one of these was actually built, in 1669–1671. It is the Oosterkerk (fig. 5), on the new islands in the eastern harbor, designed by Daniel Stalpaert, the city architect. The other three churches in this area were never built. Only a square wooden church, intended as temporary, was constructed in the second part of the new canal district: the Amstelkerk, of 1668, another design by Stalpaert.[18] This wooden church still stands today on the Amstelveld.

The Protestant city churches of Hendrick de Keyser are among the first new buildings erected for the new religion in the Dutch Republic. They mark a period of experimentation in ecclesiastical architecture in Holland. Searching for a new tradition in Protestant church building, architects and patrons took their inspiration from the simplicity of the early Christian basilica as well as from theoretical principles derived from the Temple of Jerusalem.[19] A contemporary description of the rather modest Zuiderkerk refers to a traditional basilican church with a central nave and side aisles but without transept and choir, since those spaces had no function in Calvinist liturgy.[20] The imposing Westerkerk may be interpreted in the same way. But this rectangular church with its two huge transepts can also be seen as two squares, each inscribed with a Greek cross. Centralized church spaces also seem to have been of great importance in this period. The first Protestant church in the northern Netherlands, commissioned by Prince Maurits of Orange in Willemstad in 1595, is a regular octagon. In 1620 Hendrick de Keyser designed his third church in Amsterdam, the Noorderkerk, on a Greek-cross plan. The fascination with centralized church models related to the contemporary interest in various interpretations of the Temple of Jerusalem, which also, from a Protestant point of view, provided the basic template for church building following King Solomon's divine inspiration.[21]

Both the rectangular Westerkerk with its two transepts and the cross-shaped Noorder-kerk became important models for later seventeenth-century churches in Holland.[22] In Amsterdam the centralized plan of the Noorderkerk was followed in the two other city churches, the Oosterkerk and the wooden Amstelkerk, both built on square plans. The Oosterkerk shows an inscribed cross inside its square, and the silhouette is much like that of the Noorderkerk. But unlike the churches of Hendrick de Keyser, with their impressive show of architectural decoration, the walls of the Oosterkerk are plain brick, as is true of many Protestant churches in the Dutch Republic in the period after De Keyser and many other public buildings from the second part of the seventeenth century.

In the late seventeenth century three churches were still to be built alongside the new canals. A final, unsuccessful attempt to fill the gap in the ring of churches came in the last decades of the seventeenth century. In 1684–1695 the Amsterdam lawyer and amateur architect Nicolaas Listingh designed a spacious and impressive central-plan church with a tall spire, to be built on the Botermarkt (today's Rembrandtplein) (fig. 6). He produced a series of engravings of this design as well as a huge wooden model. These were intended to help him present his project to the city government and perhaps encourage private donations. The prints are in large folio format, and the model itself is already the size of a small chapel.[23] The church was intended to become the principal seat of Dutch Calvinism, as Listingh showed in engravings that compared his designs with the Pantheon and Saint Peter's in Rome as well as Hagia Sophia in Istanbul. De Keyser's Zuiderkerk and Westerkerk each has a tall tower adjacent to the main building. Listingh placed his tower on top of the dome of his new church. It would thus have reached a height which was quite unusual in Protestant church architecture in Holland, surpassing the 112-meter-high Gothic tower of Utrecht Cathedral. In his text on the engravings, Listingh argued that the scale and cost of his project were not excessive, since

4. Westerkerk, Amsterdam, by Hendrick de Keyser, 1620–1636
Author photograph

the church would take the place of three that were planned. But none of these was ever funded or built.

Overseas Trade and the Navy

The harbor and activities related to shipping, such as shipbuilding, rope manufacture, and storage of goods and marine equipment, were the core business of the city and were therefore supported by the authorities. On the eastern side of the harbor three new islands were created in 1657–1660 for shipbuilding and warehouses. The first island

5. Oosterkerk, Amsterdam,
by Daniel Stalpaert,
1669–1671
Author photograph

were built in sober brick, of palatial dimensions, strictly symmetrical and with monumental pediments crowning central pavilions. The city architect Daniel Stalpaert was responsible for the design in both cases.

The admiralty of Amsterdam had its headquarters in the former Prinsenhof in the center of the old town. It used various warehouses on the harbor for naval equipment. After the first English-Dutch war (1652–1654) showed the need for a new facility, the admiralty built a central warehouse in 1655–1657 on the east side of the harbor.[24] Warehouses on the harbor were traditionally long, tall brick buildings, constructed in parallel bays with an entrance at the short end of each bay facing the water.[25] The Navy Warehouse shows a new and at that time unique composition. It is a monumental square building surrounded by water on all four sides with an open square courtyard in its center. Three wings facing the open water held naval supplies. The fourth, on the shore side, contained administration and other offices. The massive brick structure has windows and entrances on all four sides. Originally it had

was for the navy, the second was sold to private entrepreneurs, and the third was for the Dutch East India Company. Both the navy and the East India Company obtained permission to build huge warehouses, the former in 1655–1657, the latter in 1660–1661. Both

6. Nicolaas Listingh,
*Unexecuted Design for
a Central-Plan Church on
the Botermarkt, Amsterdam,*
c. 1695
From Nicolaas Listingh, *Niew
Desseyn tot een Seer Groote,
Stercke, en om te hooren, heel
bequame Coupel-Kerck met een
Hooren Tooren daer miden uyt
rysende* (Amsterdam, 1695);
Gemeente Archief Amsterdam

7. Navy Warehouse,
Amsterdam, designed by
Daniel Stalpaert, constructed
1655–1657
Author photograph

central projections crowned with broad pediments only on the front and back. In the
1740s the building received its centralized
appearance when pavilions were added on the
side facades because of serious problems
with the foundations. Although the Navy
Warehouse is a utilitarian building, its sober
but monumental classical architecture makes
it a powerful statement of the city's naval
power (figs. 7 and 8).

The Dutch East India Company was
founded in 1602 with a state monopoly in the
trade from the Cape of Good Hope to the
Strait of Magellan. Although it was a private
company, its local branch was both supported and regulated by the city government. Not only the ruling class had financial
interests in the company; many common
citizens also owned shares. The company's
prosperity was thus a public concern. It had
to finance its buildings in the same way as
any private institution, but the city building
company was involved in their design. The
company office was in the old city center,
with a warehouse in a sixteenth-century
building that had been an arsenal and a new
office wing built in 1606 by Hendrick de
Keyser. By the middle of the seventeenth
century the company used warehouses all
over the city. In 1660 it bought the greater
part of one of the new islands on the east side
of the harbor and in the same year began construction of an immense central warehouse

(fig. 9).[26] Unlike the navy warehouse, it was
not a square building with an inner court but
one elongated rectangular clock, 215 meters
long and just twenty-five meters wide, and

8. Daniel Stalpaert, *Ground
Plan of the Navy Warehouse,
Amsterdam* (constructed
1655–1657), engraving,
c. 1655
Photograph University of Utrecht

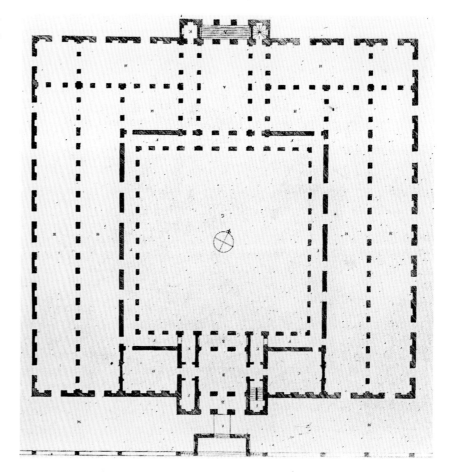

9. Jan Mulder, *Warehouse of the Dutch East India Company, Amsterdam* (constructed 1660–1661), engraving
From Caspar Commelin, *Beschrijvingen der stad Amsterdam* (Amsterdam, 1693)

10. Entrance buildings of the ropewalks of the navy (right) and the Dutch East India Company (left), Amsterdam, 1660
Author photograph

On the islands were slipways and two ropewalks, built in 1660 next to each other alongside the third island, one for the navy and one for the East India Company.[27] In these buildings, up to five hundred meters long, hemp was twisted into rope. The entrance buildings at the front, the only parts which remain today, contained storage space for recently produced rope. The brick facade of the navy's ropewalk is richly decorated with sculpted rope garlands. Its neighbor, the East India Company's ropewalk, is in plain brick with central pavilion and crowning pediment, the typical grammar of the city's architect, Stalpaert (fig. 10).

Orphanages

In the late sixteenth century the city had only one orphanage, the Burgerweeshuis, located in a former monastery on the Kalverstraat (today used as the Amsterdam Historical Museum).[28] During the first half of the seventeenth century this complex was enlarged and modernized several times, resulting in an irregular layout. The most important modernizations were Pieter de Keyser's redesign of the boys' courtyard in 1632 and, in 1634, the addition of a new girls' courtyard by Jacob van Campen. The size and layout of the new additions were restricted by the site.

This orphanage was only for children of local citizens, that is, of burghers with formal citizenship in Amsterdam. But during the seventeenth century the number of orphans grew constantly, along with the population. Many of these had been children of immigrants who were inhabitants but not official burghers. They were taken under the protection of several religious charitable institutions, such as the Diakonie and the Aalmoezeniers.[29] The city offered these groups prominent sites for their huge new orphanages. The French Huguenots were also offered a building plot in the outer parts of the most recent city extension to erect their orphanage, the Hospice Wallon, which was built in 1669–1671 by Adriaan Dortsman.[30] Several years later a home for the elderly of the Huguenot community was built on a vacant site next to the orphanage. Other religious charities, including those of the Lutherans, Baptists, and Catholics, were

five stories tall, almost completely surrounded by water. It housed all kinds of marine supplies, as well as merchandise from the Far East such as spices, porcelain, and chinaware. On the plain brick exterior, only the central pavilion had some classical decoration as well as a crowning pediment. The architecture of the elongated facade was dominated by the rhythm of three hundred windows and sixty door frames. Deepening of the surrounding canals in the early nineteenth century severely damaged the foundations, and in 1822 the building collapsed.

WEESHUYS DER DIACONYE

allowed to build their own orphanages but without any support from the city government. They had to purchase their building plots, so these buildings were much less prominent than those erected by the semi-public institutions.

The new orphanage of the Diakonie was built in 1656–1657.[31] It was intended to house 150 children, but in 1700 as many as 500 lived there. The orphanage of the Aalmoezeniers was built in 1663–1665 on the Prinsengracht. It was designed to house 800 children, but in 1700 it accommodated more than 1,300. These buildings were designed and built by the city building team, again directed by Daniel Stalpaert. Here also a less-is-more attitude toward the classical principles of architecture prevailed: a strict square brick volume, with a strictly symmetrical plan and facade (figs. 11 and 12). The Diakonie orphanage stood on the bank of the river Amstel, on Zwanenburgwal. It had two courtyards of equal size for girls and for boys, one to either side of a central axis. We find the same strictly symmetrical arrangement in the disposition of interior functions, with a wing for girls, a wing for boys, and the administration in the center. Each wing had its own dormitory, classroom, infirmary, and workshop. The same division into two almost independent departments could also be found at the Burgerweeshuis in the old city center, mentioned earlier. But in the Diakonie orphanage this functional division constituted a basic principle throughout the building. With its

two courtyards, central pavilions on the front and back facades, and two staircases, one on each of the side facades, this orphanage was designed as a rather modest but still impressive imitation of the new Town Hall.

The design of the Aalmoezeniers' orphanage followed the same principle in the organization of interior space, with two almost independent departments for boys and girls, each with its own courtyard, and so on. The idea of a dual function, used on a large scale here, was expressed in the huge brick facade on the Prinsengracht, which had two projections, each with a main entrance and each crowned by a pediment. This orphanage may

11. Anonymous, *Diakonie Orphanage, Amsterdam* (by Daniel Stalpaert, constructed 1656–1657), engraving
From Jan Wagenaar, *Amsterdam, in zyne opkomst, aanwas, geschiedenissen*, vol. 2 (Amsterdam, 1765)

12. Ground plan of the Diakonie Orphanage, Amsterdam, 1656, reconstruction by Eva Mennes-Wüsten, 1988

13. Anonymous, *Aalmoezeniers Orphanage, Amsterdam* (by Daniel Stalpaert, constructed 1663–1665), engraving
From Jan Wagenaar, *Amsterdam in zyne opkomst, aanwas, geschiedenissen*, vol. 2 (Amsterdam, 1765)

thus be regarded as adjacent twin buildings (fig. 13).[32]

Homes for the Elderly

The semipublic charitable institutions supported not only children without parents but also the impoverished elderly without children or other relatives to take care of them. Those who still could live in their own homes but could not afford food or fuel were the concern of the Huiszittenmeesters. There were two boards of Huiszittenmeesters, each connected with one of the two medieval city churches, the Oude Kerk

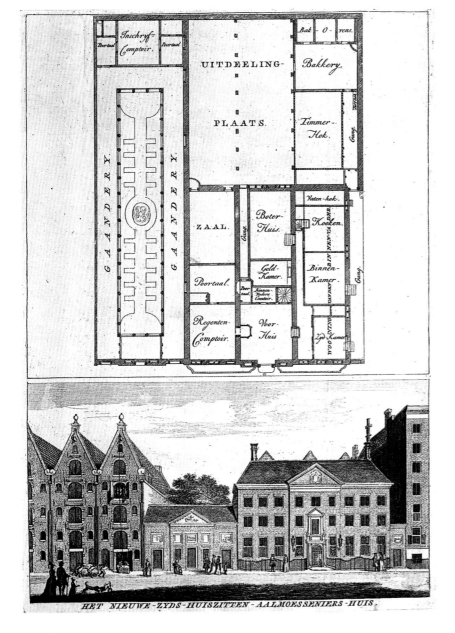

HET NIEUWE-ZYDS-HUISZITTEN-AALMOESSENIERS-HUIS.

on the east side and the Nieuwe Kerk in the western part of the city. In earlier times distribution of bread, butter, and cheese, as well as peat in wintertime, took place in these churches. Each board had its own warehouse. In the mid-seventeenth century two new buildings were constructed for the administration of both agencies as well as for the distribution of food. From then on, the poor and elderly had to go to a so-called *huiszittenhuis* for food and peat: either to the new extension on the west side, where the Nieuwezijds Huiszittenhuis was built in 1649 on the Prinsengracht, or to the office on the east side, where the Oudezijds Huiszittenhuis was built in 1654–1655 next to the existing warehouses of the institution, dating from 1610.[33] Each of these offices consisted of an administration building, which included a bakery, and an adjacent spacious courtyard. Alongside the courtyard was a cloisterlike covered passage. The poor entered at one end, received bread at the bakery counter, and exited at the other end. At the Nieuwezijds Huiszittenhuis the courtyard was beside the main building (fig. 14); at the Oudezijds Huiszittenhuis it was at the back (fig. 15).

Those who could no longer stay in their own houses could live in homes for the elderly. The first modest, purpose-designed home was built in the mid-sixteenth century to house twelve men and twelve women. From the early seventeenth century the Diakonie used a new complex that accommodated almost two hundred elderly people, housed in separate sections for men and women.[34] Founded in 1602 and known as the Oudeliedenhuis, it was erected on land that had once been a convent orchard, in the southeastern part of medieval Amsterdam. In this city of sailors there were far more impoverished elderly widows than widowers. For this reason, in the second half of the seventeenth century the Huiszittenmeesters as well as the Diakonie founded homes for elderly women. In 1649–1650 the two boards of Huiszittenmeesters together built the Kartuizerhof, a home for widows, on the site of a former monastery, in the Jordaan area. Designed by Daniel Stalpaert, it consisted of fifty-four one-room apartments on two levels around a central courtyard. Each door gave entry to four rooms, two on the ground

floor and two on the upper.[35] The inhabitants lived under protection and supervision of a board but to a degree independently.

In 1681–1683 the Diakonie founded the Oude Vrouwenhuis, an elderly women's home, on the Amstel, not far from their orphanage.[36] The city's master carpenter, Hans Jansz van Petersom, designed the vast rectangular building with three courtyards: one big, square center court and two narrow rectangular courts, one to each side. In a central position on each of the front and back sides is a spacious room for general use, the dining room (on Sundays used also for worship) on the front and an infirmary at the back. Living rooms were located in the four perpendicular sections between front and back. Four women shared a room in which each had only a cupboard bed as private space. The rooms looked either outside or into the spacious center court. Corridors ran alongside the narrow courtyards. In this building we find the same principles of architecture and logical organization of interior space as in the orphanages, but since this is a home for the elderly, there is only one upper floor. As a result this building, designed for almost four hundred people, is a low, broad complex with an extensive facade

along the river. A modest but impressive pediment crowing the central projection enhances its appearance to the city (figs. 16 and 17).

The civic buildings erected in the second half of the seventeenth century were designed according to more or less the same sober classical principles and built by almost the same group of architects and engineers. They are all constructed in plain brick, strictly symmetrical, with central projections crowned by pediments, usually displaying the city coat of arms. Although all these buildings were more or less utilitarian, built to store goods from the Far East or naval cannon or to house orphans or elderly people, they were under the control of the city. They therefore needed a certain degree of decorum to embody civic dignity and authority.

The Town Hall

The zenith of all this building activity was the new Town Hall, built in 1648–1665 on the Dam, the city's central square. As had been the case with no other public buildings, the decision to erect a new town hall on a grand scale met with opposition in some

16. Diakonie Elderly
Women's Home, Amsterdam,
by Hans Jansz van Petersom,
1681–1683
Author photograph

circles. The more orthodox Calvinist faction within the city government did not want to create a worldly monument to civic pride, which they regarded as a sign of presumption and prodigality. Instead they proposed to build a tall tower at the main entrance of the Gothic Nieuwe Kerk, the city's most important church.[37] In 1645 a fire caused serious damage to the medieval structure, and while restoration was under way several designs as well as wooden models were made for a new tower in front of the church. Nonetheless, work on the new Town Hall began in 1648. When the leader of the orthodox Calvinists died in 1652, work on

the tower was called to a halt, and all resources were devoted to the Town Hall.

In the architecture of the Town Hall we can recognize the same classical design principles evident in other public buildings, but here with a maximum demand for magnificence. Instead of brick, the facades are constructed in stone and the interiors are marble. The pediments and the interior walls display a rich marble sculptural program.[38] The pediment on the front facade shows the four oceans paying tribute to the personification of Amsterdam. Bronze allegories stand as acroteria: Justice and Prudence left and right and Peace at the apex (fig. 18). The

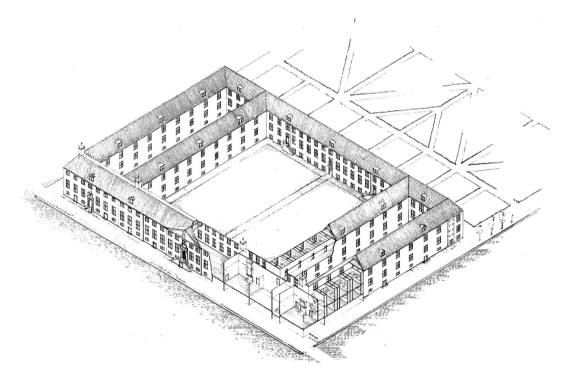

17. Diakonie Elderly
Women's Home, by Hans
Jansz van Petersom,
Amsterdam, 1681–1683;
drawing by R. Royaards-ten
Holt, 1982
Collection Rijksdienst voor de
Monumentenzorg, Zeist

corresponding pediment sculpture on the rear shows the four continents. The building is indeed a monument to the Peace of Westphalia, which gave the Dutch Republic its independence and its wealth. In fact, it is a palace for a republican city government.[39] The burgomasters and council had their rooms at the front side, on the Dam. The court of justice, with the sheriff and aldermen, had its seat just at the other side. Four important financial institutions, regarded as the cornerstones of the government, took their positions in the four corner apartments. The space with the most solemn ceremonial function, the room where the death sentence was proclaimed, was the Vierschaar, at the center of the front side on the ground floor, where three arches open to the Dam (fig. 19).

At the center of the building is the hall known as the Burgerzaal (Citizens' Hall), with a courtyard to either side. Since Amsterdam

was regarded in contemporary poems as the new Rome, the members of the city council identified themselves with the ancient Roman Senate and the burgomasters with consuls. The Town Hall itself can be interpreted as their forum, as described by Palladio and Scamozzi following Vitruvius, including a curia, a treasury, a prison, galleries, and a basilica.[40] The Burgerzaal is the basilica of this palace. Like an ancient basilica, it was a public meeting room. It was regarded as the very center, not only of the city but also of the world, a map of which is inlaid in marble in its floor (fig. 20 and page 8).

Conclusion

The development of several new or, rather, modernized building types in seventeenth-century Amsterdam was the result of the city's attempt to maintain control over its unprecedented growth. These new public

18. Town Hall (now the Royal Palace), Amsterdam, by Jacob van Campen, 1648–1665
Photograph by Jan Derwig, with permission of the Stichting Koninklijk Paleis te Amsterdam

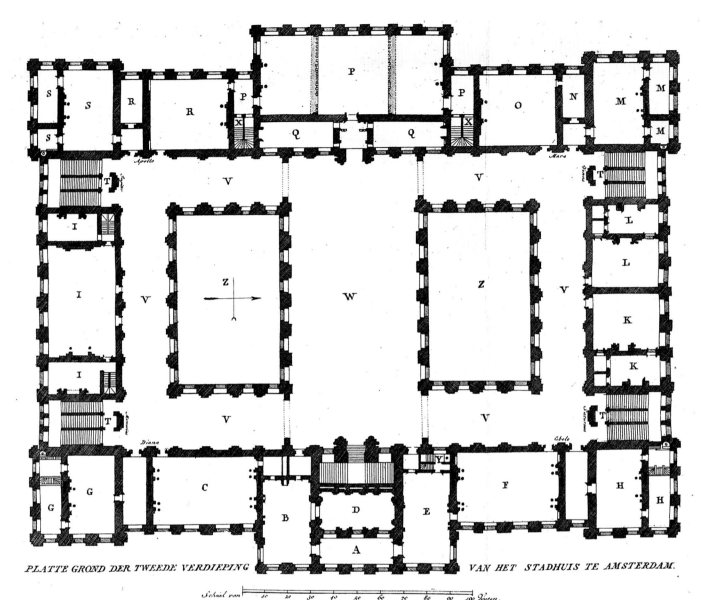

PLATTE GROND DER TWEEDE VERDIEPING   VAN HET STADHUIS TE AMSTERDAM.

Schaal van   10   20   30   40   50   60   70   80   90   100 Voeten.

A. De Puije.
B. Burgemeesters kamer.
C. Derzelver vertrek.
D. De Regtbank.
E. Justitie kamer.
F. Raads kamer.

G. Thesaurie Ordinaris en vertrekken.
H. Weeskamer en vertrekken.
I. Secretary en vertrekken.
K. Assurantie kamer en vertrekken.
L. Desolate Boedelkamer en vertrekken.
M. Rekenkamer en vertrekken.

N. Schouts kamer.
O. Schepenen Extraordinaris.
P. Schepenen Ordinaris.
Q. Vertrekken der Advocaten en Procur.s
R. Commissarissen van kleine zaken.
S. Thesaurie Extraordinaris.

T. Gemeene Trappen.
V. Galleryen.
W. Groote Zaal.
X. Trap naar de Krygsraadskamer.
Y. Trap naar de Toren.
Z. Opene plaatzen.

19. Anonymous, *Ground
Plan of the Main Floor of the
Town Hall, Amsterdam*,
engraving
From Jan Fokke, *Geschiedkundige
beschrijving van het vermaarde
stadhuis van Amsterdam*
(Amsterdam, 1808)

20. Burgerzaal (Citizens' Hall), Town Hall (now the Royal Palace), Amsterdam, by Jacob van Campen and Daniel Stalpaert, 1648–1665
Photograph by J. Wester, with permission of the Stichting Koninklijk Paleis te Amsterdam

and semipublic buildings were an organized response to the needs of expanding trade and aspects of social life in the rapidly growing city community. The Town Hall stands at the top of the hierarchy of building types in this republican city state, but architectural expression of the city's authority was not restricted to the seat of government. Utilitarian public buildings also had a role in formal representation of the city's power and prosperity, since they housed functions that were integral to the ruling institution. As a result, all the institutional buildings erected by the civil authority in the second half of the seventeenth century may be regarded as modest offspring of the Town Hall. These were less ornate and without costly building materials, but they were planned according to the same classical principles. The logical arrangement of functions in the interior space was also a common feature of this group of civic buildings. In seventeenth-century Amsterdam, classicism was more than an architectural style; it was an expression of an ideal of order and harmony that also dictated the planning of new urban space.

NOTES

1. Jonathan I. Israel, *Dutch Primacy in World Trade, 1585–1740* (Oxford, 1989), and Roelof van Gelder and Renée Kistemaker, *Amsterdam 1275–1795: De ontwikkeling van een handelsmetropool* (Amsterdam, 1983).

2. J. E. Elias, *De vroedschap van Amsterdam* (Haarlem, 1903–1905); Peter Burke, *Venice and Amsterdam: A Study of Seventeenth-Century Elites* (London, 1974); Bas Dudok van Heel, "Op zoek naar Romulus en Remus: Zeventiende-eeuws onderzoek naar de oudste magistraten van Amsterdam," *Jaarboek Amstelodamum* 87 (1995): 43–70; Henk van Nierop, "Politics and the People of Amsterdam," in *Rome, Amsterdam: Two Growing Cities in Seventeenth-Century Europe,* ed. Peter van Kessel and Elisja Schulte (Amsterdam, 1997), 146–155.

3. Konrad Ottenheym, "Tot roem en sier van de stad: Hollandse stedelijke en regionale overheden als opdrachtgevers van architectuur in de zeventiende eeuw," *Kunstenaars en opdrachtgevers (Utrecht Renaissance Studies)* 2, ed. Harald Hendrix and Jeroen Stumpel (Amsterdam, 1996), 119–140.

4. Constantijn Huygens to Jacobus Golius, 29 January 1655, The Hague, Koninklijk Huisarchief. The architect he promoted here was Pieter Post. Jan Terwen and Konrad Ottenheym, *Pieter Post (1608–1669): Architect* (Zutphen, 1993), 6.

5. Ruud Meischke, "Het Amsterdamse fabrieksambt van 1595–1625," *Bulletin van de Koninklijke Nederlandse Oudheidkundige Bond* 93 (1994): 100–122; Gea van Essen, "Daniel Stalpaert (1615–1676), stadsarchitect van Amsterdam en de Amsterdamse stadsfabriek in de periode 1647–1676," *Bulletin van de Koninklijke Nederlandse Oudheidkundige Bond* 99 (2000): 101–121.

6. A. W. Weissman, "Het geslacht De Keyser," *Oud Holland* 22 (1904): 65–91; A. W. Weissman, "De schoonzoon van Hendrick de Keyser," *Oud Holland* 37 (1920): 155–164; Ruud Meischke et al., *Amsterdam,* vol. 2 of *Huizen in Nederland* (Zwolle, 1995), 54–56.

7. Jan Terwen, "Il Palladianesimo in Olanda," in *Palladio: La sua eredita' nel mondo,* ed. Anna Della Valle (Milan, 1980), 73–95; Andrew Hopkins and Arnold Witte, "Van luxe architectuurtraktaat tot praktische handleiding: De Nederlandse uitgaven van Scamozzi's *L'Idea della Architettura Universale,*" *Bulletin van de Koninklijke Nederlandse Oudheidkundige Bond* 96 (1997): 137–153; Konrad Ottenheym, "Classicism in the Northern Netherlands in the Seventeenth Century," in *Palladio and Northern Europe: Books, Travellers, Architects,* ed. Guido Beltramini et al. [exh. cat., Centro Internazionale di Studi Andrea Palladio] (Milan, 1999), 150–167.

8. Simon Bosboom, *Cort onderwys van de vyf colommen door Vinsent Scamozzi geordineert en nu door Symon Bosboom Stads Steenhouwer tot Amsterdam in minuten gestelt seer gemackelick voor de jonge leerlingen en dienstich voor alle jonge liefhebbers der Bouw-Const* (Amsterdam, 1657). This work was reprinted several times in the seventeenth, eighteenth, and nineteenth centuries, the last time in 1854. Hopkins and Witte 1997, 150–153.

9. Van Essen 2000.

10. Ed Taverne, *In 't land van belofte: in de nieue stadt: Ideaal en werkelijkheid van de stadsuitleg in de Republiek 1580–1680* (Maarssen, 1978), 112–175; Boudewijn Bakker, "De stadsuitleg van 1610 en het ideaal van de volkomen stad: Meesterplan of mythe?" *Jaarboek Amstelodamum* 87 (1995): 71–96.

11. Isabella van Eeghen, "De historische ontwikkeling en het aanzien van de Herengracht," in *Vier eeuwen Herengracht* (Amsterdam, 1976), 105–143; Bas Dudok van Heel, "Regent Families and Urban Development in Amsterdam," in van Kessel and Schulte 1997, 124–145; Meischke et al. 1995; Konrad Ottenheym, "The Amsterdam Ring of Canals: City Planning and Architecture," in van Kessel and Schulte 1997, 33–49.

12. An overview of public and semipublic buildings in the third quarter of the seventeenth century is included in Gea van Essen, "Daniel Stalpaert (1615–1676): Stadsarchitect van Amsterdam," master's thesis, Utrecht University, 1998. A summary of this study was published in 2000 (see note 5).

13. Van Gelder and Kistemaker 1983, 267–269; Simon Groenveld, "For the Benefit of the Poor: Social Assistance in Amsterdam," in van Kessel and Schulte 1997, 192–208; Maarten Prak, "Velerlei soort van volk: Sociale verhoudingen in Amsterdam in de zeventiende eeuw," *Jaarboek Amstelodamum* 91 (1999): 29–54.

14. Gerrit Vermeer and W. H. van de Bos, "De Amsterdamse kloosters stedebouwkundig en architectuurhistorisch belicht," in *Amsterdamse kloosters in de middeleeuwen,* ed. Marian Schilder (Amsterdam, 1997), 21–46.

15. Arie van Deursen, "Church and City Government in Amsterdam," in van Kessel and Schulte 1997, 175–179.

16. Murk Daniël Ozinga, *De protestantsche kerkenbouw in Nederland van Hervorming tot Franschen tijd* (Amsterdam, 1929); C. A. van Swigchem, T. Brouwer, and W. van Os, *Een huis voor het Woord: Het protestantse kerkinterieur in Nederland tot 1900* (Den Haag, 1984).

17. Elisabeth Neurdenburg, *Hendrick de Keyser: Beeldhouwer en bouwmeester van Amsterdam* (Amsterdam, 1930); Walter Kramer, *De Noorderkerk in Amsterdam* (Zwolle, 1998).

18. Johan Jacobs, "Vitruvius moet wel geacht maar niet alleen geloofd werden: De Amstelkerk en de architectuur van de 17de eeuw," in *Jaarboek Monumentenzorg 1990* (Zwolle, 1990), 48–70.

19. See Joris Snaet, Belgium, forthcoming dissertation on concepts of ecclesiastical architecture in the Low Countries during the late sixteenth and early seventeenth centuries, Catholic University, Leuven, Belgium, 2005.

20. Cornelis Dankerts and Salomon de Bray, *Architectura Moderna ofte Bouwinge van onsen tijt* (Amsterdam, 1631).

21. The octagon refers to the medieval pictorial tradition of representing the Temple, in fact based on the Islamic Dome of the Rock on the Temple Mount in Jerusalem. The square plan used in Holland from the 1640s onward was based on a scientific reconstruction of the Temple published by the Jesuit scholar Villalpando in 1598–1604. Helen Rosenau, *Vision of the Temple: The Image of the Temple of Jerusalem in Judaism and Christianity* (London, 1979); C. J. R. van der Linden, "De symboliek van de Nieuwe Kerk van Jacob van Campen te Haarlem," *Oud Holland* 104 (1990): 1–31.

22. Ozinga 1929.

23. The immense model survives (collection Oude Kerk, Amsterdam). Ozinga 1929, 141–142; Robert Tieskens, "Koepelkerk op de Botermarkt, het huidige Rembrandtsplein, Amsterdam," in *Het kleine bouwen: Vier eeuwen maquettes in Nederland,* ed. Robert Tieskens, Derk Snoep, and Gerard van Wezel [exh. cat., Centraal Museum Utrecht] (Zutphen, 1983), 82–83; Konrad Ottenheym, "Model for a Central-Plan Church on the Botermarkt in Amsterdam; 1684–95" and "Perspective View for a Central-Plan Church on the Botermarkt in Amsterdam," in *Triumph of the Baroque: Architecture in Europe, 1600–1750,* ed. Henry A. Millon [exh. cat., Palazzina di Caccia di Stupinigi] (Turin, 1999), 566–567 (catalogue entries 527 and 528).

24. Sjoerd de Meer, *'s Lands Zeemagazijn* (Zutphen, 1994).

25. Magda Révész-Alexander, *Die alten Lagerhäuser Amsterdams* (The Hague, 1954).

26. J. C. Overvoorde and P. de Roo de la Faille, eds., *De gebouwen van de Oost-Indische Compagnie en van de West-Indische Compagnie in Nederland* (The Hague, 1929), 17–55; Henk Zantkuijl, *Bouwen in Amsterdam: Het woonhuis in de stad* (Amsterdam, 1975–1992), 404–405; J. B. Kist, *Van VOC tot Werkspoor: Het Amsterdamse industrieterrein Oostenburg* (Utrecht, 1986).

27. Overvoorde and de Roo de la Faille 1927; Zantkuijl 1975–1992, 402–403; Kist 1986.

28. Ruud Meischke, *Amsterdam Burgerweeshuis, Nederlandse Monumenten van Geschiedenis en Kunst* (The Hague, 1975).

29. Simon Groenveld, Jeroen Dekker, and Thom Willemse, *Wezen en boefjes: Zes eeuwen zorg in wees- en kinderhuizen* (Hilversum, 1997), 58–69, 130–151.

30. Built on the corner of the Vijzelgracht and the Prinsengracht. Today it houses the consulate of France and the Maison Descartes.

31. Eva Mennes-Wüsten, *Het weeshuis van de Diaconie*, master's thesis, Leiden University, 1988.

32. The orphanage of the Diakonie was demolished in 1888. The Aalmoezeniers orphanage was completely altered in 1825–1826 when it became the Court of Justice.

33. Zantkuijl 1975–1992, 223, 347–349.

34. Ruud Meischke, "De geschiedenis van het terrein van het St. Pieters- of Binnengasthuis te Amsterdam," *Bulletin Koninklijke Nederlandse Oudheidkundige Bond* 8 (1955): 1–19 and 49–84 (esp. 53–59).

35. Zantkuijl 1975–1992, 337–338.

36. Ruud Meischke, *Amstelhof 1683–1983* (Amsterdam, 1983).

37. Thomas von der Dunk, "Hoe klassiek is de gothiek? Jacob van Campen en de toren van de Nieuwe Kerk te Amsterdam, een nieuwe benadering van een oude kwestie," *Jaarboek Amstelodamum* 85 (1993): 49–90; Konrad Ottenheym, "Model for the Tower of the Nieuwe Kerk," in Turin 1999, 540 (catalogue entries 402 and 403).

38. Katherine Fremantle, *The Baroque Town Hall of Amsterdam* (Utrecht, 1959); Eymert-Jan Goossens, *Treasure Wrought by Chisel and Brush: The Town Hall of Amsterdam in the Golden Age* (Amsterdam and Zwolle, 1996); Pieter Vlaardingerbroek, "The Town Hall of Amsterdam," in Millon 1999, 537–540 (catalogue entries 389–401); Pieter Vlaardingerbroek, *Het Stadhuis van Amsterdam: De bouw van het Stadhuis, de verbouwing tot koninklyk paleis en de restauratie*, Ph.D. diss., Utrecht University, 2004.

39. Sjoerd Faber, Jacobine Huiskens, and Friso Lammertse, *Of Lords, Who Seat nor Cushion Do Ashame: The Government of Amsterdam in the Seventeenth and Eighteenth Centuries* (Amsterdam, 1987).

40. Jan Terwen, "De herkomst van de Amsterdamse stadhuisplattegronden," in *Miscellanea I. Q. van Regteren Altena* (Amsterdam, 1969), 123–125, 321–322; Konrad Ottenheym, "Architectuur," in *Jacob van Campen: Het klassieke ideaal in de Gouden Eeuw*, ed. Jacobine Huisken et al. (Amsterdam, 1995), 155–199 (esp. 190–194).

FERNANDO MARÍAS
Universidad Autónoma de Madrid

From Madrid to Cádiz: The Last Baroque Cathedral for the New Economic Capital of Spain

By about 1680 Cádiz eclipsed Seville as the port of the Carrera de las Indias (trade with Spain's American and Asian colonies) because the newer commercial galleons, of greater tonnage and draft than those of earlier years, could not navigate the Guadalquivir River to the port of Seville. By the end of the century, Cádiz had transformed itself into a first-rate economic and mercantile center. Its position as such was officially sanctioned by a royal decree of 12 May 1717 that transferred the Casa de la Contratación, the official headquarters of New World trade, from Seville to Cádiz.[1] This relocation was a kind of reward to the city for its loyalty during the War of the Spanish Succession, during which it had suffered two sieges, in 1702 and 1704.[2] As the "emporium of the orb"[3] and an eternal drain on colonial trade revenues that earned the epithet "gullet of the Americas,"[4] Cádiz had become the new economic capital of the Spanish kingdoms. The political capital and seat of court of the new Bourbon dynasty, however, remained in Madrid. There, no great architectural initiatives were undertaken until the arrival of Filippo Juvarra (1678–1736) in 1735 and, in the following year, that of Giambattista Sacchetti (1690–1764), who embarked on the construction of a new royal palace, designed in the Italian manner, for the French Philip V and his Italian wife, Isabella Farnese.

The larger picture of Spanish architecture around 1700 would remain incomplete if viewed only through the works of these two Italian architects or Robert de Cotte's projects for Philip V in Madrid, or in light of Fernando Galli da Bibiena's presence in 1708–1711 at the court of the Hapsburg Archduke Charles in Barcelona. All of these represented a new direction in Spanish architecture, marked by the importation into Spain of foreign architects and artists who worked in the architectural field. To the list of those who arrived around 1700 one could add the painters Filippo Palotta, Andrea Procaccini, and Sempronio Subisati (the latter two from Rome), who arrived around 1720 and worked at the royal palace of La Granja de San Ildefonso in Segovia,[5] and Giacomo Bonavia (from Piacenza), who arrived in 1731 and would design the church of Santos Justo y Pastor (now San Miguel) in Madrid in 1739. The first signs of what George Kubler called the "rupture of the plane" in Spanish architecture[6] came from the hands of the Austrian sculptor Conrad Rudolf, called El Romano, who designed the undulating surface of the facade of Valencia Cathedral (1701/1703–1735).[7] Having presented his inventive design in a wax model, he left to Spanish master stonemasons the translation of his vision into stone.

Spanish architects had also attempted the rupture of the plane around those same years, and not only on the basis of what Italians were doing or the play of convex and concave planes. The Spanish tradition of perspectival

1. Model of Cádiz, 1777–1779
Cádiz, Museo de la Ciudad

construction, foreshortening, and oblique composition, related to sixteenth-century Castilian retables, introduced important elements that energized their designs and impelled the spectator into movement in order to arrive at a complete understanding of the architectonic work.[8] Narciso Tomé, for example, joined this vernacular tradition with Bernini's *bel composto* in his transparente in Toledo Cathedral (1720/1721–1732) for the archbishop Diego de Astorga y Céspedes, who was buried at its foot.[9] The importance of this work notwithstanding, others, more complex in construction, typology, and composition, might still better represent the Spanish tendency that, in translating these forms into stone, combined the foreign and the familiar and modernized national traditions that were still seen as entirely valid.

So let me now come to windy Cádiz, a city on the southern tip of Spain, close to the Strait of Gibraltar, in order to study its cathe-dral and the cathedral's first architect, Vicente Acero y Acebo, whose published writings on the building will be our guide. Acero (Cabárceno [Penagos, Santander], c. 1685–Seville, 1739) was a squire and a man of strong opinions who ironically, at one point in his life, thought of entering a Carthusian monastery and never uttering another word.

As evidence of the dual economic and military importance of Cádiz—situated on an isthmus and almost completely surrounded by the Atlantic Ocean—is that it was the first and only city for which a gigantic model was made, by royal order of Charles III in 1777–1779 (fig. 1). Inspired by French *plans-reliefs*, the model, measuring 86 square meters (692 by 1,252 centimeters) including a minimal representation of the surrounding sea, represented on a scale of 1:250 a city of about 500 hectares, including the locations of future neighborhoods, models of various military and civic buildings already constructed or under way (like the cathedral

2. Cádiz Cathedral, detail
from the model of Cádiz,
1777–1779
Cádiz, Museo de la Ciudad

3. Vicente de Acero y Acebo,
*Project for Cádiz Cathedral,
Elevation*, 1725, pen and ink
Cádiz Cathedral Archive

ELEBACION GEOMETRICA EXTERIOR DELA SANTA IGLESIA DE CADÍZ AÑO DE 1725

itself), and projects planned for the immediate future, with some buildings that could
be opened to reveal their interiors.

The design of the topographic relief was
based on the ground plan of the city made
in 1749 by military engineers and with the
aid of telescopes, a camera obscura, and four
workmen in charge of measuring lengths
and heights. The construction of the city

model was directed by the sculptor Francisco
Gamberini, who worked with two other
assistants, four cabinetmakers, six carpenters,
and a team that sometimes numbered as
many as forty-eight, all under the supervision
of a military engineer, Alfonso Jiménez. The
materials included various types of wood—
acana, mahogany, cedar, ebony, beech, sandalwood, Flemish pine, guaiacum, palo santo,
and pear—as well as ivory and bone for the
cathedral and other important buildings.
The black paper used in making fans was
used for the windows, and originally silver
was used for the sea and some details.[10]

The use of expensive materials—ivory and
bone—for the new cathedral (fig. 2) attests to
the importance to the city and the kingdom
of a building meant to express "to country-
men and foreigners alike . . . the perfection
of our arts and the robustness of the principal nerve of the State, which is commerce."
By the time the city model was made, the
cathedral had been modified and reduced in
size from the original design of 1721. The
cathedral's original dimensions, known
through four drawings by its architect made
in 1725 (figs. 3–6), reveal the building as an
enormous structure, its towers equaling in
height and surpassing in richness of materials
the legendary Giralda of Seville Cathedral,
the stone and brick symbol of the city that
formerly rivaled Cádiz in the commerce
with the Indies. Moreover, the exterior of
Cádiz Cathedral wore a dress of white marble brought from Genoa and from Spanish
quarries.

The building, which was inaugurated in
1838 and was under construction until 1853,
was to stand as the last and most modern
link in the chain of Spanish cathedrals, and
especially of the series of Andalusian cathedrals *a la romana*. Even so, it has not until
now received the attention it deserves, not
even in Spain, being a monument cursed
from the beginning of its construction.[11]
The second story of the facade was modified
first by Gaspar José Cayón de la Vega (1687–
1769) and then, in a more important revision,
by his nephew Torcuato Cayón Orozco de la
Vega (1725–1783), who succeeded Acero, in
1731 and 1759, respectively. The height of
the facade was reduced by smaller towers
that were subordinated to the dome, which

SECCION GEOMETRICA DE LA SANTA IGLESIA DE CADIZ: AÑO DE 1725

was also reduced in size; thus the profile of the building was entirely reordered (figs. 6 and 7). Its double dome, which, as we shall see, drew criticism as early as 1727, gave way to a simplistic and insipid neoclassical hemispherical dome, completed in 1844 by the military engineer Juan Daura.

Just as professional criticism substantially altered Acero's design, written criticism aligned itself with the opinions of the dogmatists of the Real Academia de Bellas Artes de San Fernando (the royal academy of fine arts) in Madrid, men like Antonio Ponz, secretary of the academy. He thought that there was "no solution other than to demolish the church and simply say that it had been swept away by the sea";[12] a little later, Spanish architecture's first academic historian exclaimed: "May God forgive him [Acero]."[13]

Despite these assessments, the cathedral of Cádiz emerged with the pretension that it would be highly representative of contemporary Spanish architectural culture.

Acero was doubly conscious of this ambition when he set out to defend his idea. Acero's project had been selected in a competition whose principal judge was Francisco del Orbe, professor of mathematics of the Real Colegio de Guardamarinas (the royal naval academy).[14] Upon examining the architect and finding that he possessed the necessary knowledge, Orbe recommended that Acero execute a wooden model of the projected building.[15] The project also received the approval of the sophisticated Bishop Lorenzo Armengual del Pino de la Mota (1715–1730).[16] The owner of an important library and a distinguished art collection,[17] he was in attendance when the cathedral cornerstone was laid on 3 May 1722, feast of the Finding of the Holy Cross, to which the cathedral was dedicated. Acero immediately proceeded to lay the foundation and, in 1721–1726, constructed the crypt of prelates and canons— "the pantheons," as he called it—fifty-seven feet in diameter as compared to the sixty-

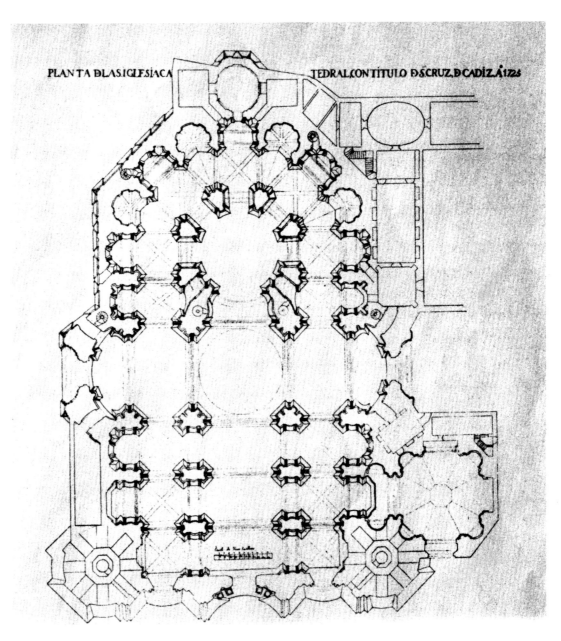

PLANTA DLASIGLFSIACA   TEDRAL,CONTÍTULO DSCRUZ,DCADIZ,Á1725

three-foot diameter of the rotunda above and topped by a very flat dome on flat arches, in the manner of some of the vaults of the legendary monastery of the Escorial (figs. 7 and 8). Acero's stonecutting for the dome, praised by the Flemish military engineer Prosper Verboom in 1724, still stands as one of the most important examples of stereotomy in modern Spanish architecture.

As we shall see, when Acero defended his profession, he called masonry the "plainsong" of architecture, "which with certain propriety can be called Music, for the consonance, that the terrain must make with the Foundations, and those with the Plan, [and]

that with the Elevation, to which must correspond the profiles," whereas stonecutting was the "counterpoint, for the variation in the quality of the material . . . and for the extraordinary cuts that come together." Acero also indicated his contributions to this field from his youth: inventions (*inventibas*) of new, ingenious cutting schemes, new instruments to facilitate the work, and the search for new *saynetes* (playful jokes) for moldings. With these inventions he had not only reduced the costs but also provided "steadfast rules" for designing Solomonic columns *de roscas a una mano o a dos* (which turn this way and that).[18]

6. Vicente de Acero y Acebo,
Facade of Cádiz Cathedral,
c. 1725, pen and ink
Madrid, Biblioteca Nacional de
España

Three drawings in the cathedral archives, dated 1725 and in a poor state of conservation, are testimony of this first phase and of Acero's first projects for the cathedral. Whether they are Acero's or the work of his draftsman, Francisco Medrano, has been a subject of debate; Kubler thought they were Acero's and René Taylor considered them to be Medrano's.[19] They are copies, probably made when a set of plans ("la Planta y Alza-

dos") was delivered to the *canónigo maestro* Zuloaga in Madrid, only to be submitted, as we shall see, to the judgment of experts. The drawings consist of a ground plan; an exterior elevation, or "geometric elevation"; and a "geometric" section. They are better known from tracings made in 1928 by Pablo Gutiérrez Moreno (see figs. 3–5) than from the photographs published by Pablo Antón Solé in 1976.[20] A fourth drawing of the north facade, made around the same time, is preserved in Madrid (see fig. 6).[21]

Unfortunately, on 11 April 1726, at about the time Acero's designs were being judged in Madrid, the dome of the conventual church of Santo Tomás in Madrid collapsed, killing eighty people. Consequently, the city of Cádiz became fearful of building a dome that would be the highest and most daring in the history of Spanish architecture and would, moreover, be of stone instead of brick and plaster.

The criticisms of Acero's project are known to us principally through three pamphlets printed in Cádiz. The first of these was published in 1728 by Acero himself, with a purpose explained by its title: "Don Vicente de Azero, provoked by the stated opinions [of various architects of Madrid and Seville] . . . answers the reports in which the plan and elevation have been criticized" (fig. 9).[22] The second was published by José Gallego y Oviedo del Portal (Salamanca, 1686–Jaén, 1736), master builder of the cathedral of

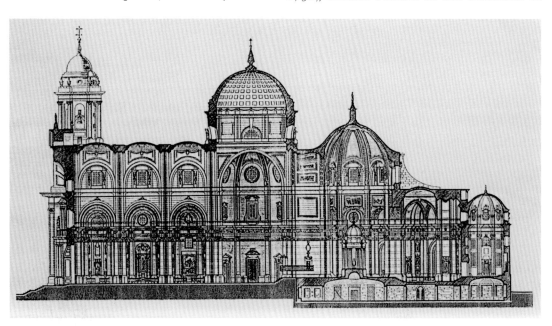

7. Otto Schubert, *Section of
Cádiz Cathedral*, c. 1908
From Otto Schubert, *Geschichte des
Barock in Spanien* (Esslingen, 1908)

Jaén, as a "manifesto to the public" containing his "judgment on the building of the Temple of Cádiz."[23] The third pamphlet, anonymous and also dated 1730, was presented as an "extract of the opinions expressed by masters consulted with regard to the doubts voiced about the foundations, ground plans and elevations of the cathedral church."[24] Its purpose seems to have been to exonerate Acero of blame for the added expense and construction delays that might have resulted from concerns about the solidity of the foundations and the stability of the dome, and to "satisfy the benefactors, supporters and friends of Truth." In other words, it seems to have been Acero's last plea before the court of public opinion, after he had left the building site in 1729, offended by the misgivings of the cathedral chapter, which, on its side, had accused him of being "stubborn," of "inconstancy and inequality in the handling of the construction," and of "being politically inept." Acero was thus the first polemicist in Spain to have gone to press with the defense of an architectural project. The only precedent of which I am aware is that of Juan Gómez de Trasmonte, an architect in Mexico City, who in 1635 published his defense of proposed changes to the cathedral of that city in

the form of a letter including a drawing of one of the new pillars that were to be introduced, under the explanation, "Juan Gómez de Trasmonte, master builder of the Cathedral, and Royal houses of this City . . . suggests as appropriate . . . the removal of the four Pillars of the Crossing, for being of little thickness for their function."[25] Both of these architects, filled with personal pride, went so far as to put into print works addressed not only to the authority of the viceroy or to the cathedral chapters, but to a much larger segment of the population, thereby soliciting the support of what today we would call public opinion.

On the margins of the debate about structural soundness, and demonstrating the importance of scientific as opposed to artistic arguments in architecture, the first of the three pamphlets, together with some of the information from the other two, is a valuable resource on the history of the cathedral and its architect. These texts indicate that as soon as the crypt and the underground vaults were finished, the "malice of two [unidentified] men" directed criticism to the proportions of the building that was beginning to rise—to "the eyes of those who see less, even though they are always looking." The cathedral chapter decided that plans would be sent to Madrid to be appraised by the leading architects of the court. On their request, drawings of the foundations of the new cathedral were also sent. In 1727 three architects issued reports: the municipal chief mason Francisco Ruiz on 25 July;[26] the city's chief architect, Pedro de Ribera (1681–1742), on 21 August;[27] and Francisco José de Silva, a Theatine and regular cleric of the order of Saint Cajetan, on 23 August. All three approved the design of the foundations, citing different authoritative models.[28] Nonetheless, they insisted on the strengthening of the main piers (*machos torales*) in order to support the height of the highest cupola. For his part, Ruiz "praised" especially the "contrast created by the columns placed in the diagonals of the piers, or pillars, because the author shows what he thinks they should be, according to the order of the plan; otherwise the plan should be changed" (*demuestra los que le parece deben ser, siguiendo el método de la Planta, la que confiessa sería mejor mudar en tal caso*). Actually, Ribera and Silva, as we shall see, each dared to draw his own design, and Silva even praised the design by his colleague from Madrid.

Other assessments of the foundation design in Cádiz itself were requested, in addition to these reports from the court. Leonardo de Figueroa (c. 1655–1730), chief architect of the Colegio de San Telmo in Seville,[29] and the Jesuit Francisco Gómez (1678–1749)[30] examined the plans and the construction as it stood in 1728 and signed their respective reports on 19 and 21 July. They praised the "Pantheon, of great capaciousness, and openness, supported partly by flat arches and partly by vaults (*parte a Regla y parte de Bóbedas*), embedded, secure, and executed according to the precepts of masonry." Figueroa considered the height of the crossing tower over the principal nave (250 feet, and thus 97 feet higher than the vaults of the cathedral of Seville) to be excessive and recommended that it be replaced by a sail vault. He also thought that the height of the flanking towers, which he understood to be thirty feet taller than the Giralda in Seville,[31] was excessive in proportion to their width and advised that their height not exceed five times their diameter. Gómez, on the other hand, rejected the dome—"the crossing tower

with its dome shown in the plan cannot survive"—and the proportion of the dome's triangular pillars[32] to the span of the supporting arches, also recommending a sail vault in its place. With regard to the flanking towers, he allowed for a height of six times the width, the proportions of the minaret of the mosque-cathedral of Córdoba, but reduced their diameter and corresponding height from 300 to 216 feet. The main problems that Gómez found, however, were with the foundations. He recommended that the iron frame (*pilotaje de acero*) be

9. Opening page of Vicente de Acero y Acebo, *Probocado Don Vicente de Azero . . .* (Cádiz, 1728) Mexico City, Collección Guillermo Tovar de Teresa

replaced by wooden pilings and a Roman-style rubble masonry of coarse wet sand or stone rubble.

For his part, Acero thought that he had surpassed the other architects and great craftsmen who had contributed to the design of his cathedral, even though some might have impugned his authorship of the facade and towers. Diego de Landa refuted this particular charge, and the mathematician Lucas de Valdés praised Acero's own "ingenuity."[33] Nor had Acero "fainted" at the idea that the

10. Cádiz Cathedral, facade
Author photograph

cathedral would be thought of as "an undertaking, that was to remain in the sight of the whole World: such is Cádiz, in the variety of Nations that come to her." In spite of the criticisms, Acero had already given proof of his "daring" architecture in the "Pantheon," or crypt (see fig. 8), designed and constructed like a "Rotunda," "without Supports, or common keystone." He trusted in Divine Providence to provide the cathedral chapter with the resources and himself with "life enough to perfect the Temple unto the last Molding," although "with little gray hair to comb (as someone said) there is no need for a miraculous intervention." Nevertheless, "in case God should call him to judgment," Acero offered "with the greatest care, [to] dedicate [himself] to putting forth true demonstrations, and secure Rules, and Guidelines, so that the cathedral will be finished as it was planned, and designed."[34]

Elsewhere, Acero tells us of his training as a stonemason under Francisco Hurtado Izquierdo during the construction of the Sagrario of Granada and of his work as the master builder for the cathedral of Guadix[35] and the charterhouse of El Paular (Rascafría, Segovia), not far from Madrid.[36] He also writes about what he has read, of his trips through Spain and, "to enrich himself with [knowledge of] examples and specimens," his trips through "the Provinces of Italy, seeing . . . the most celebrated buildings, that are also living texts and not only mute masters."[37]

His interests, however, do not seem to have been drawn either to the works of architects whom he called the "second Ancients," such as Bramante at Saint Peter's or Juan de Herrera at the Escorial, or to his own contemporaries. Instead he singled out as "modern" and "heroes of the discipline" Vignola (citing D'Avilier's print of the Gesù in Rome)[38] and Pellegrino Tibaldi (citing Andrea Pozzo's print of San Fedele in Milan),[39] as well as Michelangelo's work at Saint Peter's. For Acero, a fundamental idea and goal was the general need—noted even for certain Gothic buildings—to reduce the thickness of the pillars, allowing for greater capacity within the building and consequently "greater beauty." If Bramante had given birth to the brilliant idea of the domed drum (a rotunda with a round clerestory, hemi-spherical dome, and lantern over four main arches, as Acero put it) and had at the time been accused of being "bold in his intent to put into practice his never before imagined thought," Acero asked himself who would be "so brash, as to be governed by the rules of the first and second Ancients, while in the moderns one has the experience of their Works by their pens both written and designed."[40] On the basis of these models, it was possible to arrive at the solution he proposed for the cathedral dome, with two shells and two lanterns, taken, also through Pozzo, from the project that the Jesuit mathematician Orazio Grassi had designed in 1626 for the dome of Sant'Ignazio in Rome.[41]

Acero's contemporaries, on the other hand, could supply a new decorative repertory, beginning with Francesco Borromini's fluted decorations for the Collegio di Propaganda Fide,[42] or with Pozzo's windows with inverted pediments; or they could supply new syntactical ideas, such as those for the design of elliptical pillars with obliquely placed columns. But these elements could also be based on the works of architects of greater authority—"classic architects," Acero called them—such as Michelangelo's Cappella Sforza at Santa Maria Maggiore,[43] while the freestanding pillars could be based on Tibaldi's San Fedele[44] and the ample "butterfly" piers with oblique columns in Raphael's project for Saint Peter's, published by Sebastiano Serlio.[45]

But it was not only Italian architects who enjoyed classic status in Acero's eyes; he also admired the "great Diego de Siloé [Burgos, c. 1490–Granada, 1563], Spaniard[;] . . . as a Prince in the profession of Architecture, we should take off our hats when we speak of him, as the Italians do for Michelangelo Buonarroti." Siloé's importance resided in inventing solutions that, consecrated by use, had enabled the progress of architecture. His stature could be verified by his cathedrals at Granada and Málaga[46] and, among the modern works that carried on the development, by those of Jaén and Guadix and the Sagrario of Granada (1705–1738), by Acero's master Francisco Hurtado Izquierdo.[47] Hurtado himself had attempted to "disguise," in the typical manner of the Granada cathedral, the basic structure of Saint Peter's;

11. Cádiz Cathedral, aisle
Author photograph

in Cádiz, Acero, in turn, seems to have tried to merge the plans of the Sagrario and the cathedral of Granada.

In Cádiz Cathedral, a curvilinear rather than an undulating facade (fig. 10; see also fig. 6), modified from the original design by Acero's successors, opened into a church that "stretched" the Sagrario and, for its pillars with columns at right angles to each other, substituted elliptical pillars with oblique columns (figs. 11 and 12) whose diagonals mirrored the pattern of the groin vaults—almost Gothic in style—over the

12. Cádiz Cathedral, nave vaults
Author photograph

ambulatories, Acero did not (as Baldassare Longhena had done at the Salute in Venice) insert a sixteen-sided polygon between the exterior wall of the chapels and the exterior wall of the rotunda, but kept the octagon active, making some of the chapels coincide with its angles and causing the facades of the chapels to break forward into the ambulatory (fig. 18).

In contrast to the convention, in secular buildings, of openings in a flat wall, Acero's chapels and the windows above them open on corners (figs. 18 and 19), reminding us of certain solutions in fifteenth-century Valencian Gothic and sixteenth-century Andalusian architecture (fig. 20). What is more, and as if to complicate matters further, the vaults of some chapels and bays abandon a concave shape for a convex one, echoing, for instance, the curvilinear forms of the pillars of the main arches that join the dome and the rotunda (see figs. 12 and 15), interconnecting rather than separating these spaces for the celebration of the Mass and for prayer. Curves, angles, and corners dominate this new progression from Siloé's and Hurtado's personal styles, characterized by Acero himself as *arquitectura crespa*—choppy, or spiky, architecture—as if it were part of a seascape in the whitecaps of Atlantic waters (see figs. 11, 12 , and 14). It was from the sea that one would first see the cathedral, sited on the so-called Frente del Vendaval (gale-wind waterfront) of Cádiz.[48]

It is no wonder that Acero's contemporaries judged the cathedral of Cádiz overall as a "provocation," to which the provoked Acero, proud of his deed, responded with a published statement. Spanish baroque architecture would come to be defined by various elements, including the decidedly mathematical tone of its geometrical bias; an emphasis on stonecutting and all its consequences; a taste for polygonal, irregular, and oblique forms and transverse, diagonal, and foreshortened views; and a desire to recycle specific Spanish Gothic and Renaissance models as historical references and quotations. A century before, the Flemish Jesuit and mathematician Juan Carlos de la Falla, in one of his lectures on architecture at the Imperial College of Madrid in which he criticized the limitations and lack of a systematic method in Vitruvius and Serlio, had stated:

aisles, projected by Acero but never built (fig. 13; see also fig. 5). The main altar was positioned under a dome at the crossing, and behind it, an arch with a triple curvature led to a rotunda similar to the one in the cathedral of Granada, designed to make room for the choir stalls, topped by a domical vault with lunettes and surrounded by an ambulatory (figs. 14–17). An octagonal geometry ordered the entire space of the chevet (fig. 13), rationalizing the irregular decagonal form Siloé used in Granada. Yet, contrary to medieval and modern conventions for

"It is frightful that we have put more effort into conforming to the constructions of the ancients than to their way of dressing, as if it were impossible to find a thousand types of adornments and proportions in the act of building, just as we have found different styles of dressing."[49]

It is obvious that in the era of crinolines, corsets, and frock coats, the Greek peplos and the Roman toga would be scorned not only for their sparse ornament, but also for their simplicity of design. Acero could blame his departure on those who saw "the ancients as oracles," even though his cathedral was a conscious reflection of the cultural tradition of medieval and modern *all'antica* Spanish architecture. He could be faulted not only for pretensions of architectural modernism, but also for political ineptitude. Nevertheless, his resignation as the cathedral's architect could be seen as a logical end to this story. He made architecture an economic, social, and political expression as well as an artistic one, and he took the debate about construction from the privacy of the chapter-house and the bishop's study to a public arena. And that was probably too modern.

Cádiz Cathedral: plan (after O. Schubert)

13. Otto Schubert, *Plan of Cádiz Cathedral*, c. 1908
From Otto Schubert, *Geschichte des Barock in Spanien* (Esslingen, 1908)

15. Cádiz Cathedral, main
arch under the dome
Author photograph

16. Cádiz Cathedral, interior
of the dome
Author photograph

17. Cádiz Cathedral, rotunda
from the ambulatory
Author photograph

18. Cádiz Cathedral, facades
of ambulatory chapels
Author photograph

19. Cádiz Cathedral, window
over ambulatory chapels
Author photograph

20. Iglesia de El Salvador,
Úbeda (Jaén), entrance to the
sacristy
Author photograph

NOTES

1. At that time, when Spain was still the major world power but not the leading European power, Cádiz was its fourth most populous city. With about 72,000 inhabitants, it trailed Madrid, Barcelona, and Seville. The Casa de Contratación was returned briefly to Seville in 1725. Cádiz lost its monopoly over the Carrera de las Indias in 1778, with King Charles III's Decree of Free Trade. Antonio García-Baquero González, *Cádiz y el Atlántico (1717–1778)*, 2 vols. (Seville, 1976).

2. Henry Kamen, *La Guerra de Sucesión en España 1700–1715* (Barcelona, 1975), and Henry Kamen, *Felipe V, el rey que reinó dos veces* (Madrid, 2000), 44–131.

3. "Emporium of the orb" is from the title of a book by Fray Jerónimo de la Concepción, *Emporio del orbe, Cádiz ilustrada* (Amsterdam, 1690).

4. This characterization was accurate at least of the cathedral, which fed itself, so to speak, on American commerce. "Gullet of the Americas" (garganta de las Américas) is from the minutes of a cathedral chapter meeting of 1793 (Archivo catedralicio, actas generales, libro de actas de 1793). A tax assessment was awarded to the cathedral by royal decree on 25 November 1726 and remained in force until the revolutionary wars of 1793. The tax equaled 25 percent of the riches aboard the first three commercial galleons arriving from America with the city of Cádiz as their destination. On the financing of the cathedral, see Lorenzo Pérez del Campo, *Las catedrales de Cádiz* (Madrid, 1988), 30–31. This tax on American commerce constituted 72.23 percent of the revenue for construction. In 1770 it was calculated that 14 million reales had been spent on construction, of which almost 75 percent came from the tax. Pascual Madoz, *Diccionario geográfico-estadístico-histórico de España y de sus posesiones de ultramar*, 16 vols. (Madrid, 1845–1850), 5:171, adds other data on the basis of what Javier de Urrutia presents: as much as 24,829,796 reales had been spent by 1793, of which 20,780,443 came from the tax, and as much as 27,384,233 reales had been spent by 1843. Javier de Urrutia, *Descripción histórico-artística de la catedral de Cádiz* (Cádiz, 1843).

5. Delfín Rodríguez Ruiz, ed., *El Real Sitio de La Granja de San Ildefonso. Retrato y escena del rey* (Madrid, 2000).

6. George Kubler, *Arquitectura de los siglos XVII y XVIII* (Madrid, 1957), 165–172. On Italianisms in Spanish baroque architecture, see also the following works by Alfonso Rodríguez G. de Ceballos: "Francisco Borromini en España," in *Borromini*, ed. Giulio Carlo Argan (Madrid, 1987), 7–58; "La huella de Bernini en España," in *Bernini*, ed. Howard Hibbard (Madrid, 1982), vii–xxx; and "El 'bel composto' berniniano a la española," in *Figuras e imágenes del Barroco: Estudios sobre el barroco español y sobre la obra de Alonso Cano*, ed. José Alvarez Lopera et al. (Madrid, 1999), 67–86.

7. Joaquín Bérchez, *Arquitectura barroca valenciana* (Valencia, 1993), 78–86; Joaquín Bérchez and Arturo Zaragozá Catalán, *Valencia: Arquitectura religiosa*, ed. Joachín Bérchez, Monumentos de la comunidad valenciana, vol. 10 (Valencia, 1995), 44–48; Fernando Pingarrón, "La fachada barroca de la catedral de Valencia: Los contratos originales y otras noticias de la obra en torno al año 1703," *Archivo de arte valenciano* 67 (1986): 52–64; and Fernando Pingarrón, *Arquitectura religiosa del siglo XVII en la ciudad de Valencia* (Valencia, 1998), 130–142. Rudolf was in Madrid in 1701 after studying in Paris and Rome. He went back to Austria with the archduke.

8. Fernando Marías, "Elocuencia y laconismo: La arquitectura barroca española y sus historias," in *Figuras e imágenes del barroco: Estudios sobre el barroco español y sobre la obra de Alonso Cano*, ed. Delfín Rodríguez Ruiz (Madrid, 1999), 87–112.

9. Nina Ayala Mallory, "El Transparente de la catedral de Toledo," *Archivo español de arte* 42 (1969): 255–288; José María Prados, "Las trazas del Transparente y otros dibujos de Narciso Tomé para la catedral de Toledo," *Archivo español de arte* 49 (1976): 387–416; José María Prados, "Los Tomé: Un familia de artistas españoles del siglo XVIII" (Ph.D. diss, Universidad Complutense de Madrid, 1991), 1:56–425.

10. According to the inscription on the model, Charles III commissioned it through his secretary of state, the conde de Ricla Ambrosio Funes de Villalpando, as part of "a general collection of relief models of all the cities and sites of his kingdoms." The commission was given to Francesco Sabattini, general manager of the corps of engineers and chief architect to the king, who turned it over to Jiménez, with a yearly budget of 6,000 escudos. It seems that the budget rose to 213,397 reales. The only models created were that of Cádiz (and one of the fort of La Concepción, now in the Museo del Ejército, Madrid), probably because of the city's vulnerable military position. Made to be assembled and dismantled, these models were destined for one of the royal residences of the court in Madrid (they ended up at the Casón de Buen Retiro), where they were to be kept with the preparatory plans and outlines.

The characteristics of the city model, such as its scale (7 *varas* per Castillian *pulgada*), its formal aspects, the fact that principal buildings were not fixed to the base and thus were changeable, and the richness of the materials—the ships made of mahogany and pear with artillery of ebony or brass, the sandalwood, Flemish pine, guaiacum, palo santo, marble, and black paper—suggest a difference in intention, even if the king was inspired by French *plans-reliefs*. Jiménez based his model on the ground plan of the city (Cádiz, Archivo Municipal) that had been drawn by the military engineer Ignacio Sala and on the plans of the cathedral under construction.

On the model, see César Pemán, "El plano relieve de Cádiz de 1777–1779," in *Actas del XXIII C.I.H.A: España entre el Mediterráneo y el Atlántico*, 3 vols. (Granada, 1976), 3:651–665; Ricardo Moreno Criado, *La maqueta de Cádiz* (Cádiz, 1977); Antonio Bonet Correa, *Cartografía de plazas, fuertes y ciudades españolas, siglos XVII–XIX: Planos del Archivo Militar Francés* (Madrid, 1991), xlviii; José Luis Sancho, "La colección de relieves de las fortificaciones del Reino, y el 'Modelo' de la Ciudad de Cádiz," in *Francisco Sabatini 1721–1797*, ed. Delfín Rodríguez (Madrid, 1993), 510–511; Fernando Marías, "From the 'Ideal City' to Real Cities: Perspectives, Chorographies, Models, Vedute," in *The Triumph of the Baroque: Architecture in Europe, 1600–1750*, ed. Henry A. Millon [exh. cat., Palazzina di Caccia di Stupinigi] (Turin, 1999), 218–240. On *plans-reliefs*, see Antoine de Roux, Nicolas Faucherre, and Guillaume Monsaingeon, *Les Plans en relief des places du roy* (Paris, 1989); Isabelle Warmoes, *Le Musée des plans-reliefs: Maquettes historiques de villes fortifiées* (Paris, 1997).

11. *Descripción de la Nueva Iglesia Cathedral de Cádiz y estado de su Fábrica hasta el día presente* (Cádiz, 1770); Antonio Ponz, *Viaje de España* (Madrid, 1947), 1565–1566; Javier de Urrutia, *Descripción histórico-artística de la catedral de Cádiz* (Cádiz, 1843); Pablo Gutiérrez Moreno, "La cúpula del maestro Vicente Acero para la nueva catedral de Cádiz," *Archivo español de arte y arqueología* 12 (1928): 183–186; Pablo Antón Solé, *La catedral de Cádiz: Estudio histórico-artístico de su arquitectura* (Cádiz, 1975); Pablo Antón Solé, *Catálogo de planos, mapas y dibujos del Archivo catedralicio de Cádiz* (Cádiz, 1976); *La catedral nueva de Cádiz* (Seville, 1993); Pérez del Campo 1988; Lorenzo Pérez del Campo, "Bases materiales de la arquitectura andaluza: El comercio americano y la financiación de la catedral de Cádiz," *Boletín de arte de la Universidad de Málaga* 6 (1985): 135–148. René Taylor, "La fachada de Vicente Acero para la catedral de Cádiz," *Archivo español de arte* 42 (1969): 302–305; Antonio Bonet Correa, *Andalucía barroca: Arquitectura y urbanismo* (Barcelona, 1978), 131–138; Pedro Navascués Palacio, "Nuevas trazas para la catedral de Cádiz," in *Miscelánea de Arte* (Madrid, 1982), 174–176; Delfín Rodríguez Ruiz, "Tradición e innovación en la arquitectura de Vicente Acero," *Anales de arquitectura* 4 (1992): 37–49; Marías 1999, 87–112.

12. Antonio Ponz, *Viaje de España*, 18 vols. (Madrid, 1791–1794), 16–18: 37.

13. Eugenio Llaguno y Amírola, *Noticias de los arquitectos y arquitectura de España desde su restauración*, 4 vols. (Madrid, 1829), 4:100.

14. The Real Colegio de Guardamarinas, or Academia de Guardias Marinas, was founded in 1717 to train Spanish sailors. The academy taught geometry, trigonometry, cosmography, geography, hydraulics and fluids, fortification, naval construction, navigation, and sailing maneuvers. See Francisco José González, "El Real Observatorio de la Armada y su faceta docente: Los estudios superiores (siglos XVIII y XIX)," *Gades* 18 (1988), and, in the same issue, Manuel Ravina, "Notas sobre la enseñanza de las matemáticas en Cádiz a fines del siglo XVII."

15. A model (or models) and original drawings by Acero seem to have been given to the Academia de Nobles Artes de Cádiz in 1813, once they were thought no longer to be operative for the building. See Antón Solé 1976, 70–73.

16. Armengual (Málaga, 1663–Chiclana [Cádiz], 1730) was the son of a fisherman who was granted the title marques de Campoalegre in 1715 for his political service under Philip V. He was also the supervisor and vicar general of the diocese of Zaragoza, canon of Santiago de Compostela, and auxiliary bishop of Zaragoza. In 1705 he went to Madrid as governor of the Real Consejo de Hacienda. In 1707 he was named councilor and *camarista* of the Consejo Supremo de Castilla and general director of the Real Hacienda, where he remained until 1715, the year in which he was named bishop of Cádiz, taking his seat in 1717. As bishop of Cádiz, he was also the head chaplain and vicar general of the Real Armada del Mar Océano. See Pablo Antón Solé, *La iglesia gaditana en el siglo XVIII* (Cádiz, 1994), 151–163.

17. The collection of 672 items (179 religious scenes, 258 landscapes and still lifes, 14 mythological scenes, 51 portraits, and 58 genre scenes) included paintings by El Greco, Alonso Cano, Bartolomeo Esteban Murillo, Juan Carreño de Miranda, and Hieronymous Bosch and copies by Rubens and Annibale Carraci. See Arturo Morgado García, *Iglesia y sociedad en el Cádiz del siglo XVIII* (Cádiz, 1989), 47–54. The inventory of the collection is in the Archivo Diocesano, Cádiz (A.D.C.): Varios, Leg. 2296.

18. Fernando Marías, "Alonso Cano y la columna salomónica," in *Figuras e imágenes del barroco: Estudios sobre el barroco español y sobre la obra de Alonso Cano*, ed. Delfín Rodriguez Ruiz (Madrid, 1999), 291–321. For the quotations from Acero, see note 22, below.

19. José de Ceballos Bustillo, Seville, c. 1740, to Fray Tomás del Valle, bishop of Cádiz, Archivo catedralicio, cuentas de fábrica, legajo sin numerar; quoted in Taylor 1969.

20. The three drawings are catalogued in Antón Solé 1976 as follows. Plan (fig. 5; numbered 1 in the catalogue: 104 by 86 centimeters; inscription, recto: *Planta de la Sta. Iglesia Catedral con título de Sta. Cruz de Cádiz. A° 1725 / Escala de Varas Castellanas*; inscription, verso: *Como Diputados actuales de la nueva Catedral certificamos que el Plano de la Buelta se hallaba en la Contaduría del Illmo. Cabildo tenido por de Dn. Vicente Acero. Cádiz, 31 en° de 1788. Dn. Juan Quintian Ponte. Pedro Ignacio del Campo. Dn. Pedro Juan Sánchez.* Elevation (fig. 3; numbered 3 in the catalogue: 93.5 by 103 centimeters; inscription, recto: *Elebación Geométrica exterior de la Sta. Iglesia Catedral de Cádiz. Año de 1725 / Escala de Varas Castellanas*; inscription, verso: *Como Diputados actuales de la nueva Catedral certificamos que el Plano de la Buelta se hallaba en la Contaduría del Illmo. Cabildo tenido por de Dn. Vicente Acero. Cádiz, 31 en° de 1788. Dn. Juan Quintian Ponte. Pedro Ignacio del Campo. Dn. Pedro Juan Sánchez.* Section (fig. 4; numbered 2 in the catalogue: 100 by 108 centimeters; inscription, recto: *Sección Geométrica de la Sta. Iglesia de Cádiz.*

Año de 1725 / Escala de Varas Castellanas; inscription, verso: *Como Diputados actuales de la nueva Catedral certificamos que el Plano de la Buelta se hallaba en la Contaduría del Illmo. Cabildo tenido por de Dn. Vicente Acero. Cádiz, 31 enº de 1788. Dn. Juan Quintian Ponte. Pedro Ignacio del Campo. Dn. Pedro Juan Sánchez.*

21. Madrid, Biblioteca Nacional de España, AB 877. It was first published as a photograph (see Taylor 1969); it is possibly a copy (29.7 by 14 centimeters; pencil, pen, and gray and black wash) rather than an original, as Delfín Rodríguez Ruiz supposed. See his "Álbum de Antonio García Reinoso," in *Dibujos de arquitectura y ornamentación de la Biblioteca Nacional: Siglos XVI y XVII*, ed. Elena Santiago Páez (Madrid, 1991), 324–325.

22. Vicente Azero [*sic*], *Probocado Don Vicente de Azero, de los dictámenes, que dieron el R. P. Don Francisco Joseph de Silva, D. Pedro de Rivera, y D. Francisco Ruiz, Maestros de Arquitectura en la Villa, y Corte de Madrid; y el P. Francisco Gómez de la Compañía de Jesús, y D. Leonardo de Figueroa, assimismo Maestros en la Ciudad de Sevilla, responde á los papéles, en que han contradicho el plano, y alzado dispuesto por Don Vicente, para la nueva Cathedral de Cádiz, cuya Fábrica está á su cargo, como Maestro Mayor de la obra de dicho Templo*, n.p., n.d. [Cádiz, 1728], Mexico City, Colección Guillermo Tovar de Teresa. The date is inferred from the narration of events. On the pamphlet, see Rodríguez Ruiz 1991, 322, note 33, and Rodríguez Ruiz 1992, 37–49.

23. José Gallego y Oviedo del Portal, *Papel manifiesto que da al público don J. Gallego y Oviedo del Portal Maestro mayor de la Fábrica Nueva de la S. I. Catedral de Jaén, sobre el juicio que ha hecho de la Fábrica del Templo de Cádiz*, n.p., n.d. [Cádiz, 1730]. A copy is preserved in Seville, Universidad de Sevilla, Facultad de Filosofía y Letras, Laboratorio de Arte Francisco Murillo Herrera, Sig. 9.510–21.083.

24. *Extracto de los dictámenes dados por los maestros consultados sobre dudas que se han ofrecido en cimientos, plantas y alzados de la Iglesia Catedral que se está fabricando en esta ciudad de Cádiz, con que se informa a todos y satisfacen a los bienhechores afectos y amigos de la verdad* (Cádiz, [1730]). A copy is preserved in Seville, Universidad de Sevilla, Facultad de Filosofía y Letras, Laboratorio de Arte Francisco Murillo Herrera, Sig. 9.510–21.083. I thank Dr. Fátima Halcón for the copies of this and the pamphlet cited in the preceding note.

25. The drawing was first photographed by Luis G. Serrano; see Serrano, *La traza original con que fue construida la catedral de México* (Mexico City, 1964). See also Fernando Marías, "Reflexiones sobre las catedrales de España y Nueva España," *Ars Longa* 5 (1994): 45–51, and Martha Fernández, "Juan Gómez de Trasmonte en la catedral de México," *Arquitectura y creación* (Mexico City, 1994), 39–72. It was also analyzed by Joaquín Bérchez; see Bérchez, *Arquitectura mexicana de los siglos XVII y XVIII* (Mexico City, 1992)

26. Little is known about Francisco Ruiz. Between 1726 and 1735 he worked on the reconstruction of the Dominican church of Santo Tomás in Madrid.

27. For the little that is known about Ribera, see Matilde Verdú Ruiz, *El arquitecto Pedro de Ribera (1681–1742)* (Madrid, 1998), 189.

28. In his discussion, Silva referred to the church of San Cayetano in Madrid, designed by Ribera, and to the college of the monastery of San Cayetano at Salamanca, a work by Silva himself (1702–1709) under the direction of Domingo Pérez. See María Nieves Rupérez Almajano, *Urbanismo de Salamanca en el siglo XVIII* (Salamanca, 1992), 112–114 and 262.

29. On Leonardo de Figueroa (Utiel, Cuenca, c. 1660–Seville, 1730), see Antonio Sancho Corbacho, *Arquitectura barroca sevillana del siglo XVIII* (Madrid, 1952) and Jesús Rivas Carmona, *Leonardo de Figueroa: Una nueva visión de un viejo maestro* (Seville, 1994).

30. Francisco Gómez (Fregenal de la Sierra [Huelva], 1678–Bogarra, 1749), a lay member of the Society of Jesus and referred to as *architectus* only beginning in 1717, lived and worked in Andújar (1717); Córdoba (1722–1726); Baeza (1727–1735 and 1738); and Seville, Fregenal, and Granada (1740–1749). It is possible that he designed, in 1739, the magnificent facade of the Jesuit College of San Justo y Pastor in Granada and the staircase of the Jesuit College of Santa Catalina in Córdoba. See Antonio Gallego y Burín, *El Barroco granadino* (Granada, 1956), 46–47; Alfonso Rodríguez G. de Ceballos, *Bartolomé de Bustamante y los orígenes de la arquitectura jesuítica en España* (Roma, 1967), 182; Jesús Rivas Carmona, *Arquitectura y policromía: Los mármoles del Barroco andaluz* (Córdoba, 1990), 120–121 and 126; and René Taylor, "El Sagrario de la Catedral de Granada y la Junta de maestros de 1737," *Anuario del Departamento de Historia y Teoría del Arte* [Universidad Autónoma de Madrid] 7–8 (1995–1996): 179, note 45.

31. In Acero's drawings of 1725 the height of the towers was actually 300 feet, equal to that of the Giralda of Seville.

32. On that topic see Fray Lorenzo de San Nicolás, *Arte y uso de architectura* (Madrid, 1639), chap. 21, and Fernando Marías, "Piedra y ladrillo en la arquitectura española del siglo XVI," in *Les chantiers de la Renaissance*, ed. Jean Guillaume (Paris, 1991), 71–84.

33. Acero [1728], 21. Lucas de Valdés (1661–1725), a son of the painter Juan de Valdés Leal, came from Seville, where he had worked also as a painter, to Cádiz in 1719 to teach mathematics at the royal naval academy.

34. Acero [1728], 16–19.

35. Carlos Asenjo Sedano, *Guía de Guadix* (Granada, 1989), 161–163.

36. See René Taylor, "Francisco Hurtado and His School," *The Art Bulletin* 32 (1950): 25–61, and René Taylor, *Arquitectura andaluza: Los hermanos Sánchez de Rueda* (Salamanca, 1978).

37. Acero [1728], 16–19. Acero had been in Italy to perfect his training, according to the military engineer Andrés de los Cobos, writing in 1733. Cobos pointed to Acero as one of the most "able" architects, since he possessed "sufficient knowledge of theory in the parts of Mathematics that concern his profession . . . and mastered with excellence the practice of stonecutting, he had a special taste in all the works I have seen and I know he built [y un especial gusto en quanto le he visto y he sabido ha executado], and he is so devoted to his faculty, that once he knew architecture well, he went without necessity to Italy to enrich himself in [knowledge of] specimens. . . . " Andrés de los Cobos to José Patiño, 1733, transcribed in María Jesús Callejo, "El Real Sitio de San Ildefonso" (doctoral thesis, Universidad Complutense de Madrid, 1988), 3:973–974.

The chronology of Acero's trip is unclear. The years 1700–1707 have been proposed for this Italian journey, but it more likely took place between 1710 and 1713, coinciding with Cobos' time there, spent mainly in Milan, between 1710 and 1712. René Taylor speculated that Acero would have traveled to Italy between 1716 and 1719, after he was named chief architect (according to Taylor) of the cathedral of Guadix and before he developed his supposed intention to enter the charterhouse of El Paular as a lay brother in 1719. See Taylor 1995–1996, 179, note 38.

38. Augustin-Charles D'Aviler, *Cours d'architecture* (Paris, 1691 and 1720).

39. Andrea Pozzo, *Perspectiva pictorum et architectorum . . .* (Rome, 1693–1698 and 1700–1702).

40. Acero [1728], 12.

41. The Jesuit and mathematician Orazio Grassi (1583–1654) drew two projects for the dome of Sant'Ignazio, that of 1626, referred to here, and one in 1651. On the latter, see Richard Bösel, *Jesuitenarchitektur in Italien 1540–1773* (Vienna, 1985), 198; Joseph Connors, "Borromini's Sant'Ivo alla Sapienza: The Spiral," *The Burlington Magazine* 138, no. 1123 (1996): 679; and Vitale Zanchettin, "Il tiburio di Sant'Andrea alle Fratte: Propositi e condizionamenti di un testo borrominiano," *Annali di architettura* 9 (1997): 121–123. The first was reproduced by Andrea Pozzo (Pozzo 1693–1698 and 1700–1702, vol. 2, fig. 94) and by Alessandro Specchi for Domenico de' Rossi (d. 1729), *Studio d'architettura civile*, 3 vols. (Rome, 1702, 1711, 1721), 3:553. See Simona Ciofetta, "Lo *Studio d'architettura civile* edito da Domenico de' Rossi (1702, 1711, 1721)," in *In urbe architectus, modelli, disegni, misure: La professione dell'architettura, Roma 1600–1750*, ed. Bruno Contardi and Giovanna Curcio (Rome, 1991), 214–228, and Gianfranco Spagnesi, *Alessandro Specchi, alternativa al borrominismo* (Turin, 1997), 14–19. Grassi's solution derived from that for the church of Santa Maria di Loreto in Roma, by Antonio da Sangallo the Younger and Giacomo del Duca, reproduced in Gian Giacomo de Rossi [Jo. Iacobo de Rubeis], *Insignium Romae Templorum Prospectus exteriores interioresque a celebrioribus Architectis inveni* (Rome, 1684). It does not seem to have been influenced by the solutions proposed by François Mansart in his project for the Chapelle Bourbon in Saint-Denis, by Christopher Wren's design for the dome of Saint Paul's, London, or by Jules Hardouin Mansart's dome for the Invalides in Paris.

42. Illustrations of the Collegio de Propaganda Fide were published by Alessandro Specchi in Domenico de' Rossi, *Studio d'architettura civile*, 3 vols. (Rome, 1702, 1711, 1721), vols. 1 and 2.

43. Michelangelo's design for the Cappella Sforza was published in Gian Giacomo de Rossi, *Disegni di varii altari e cappelle . . . di Roma* (Rome, n.d.), plate 13.

44. On San Fedele, see Giuseppe Dardanello, "Esperienze e opere in Piemonte e Liguria," in *Andrea Pozzo*, ed. Vittorio De Feo and Vittorio [Valentino] Martinelli (Milan, 1996), 24–41.

45. Raphael's Saint Peter's project was published in Sebastiano Serlio, *Il terzo libro dell'archittetura* (Venice, 1540) and in the Spanish edition, *Tercero y quarto libro de architectura* (Toledo, 1552, 1563, 1573), xxi.

46. Earl E. Rosenthal, *The Cathedral of Granada: A Study in Spanish Renaissance Architecture* (Princeton, 1961); Fernando Marías, *El largo siglo XVI: Los usos artísticos del Renacimiento español* (Madrid, 1989); Marías, "'Trazas' e disegni nella architettura spagnola del Cinquecento: La cattedrale di Granada," *Annali di architettura* 9 (1997): 200–217.

47. Taylor 1995–1996, 149–179.

48. Even Acero's scrolled buttresses seem to distance themselves—in a choppy way—from those used by Baldassare Longhena in Santa Maria della Salute in Venice as well as from his most likely source, Sangallo the Younger's project for San Giovanni dei Fiorentini in Rome, engraved by Antonio Labacco.

49. Jean-Charles de La Faille, *Tratado de la Architectura* (1636), Biblioteca del Palacio Real de Madrid, Ms. 3729, 2.

WALTER ROSSA
University of Coimbra

Lisbon's Waterfront Image as an Allegory of Baroque Urban Aesthetics

A comparison of sixteenth- and eighteenth-century views of Lisbon reveals a striking fact. Take, for instance, a late-sixteenth-century ink and watercolor view and a late-eighteenth-century pencil drawing, both panoramas of the city from the south bank of the Tagus (figs. 1 and 2). In the first example the Terreiro do Paço—the large space open to the Tagus and in front of the royal palace, the Paço da Ribeira—is at the center of the image. The rest of the city is represented by recognizable depictions of a handful of important buildings emerging from an otherwise highly stereotyped view of houses and public spaces. The pencil view, by contrast, shows the waterfront as a whole with the city behind it. We can easily recognize specific houses, palaces, and churches in a realistic cityscape.

Many such views exist, and in all of them the difference between earlier and later representations is clear. With the exception of engravings by the Flemish artist Dirk Stoop from the 1660s, not until the beginning of the eighteenth century was Lisbon portrayed with more than a very superficial interest in anything except the Terreiro do Paço area and one or two buildings in the background. Only after 1700 did views include detailed representations of other parts of the city, exhibiting a special concern for realism in addition to using an expanded range of techniques and supports.

It is my conviction that this relatively late change in representations of Lisbon reflects the modernization of the city itself and of the Portuguese monarchy's idea of the relationship between Portugal's empire and its capital city. The modernization of Lisbon began after 1650 and culminated in a project for the redevelopment of Lisbon's waterfront in the second and third decades of the eighteenth century. These changes were fundamental to the rise and development of Portuguese architecture and urbanism. The earthquake of 1755 razed the few structures realized under that plan, but the formal concept survived in the lesser-known plans for Lisbon's expansion beyond the area known as Baixa, under the regime of Sebastião José de Carvalho e Mello, marquis of Pombal.[1]

An interest in defining the image of Lisbon dates from the beginning of the sixteenth century. Although the same may be said of the most important cities of Europe, Lisbon's new position as a commercial interface with the East and the New World engendered both curiosity and fascination among Europeans. Representations of Lisbon before the eighteenth century are more numerous than those of other Portuguese towns or landscapes; they are also, for the most part, the work of foreigners, specifically, from northern Europe.[2] In fact, it seems that, from the

Anonymous, *View of Lisbon*, c. 1775, pencil (detail)
Academia Nacional de Belas Artes, Lisbon

era of colonial expansion until the Enlightenment, the Portuguese had no interest in representing their own urban spaces, except for political or military purposes. These representations were usually technical or codified (maps, plans, schemes, and so on) rather than pictorial, naturalistic, or realistic.

The real concern of the Portuguese seems to have been with the material culture of their cities. The most flattering descriptions of Lisbon from the discoveries era deal essentially with the cosmopolitan, commercial, functional, and festive patterns of urban life, not with architectural or urban space. Even references to selected buildings are guided mainly by the symbolic significance of structures and their functions in the rule of the overseas empire.

An example is the well-known *Urbis Olisiponis Descriptio* (1554),[3] a laudatory work in which Damião de Goís (1502–1574) highlighted seven buildings. Only one of these was a church—the Misericórdia, a building of modest scale in the Manueline style— and another was a palace, the Paço dos Estaus, the small and architecturally unremarkable guest residence for eminent visitors built in the first half of the fifteenth century. The other buildings had trade and shipping functions, with the exception of the Hospital de Todos-os-Santos (All Saints Hospital), perhaps the only one that, in architectural and urban terms, deserves special attention. For

obvious reasons, the exclusion of the royal palace from Goís' list is most significant for this discussion.

The reality is that the kings who ruled during the Age of Discovery—John II (r. 1481–1495), Manuel I (r. 1495–1521), and John III (r. 1521–1557)—did not undertake monumental programs for the capital of the new empire. Their efforts were limited to measures and reforms that improved sanitation, regulated the expansion of the city in some areas, and cleared its center. The two principal public spaces of Lisbon to this day—the Terreiro do Paço and the large square known as Rossio—were defined by a series of unrelated decisions, not in accordance with a plan.

The last of those decisions was the siting of a large church (Saint Sebastian) on the southern edge of the Terreiro do Paço with its rear facing the river. If the church had been built, it would have established the precedent of a closed square in place of the open space toward the river. It never rose above the foundations, and Philip II of Spain (r. 1580–1596) abandoned the project as soon as he ascended the Portuguese throne.

In fact, the church drew one of the many criticisms that Francisco d'Holanda (1518–1584) reported to King Sebastian (r. 1557–1580) in 1571 in his *Da Fabrica que falece ha Cidade De Lysboa* (The building program that Lisbon needs).[4] The context for d'Holanda's negative critique consisted basi-

1. Simon de Miranda, *View of Lisbon*, c. 1575, ink and watercolor
Archivo di Stato, Turin

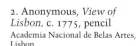

2. Anonymous, *View of Lisbon*, c. 1775, pencil
Academia Nacional de Belas Artes, Lisbon

cally of an illustrated list of monuments that, by their scale, classical architectural language, and functionality would have transformed Lisbon's image into something corresponding to the importance of the city. Like Goís, d'Holanda was a humanist and well traveled. He was also an artist, and it was in that regard that he had visited Italy three decades before at John III's order and expense. Unlike Goís, however, d'Holanda had never visited any of the large mercantile cities of northern Europe, such as Danzig, Brussels, Rotterdam, or Antwerp, which were Goís' principal references.[5] The difference makes very clear the real inspiration of d'Holanda's recommendations for Lisbon. (As in other fields of history, when we deal with opinions about urbanism we should understand their contemporary cultural biases.) These two Portuguese Renaissance intellectuals represented, to put it very simply, a liberal and mercantile viewpoint in one case and an artistic, classicist, and erudite one in the other.

A detailed evaluation of the architectural and urbanistic foundations of the mythical image of Lisbon in the Age of Discovery, based on both visual and written sources, is the subject of ongoing study.[6] What matters is that history has formed an image of Lisbon inspired by its activity as a city of international significance, not by its artistic or monumental reality.

As a whole, the Lisbon of the discoveries period was spatially and aesthetically uninteresting to classically educated and Italianized Portuguese intellectuals. No important districts or buildings date from that era. Concepts of planning were late medieval. A Renaissance modernization of royal buildings and public spaces after the 1540s was of limited interest and impact in a city in which the king did not actually reside.

Philip II of Spain became king of Portugal in 1580, and it seems that in a short time he understood all this.[7] In spite of his initial intention of making Lisbon a capital, the city developed as simply another pole of his empire. But he succeeded in leaving his stamp at the center of the usual image of Lisbon: the towerlike pavilion that would be the marker of Lisbon's royal palace until the earthquake of 1755.

In the seventeenth century panoramas of Lisbon were rare, but Philip II's intervention on the western edge of the Terreiro do Paço originated a new theme in the city's imagery. The east facade of that reworked wing of the palace became the focus of new and more detailed views. But the rest of the city remained conspicuously absent from artistic consideration and production (fig. 3).

The restoration of independence from Spain in 1640 brought about a radical transformation. The city was redefined, first in military terms, with plans for a fortified ring known as the Fundamental Line of Fortification (1650). Although it enclosed such a large area that it could not be completed, it functioned as the city's limit until the middle of the nineteenth century.

At the same time the first rigorous survey of the center of Lisbon at usable scale was drafted. It confirms, incidentally, that the city's waterfront was in fact reclaimed land, choked by an unplanned, organically evolved, and disorderly assemblage of shipping and harbor facilities. The plan also shows that the Terreiro do Paço was only a large yard, similar to the one in front of the Alcazar in Madrid, suitable for military displays and pageantry but of little meaning to the city's day-to-day life. The royal palace, depicted only to show Philip II's changes, appears as an obscure and confused structure to the north of that space (fig. 4).

Otherwise Lisbon remained a city distant from its river. Its everyday life centered on its other principal public space, the large square known as Rossio, north of the Terreiro

7

3. Gustavo de Matos
Sequeira, project director,
*Model of Lisbon before the
Earthquake of 1755*, detail
showing the Paço da Ribeira
on the Terreiro do Paço,
1955–1959, wood and plaster
Museu da Cidade, Lisbon

do Paço and near the Hospital de Todos-os-Santos, which served as a marketplace in the eighteenth century.[8]

Among other structural causes, the sixty years of Spanish domination (1580–1640) and the consequent deep economic and social depression, followed by the post-restoration effort of reassuming power over an empire dispersed all over the planet, excluded the Portuguese from the artistic and aesthetic mainstream. The period after the restoration saw an eclectic return to the architecture of Portugal before the union with Spain, a revival considered to be an expression of sovereignty.[9] For this and other reasons, the development of a Portuguese baroque was long delayed.

The prolonged state of war with Spain had led to the development of an aesthetic of austerity based not only on mathematical knowledge and Cartesian method, but also on a strong tradition of minimal architectural expression. It also reflected the dominant role of military engineers in supervising major architectural works. The rebirth of Portugal as an independent state was simultaneous with the birth of the so-called Portuguese school of military architecture and engineering, which was realized through the establishment of academies of fortification all over the empire.

The recovery of independence did not mean the resumption of former sovereignty over all the possessions of the empire as it had existed in the golden sixteenth century. Therefore, after the restoration and during the subsequent war with Spain (1640–1668), Portuguese diplomacy established important channels of communication and a policy of alliances with several European monarchies.[10] Four royal weddings were particularly important in this context, for they involved the arrival in Portugal of foreign princesses and their retinues.[11] Queen Maria Francesca of Savoy came to Portugal after she married Alfonso VI in 1666 and remained after his early death to marry Peter II in 1668. Catherine of Bragança, queen of England, returned to Portugal after the death of her husband, Charles II, in 1685. Maria Sofia of Neuburg, the second wife of Peter II, arrived in Lisbon in 1687. Twenty-one years later Maria Ana of Austria would marry John V. Around 1720 the Portuguese and Savoyard diplomats in Lisbon and Rome

4. João Nunes Tinoco, *Plan of Lisbon*, 1650, ink
Museu da Cidade, Lisbon

explored a possible marriage between a Portuguese princess and the duke of Savoy.

Through the exchange of ambassadors and court personnel, these royal marriages brought the court of Lisbon into direct contact with two of the major examples of urban renovation and monumental upgrading in late-seventeenth-century Europe: London and Turin. After the earthquake of 1755, Manuel da Maia (1678–1763), the crown's chief engineer and the strategist of Lisbon's reconstruction, would cite both as examples for that undertaking in an official report to the marquis of Pombal.[12]

With the stabilization of the new dynasty after the peace with Spain in 1668 and Pope Clement IX's acknowledgment of Portuguese independence in the following year, the crown could finally attend to Lisbon's image as the capital city of the kingdom and the colonial empire. The discovery of vast gold resources in Brazil at the end of the century helped to enhance that desire and provide for the expenses. Perhaps it also stimulated fantasy.

John V was proclaimed king on New Year's Day in 1707. He was seventeen years old and would enjoy one of the longest reigns of the Portuguese monarchy, ended by his death in 1750. Within five years he had developed a policy that emphasized kingly over papal authority. The main motivation was a disagreement between the Portuguese crown and the papacy that, since the restoration, had focused on Portugal's Catholic mission in the East—the so-called Eastern Padroado (Padroado do Oriente).

The Padroado entailed a large number of exclusive rights and privileges that the papacy had conceded over time to the Portuguese crown in a series of bulls, starting with the *Inter Caetera* (1456) and culminating with the *Praecelsae Devotiones* (1514). On its side, Portugal was committed to undertaking an extensive and effective religious mission. As a small country with a small population and few resources, Portugal had never been able to support full-scale missionary activity in the overseas empire. It was explicitly for that reason that in 1622

Pope Gregory XV launched a parallel initiative through the Sacred Congregation for the Propagation of the Faith (Propaganda Fide). For decades, Rome's strategy was helped by Portugal's loss of independence, war with Spain, and the Portuguese economic crisis.[13] In spite of enormous effort during many reigns, even after Portugal recovered its independence from Spain, the Eastern Padroado was never fully restored to its former importance and territorial extent. The papacy was in fact the last of the European courts to acknowledge Portuguese sovereignty after the restoration.

Following one of his father's main commitments (as well as other objectives such as glory and kingly emulation), John V dedicated his reign largely to the renewal, growth, and ostentation of the Portuguese monarchy's world religious power. In a first step (or rehearsal), John V launched his diplomacy in Rome by obtaining the designation of collegiate church for the royal chapel. The title was conceded in the bull *Apostolatus Ministerio* of 1 March 1710. It was not coincidental that the king wanted his chapel to be dedicated to Saint Thomas, the apostle of the East, buried at Madras, a Portuguese possession, where he had founded the bishopric of Mylapore.

But that was not enough. John V's objective required an emphatic change of image—an urbanistic revision—of his capital, including its expansion. A new royal palace and a new cathedral were the cornerstones of the scheme. All he needed was a worthy architect for his architectural and planning projects.

Meanwhile, many lesser measures addressed the city's principal constraints.[14] Manuel da Maia, then a young engineer in the office of the Fundamental Line of Fortification, was charged with a comprehensive survey of Lisbon, which he finished in 1716. (Unfortunately, only a copy of the portions covering the central area has survived.) The basis for a larger-scale intervention was thus in place (fig. 5).

The survey was immediately used for one important purpose: an ecclesiastical and administrative division of the city. The approval of Pope Clement XI came with the bull *In Supremo Apostolatus Solio* of 7 November 1716. The text establishes a division between east Lisbon, the older part of

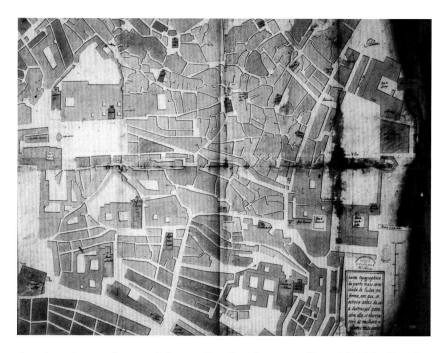

5. Manuel da Maia, *Plan of Lisbon*, original c. 1716; copy, c. 1756, ink and watercolor
Gabinete de Estudos Arqueológicos de Engenharia Militar, Lisbon

the city, clustered around the medieval cathedral, and west Lisbon, where the royal palace was located, with its chapel, the seat of the metropolitan and patriarchal designation simultaneously conferred upon Lisbon's archbishop by the pope. By that document west Lisbon became New Lisbon, a rechristening that expressed John V's strategy of renewing the city.

Thus, symbolically and ideologically, west Lisbon became the true Portuguese imperial capital, the site of the strategic fusion between patriarchy and monarchy, a new political order in which the Portuguese Padroado would presumably play a significant role. Thus also, east Lisbon was left behind as the aesthetically and urbanistically inferior part of the city, unfit for the ambitions of the king's courtiers. The city's expansion to the west—to the sea—had been a slow, organic process since the sixteenth century, but it could now be regularized and directed.

Gradually the king established customs, rituals, and a court protocol that tended to merge civic and ecclesiastic life. In the words of Angela Delaforce, "His ambition was accompanied by an ever-deepening desire to emulate the pomp and grandeur of the papal court."[15] Notwithstanding, the papacy was not the only reference in Rome. In a letter to the king attached to Manuel da Maia's survey drawing, a high-ranking court official wrote that it would be appropriate to do in

Lisbon what the Emperor Domitian had done in Rome "to everyone's applause."[16] Domitian (81–96) was responsible for constructing the principal imperial residence on the Palatine Hill and the stadium that lies under the Piazza Navona.[17] These Roman imperial evocations were a feature of John V's court as part of an overall emulation of Rome.[18] The Palatine reference has a special relevance as a token of the monarch's intentions for Lisbon. The ideological and political context of John V's attempted remaking of Lisbon was the fantasy of a "new Rome."[19]

At the foreign end of the Lisbon-Rome connection was the supernumerary ambassador Rodrigo de Sá e Menezes (1676–1733), marquis of Fontes. He had left for Rome in 1712 with orders to obtain the papal concessions already mentioned. Prime among them were the integrity and autonomy of the Eastern Padroado, which were constantly threatened by the Propaganda Fide on any pretext. They also included the diocesan division of Lisbon and the elevation of the archbishop of west Lisbon to the rank of patriarch and metropolitan, as previously recounted, and the right to nominate papal nuncios.[20]

The king's instructions to Fontes reflect the close relationship between the Portuguese and Piedmontese crowns. John V explicitly declared that he expected full support from his "friends" (and family) in Turin for his requests of the pope and, consequently, instructed his ambassador to visit them. An earlier Portuguese envoy in Rome, Andre de Melo e Castro, had received similar instructions when he left Lisbon in 1707. Correspondence from the Savoyard ambassador in Rome to his king confirms that diplomatic support.[21]

The ambassadors worked together for several years to achieve the king's objectives.[22] But it seems to have been Fontes' spectacular entry into Rome for his public audience with Clement XI in 1716, together with naval support against the Turks granted to the pope by Portugal, that, with the exception of a matter related to the Padroado (the so-called Chinese rites controversy),[23] finally won the pope's agreement, granted by the bull of 7 November 1716, to John V's suit.

The marquis of Fontes was a military engineer trained at Lisbon's academy and knowledgeable in architectural matters. He was also a distinguished connoisseur of art and antiquities. A contemporary chronicler, Filippo Juvarra's anonymous biographer, confirmed his qualifications in emphatic terms.[24] Fontes became the king's most important adviser on the arts, and his residence in Rome was of extreme importance to the renewal of the arts in Portugal as a whole.

Fontes' access to the artistic scene in Rome was facilitated not only by his personal skills, but also by contacts of the Portuguese crown with the Accademia dell'Arcadia and the Accademia di San Luca, especially with Cardinal Pietro Ottoboni, munificent patron of art and literature; the architect Carlo Fontana (1638–1714); and Fontana's disciple Filippo Juvarra (1678–1736).[25]

In fact, the development of a strategy based on Portuguese artistic patronage in Rome can be traced to the reign of John V's father, Peter II. His objectives were those that John pursued: recognition of Portugal's independence and of the importance to Christianity of the Portuguese empire, and the restoration of the Padroado.

This agenda was confirmed by the inscriptions and the iconographical program of the elaborate allegorical decorations, designed by Carlo Fontana, of the space and the central catafalque installed in 1707 at Sant'Antonio dei Portoghesi to commemorate the death of Peter II. Besides the detailed description and engravings from a booklet published for the dedication,[26] Fontana's young pupil, Filippo Juvarra, left a drawing of the catafalque,[27] and his master's plan and sketches for it are preserved in the archive of the church. Even the engravings, the text, and the sermon, also published in the booklet, clearly support the Portuguese strategy.[28]

Nine years later the same themes were employed, at a much larger scale, in the iconography of Fontes' ceremonial entry and triumphal progress through the streets of Rome as Portuguese ambassador. The depiction of Portuguese maritime exploits and colonial possessions on the gilded carriages and the three days of exuberant festivities functioned as clear and public statements of what the Portuguese king wanted from Clement XI. By its obvious quotations of earlier imperial entries into Rome, the event

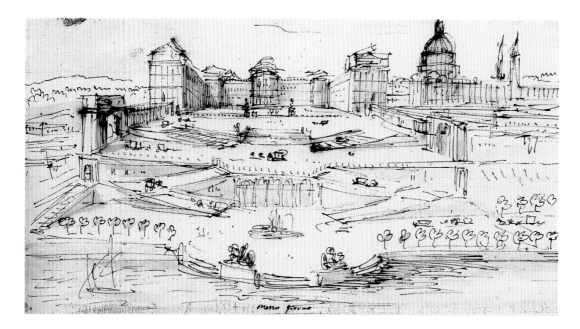

6. Filippo Juvarra, *Pensiero for a New Royal Palace and Patriarchal Church on the Terreiro do Paço: Overall View from the River,* 1717 (newly identified), ink
Musei Civici di Torino

also stressed the historical and territorial arguments for John V's claims.[29] Since the carriages were made in Rome, it seems likely that it was Fontes who devised the entire program.[30]

According to some sources,[31] from the beginning of the eighteenth century until his death in 1714, Carlo Fontana was the Portuguese royal architect in Rome. On that pretext John V invested him with the most prestigious Portuguese order, the Military Order of Christ.[32] The recognition was a way for the Portuguese king to appropriate the pope's architect. As a reward for Fontana's services, it was perhaps excessive, but in another sense it may be justified by the importance of Fontana's studio to Portuguese baroque architecture, which is evident even though his role has not yet been thoroughly documented.

Fontana's death left a void among the leadership of the Arcadian architects, as can be seen in the competition of 1715, sponsored by Pope Clement XI, for the new sacristy of Saint Peter's, to which three of Fontana's disciples—Filippo Juvarra, Tomasso Mattei, and Antonio Canevari—presented projects.[33] Each would work on John V's plans for a new royal palace and patriarchal church on a new site in Lisbon, renewal of the Paço da Ribeira, or both. Scholars who have written about this question have seen connections between each of these three architects, the competition of 1715, and the marquis

of Fontes' artistic and diplomatic activity in Rome.[34]

Ultimately, however, it would be a fourth pupil of Fontana, Johan Friedrich Ludwig (1670–1752)—known in Portugal as Frederico Ludovice[35]—who would build something related to the scheme for a royal palace and patriarchal church. Contrary to assumptions and scholarly debates of the past, today it is clear that he was also the only one of these architects who actually worked on designs and construction superintendence for the palace and convent of Mafra.

In summary, that was the context in which, in 1717, Fontes asked Juvarra to develop perspective drawings of "un modello di sua invenzione" for the new royal palace and patriarchal church of Lisbon. The episode figures in Juvarra's anonymous biography[36] and in an account by the Portuguese painter Vieira Lusitano,[37] then in Rome. A painting by Gaspar Van Wittel (Gaspare Vanvitelli) based on Juvarra's drawings was sent to John V. It seems likely that Fontes' "modello" comprised a site plan and a conceptual sketch whose purpose was better to display the virtuosity of the architect's *pensieri.*

I think that three sketches of Lisbon in Caserta's collections relate to that commission.[38] Two of them are detailed representations of the Terreiro do Paço at that time. They differ in their rapid, sketchy quality from the third, which is undoubtedly from

7. Filippo Juvarra, *Pensiero for a New Royal Palace and Patriarchal Church on the Terreiro do Paço: View of the Palace*, 1717 (newly identified), ink
Musei Civici di Torino

another hand. Thus it is very likely that they reveal the direct intervention of Fontes.

Many scholars have accepted Emilio Lavagnino's identification of a painting he published in 1940 as Vanvitelli's rendering of Juvarra's concept.[39] But that painting is only one more depiction of the Terreiro do Paço with the palace as it looked from the east after the building campaigns of Philip II, and there is no proof that it came from Vanvitelli's hands.

The image we are looking for would contain something inspired by Juvarra's drawings for the project. I share with other scholars the opinion that three Juvarra sketches of Lisbon in the collections of the Musei Civici di Torino relate to that project and not to the one he developed in Lisbon two years later (figs. 6, 7, and 8).[40] The topography shown in the Turin drawings and the relationship of the buildings to the river more closely resemble the situation of the Paço da Ribeira than the

8. Filippo Juvarra, *Pensiero for a New Royal Palace and Patriarchal Church on the Terreiro do Paço: View of the Patriarchal Church*, 1717 (newly identified), ink
Musei Civici di Torino

area on the periphery that Juvarra and the king would choose in 1719. But they were far from reality. Even with Fontes' help, it would have been difficult for Juvarra to imagine and draw the area without seeing it. Perhaps that was the main reason for a painting instead of a set of project drawings. The painting may have been intended to say that he needed to visit Lisbon.

In fact, one of the most remarkable characteristics of Juvarra's architecture is its close relation with the site and the surroundings. Those who have studied his works and *pensieri* most closely have emphasized the importance of his architecture of his long experience with scenography.[41] The little we know about his work for John V in Lisbon is enough to prove it. Unlike other architects, Juvarra could not have designed a project for a place he had never seen.

That apparent handicap should have been the reason for his invitation to Lisbon: what the Portuguese monarch wanted was a new urban image, or setting. In urbanistic terms, John V knew the projects Juvarra was building for the house of Savoy. Not only the buildings, but also their fundamental contribution to the third and final pre-Napoleonic expansion. Besides, Juvarra's Piranesian tendency toward *vedute* of ancient monuments and cities certainly increased his credit with the Portuguese monarch.[42]

The king was also aware of Juvarra's experience throughout his career with a certain type of architectural program, from his work on the Messina harbor to submissions for Concorsi Clementini at the Accademia di San Luca: "Chiesa con Canonica, collegio e Ospedali" (Church with presbytery, school, and hospital; 1702), "Palazzo Pontificio" (Papal palace; 1703), "Pubblica Curia con i suoi annessi" (Public administration building with annexes; 1704), and, later, "Progetto per una grande chiesa" (Project for a large church; 1716). Large-scale programs of this kind were standard.

Turning again to the origin of the Lisbon drawings in the collection of the Musei Civici di Torino, I would argue that if one of the projects of 1719 and related sketches were lost—perhaps in the earthquake of 1755—why not the others produced at the same time? It is most likely that those three known sketches date from 1717 and never left Italy.

In addition to Vanvitelli's lost painting, models, drawings, and other representations relating to architectural and urban planning proposals were sent from Rome to Lisbon for John V's consideration. Also completed and sent in 1717 was a project by Tomasso Mattei, another of the pupils of Carlo Fontana who had participated in the competition for the sacristy of Saint Peter's. Like the Juvarra project, it was a commission of the marquis of Fontes. Curiously, the response to Fontes stated that the king believed the project would be considerably improved with his ambassador's contribution after Fontes returned to Lisbon, which the king desired "too much."[43] It was a diplomatic way of saying that the king did not like the project. Fontes must seek another architect. Perhaps it was after this that he turned to Juvarra.

Mattei's project, which is also lost, has always been connected with the palace and convent of Mafra, but in reality it was made for the royal complex of Lisbon.[44] At that time the building of Mafra was in progress under a different director and to another design, and it would take definitive form only at the end of the 1720s. In fact, every clear primary source connects Fontes' activity in Rome with the concept, program, and project for the new royal palace and patriarchal church in Lisbon; none suggests a connection to Mafra.

Historians have made erroneous connections to Mafra because the Lisbon project has usually been overlooked. The dream of a new Lisbon as a new Rome was never much more than a royal fantasy. On the other hand, the palace and convent of Mafra are an impressive reality that has always attracted the interest of scholars. In fact, the abandonment of the Lisbon project seems to have been the main motive for the extraordinary increase of commitment to Mafra. The planning and building of Mafra were complex processes, and the problem of authorship of its evolving master plan has been the subject of many publications.[45]

Studies on Mafra devote attention to a so-called Roman architecture museum that was installed in the Paço da Ribeira, where models (some full size), plans, and views as well as sculptures, monuments, altars, and their details, sent from Rome in great numbers, were displayed in endless galleries.[46] A veritable battalion of well-known artists worked in Rome on the acquisition and transfer of these objects during most of John V's reign. Unfortunately, these collections were lost in the earthquake and fire of 1755. Recently published extracts from contemporary sources testify that the collections were intended for work and study. The means of improving Portuguese architecture was the generation of ideas nourished by images, proposals, and visiting artists.[47] With few exceptions, the buildings realized were planned and drawn in Lisbon by architects in residence there, near the king and his advisers but always with reference to the imported examples in the "Roman architecture museum."

Mattei's and Juvarra's projects were completed and sent from Rome in a year of particular importance for new developments in Portuguese culture. In addition to the decisive steps toward Lisbon's urban renovation, 1717 saw many other initiatives: the official start of construction of the Mafra complex as well as that of the library of the University of Coimbra, the cornerstone of a reform then promoted in that institution; the creation of the first academies, including the productive Royal Academy of History; and the initial publication of the first Portuguese newspaper, *Gazeta de Lisboa.*

Juvarra at last journeyed to Lisbon, where he arrived in 1719 to pursue the project to replace the accretive and confused palatine complex on the Terreiro do Paço. The palace was comfortable and even luxurious, but, despite successive remodelings, architecturally and urbanistically outdated and inarticulate. The royal chapel was far from the scale and luxury the king saw fit for a metropolitan and patriarchal see.[48] Fontes conveyed this idea to Juvarra in Rome, and the architect was expected to work on it when he arrived in Lisbon. For the journey he obtained a six-month leave of absence granted him by Victor Amadeus II of Savoy.

By the middle of March, according to the nuncio's report, Juvarra had drawn a first project for the existing palace site.[49] One month earlier, however, courtiers and specialists in areas other than architecture had been invited to confer on the location of the royal and patriarchal complex.[50] Most of them had a different view of the situation. They thought that the city's renovation should begin on new ground, not in the crowded old commercial center of Lisbon, as Fontes had in mind.[51]

That view was consistent with the east-west division of Lisbon, and the king understandably subscribed to it. In an open field he could imagine a new complex, in the nuncio's words, "larger and more appropriate" (*più vaste e confacenti*),[52] which could bring his dream of a new Lisbon closer to realization.

In search of an ideal site, John V, members of the court, and the architect made frequent excursions through the neighborhoods of Lisbon and stood for long hours on a boat on the river. Juvarra's anonymous biographer described the end of that long process in vivid terms:

It took about three months to find an adequate site for such a structure; but finally . . . the king himself with the great lords of his kingdom, the lord marquis of Fontes, and Don Filippo [Juvarra] traveled by boat some miles from Lisbon to see a place not far from the ocean, beautiful and of great amenity . . . and it was chosen as the site of the complex.[53]

The site was a wide, airy slope known as Buenos Aires, west of the city center facing the river and the harbor's entrance. According to the same passage in the biography, John V had ordered Juvarra "to make a drawing of the royal palace, the patriarchal church, the patriarchal palace, and the canonry, with the injunction that that building complex would take first place after the renowned massive structure of Saint Peter's." Juvarra presented what the nuncio described as a "new design adapted to the newly chosen site"[54] to the king two weeks after he submitted the project for the old site. The new design was for "a complex not secondary, but equal in importance to the great buildings of Saint Peter's and worthy of the greatness of the king."[55] Rome was indeed the model he strove not just to imitate, but to surpass.

Once again, both projects have been lost. With so little evidence we can hardly imagine the intended scenographic and urbanistic

9. Filippo Juvarra, *Pensiero for a Monumental Lighthouse for the Harbor of Lisbon,* 1719 (newly identified), ink
Biblioteca Nazionale Universitaria di Torino

effect, even with the inclusion in the program of an enclosed park with wild animals—a zoo.[56] But it is obvious that for both sites a scenographic dialogue with the river was the main theme of the architectural composition.

Another of Juvarra's projects for Lisbon, for which the project drawings are also lost, was a monumental and honorific lighthouse for the harbor entrance, located to the west of the future palace and patriarchal church. Significantly, it was the first thing John V asked Juvarra to do when he arrived. Once again the architect's anonymous biographer provides a description:

The first commission that he received was that of a design for the port's lighthouse, for which he conceived a column in the ancient style in imitation of those that one sees in Rome, with the arms of the king in the middle supported by two [personifications] of Fame, and a great light at the top . . . imitating the works of the ancient emperors.[57]

A *pensiero* by Juvarra in the Biblioteca Nazionale, Torino, matches this description and the contemporary appearance of that part of Lisbon's harbor (fig. 9). The drawing differs from the description only in showing, above the housing for the light, a standing male figure. Was the sketch a suggestion for portraying John V as an imperial evocation?

It is not unlikely that the prototype of Alexandria's lighthouse also occurred to Juvarra and to the king, especially since Alexandria was one of the few cities of the late Roman Empire that was the seat of a patriarch. The comparison placed Lisbon on the footing of a newly founded capital, one of the world's marvels and Europe's face to the Atlantic. The design also shows formal and symbolic connections with Lisbon's Belém Tower. Like the lighthouse, it marks a harbor, with a defensive bulwark as a basement, but it is also an architectural masterpiece of the Portuguese monarchy from the discoveries period.

Records from the period of Juvarra's stay portray the king as a dedicated and enthusiastic patron. He received and housed Juvarra with great care and distinction and spent as much time as he could with him. It seems that during Juvarra's sojourn John V did not visit the construction site at Mafra.

During his short time in Lisbon Juvarra was involved in other studies and projects, especially for ephemeral architecture for court and civic festivities.[58] When his six-month leave of absence came to an end, he left Portugal laden with gifts and honors. Among the latter was the notable distinction granted earlier to Carlo Fontana, the Military Order of Christ.

Juvarra left Lisbon for a brief European study tour supported by John V and returned to Turin to resume his projects there. Specialists have considered that trip, along with his stay in Portugal, with its most distinctive architecture, as the catalyst of important changes in Juvarra's architecture.[59] According to a letter from the nuncio in Lisbon, who kept the pope informed of the progress of John V's efforts to emulate Rome,[60] the plan was that he would return to Lisbon soon to supervise construction of his projects.

Construction of the new royal and patriarchal complex at Buenos Aires began two days before the Italian architect's departure. At the same time it was decided to bring some 300 masons from Milan. Especially important was the preparation that had to be done for Juvarra's return, at which time construction of the walls was to begin. The preparation of the site and the building of the water supply system to the palace were started. At the same time, Manuel da Maia was ordered to make a survey of a vast area between Lisbon and the city's fortified line to the west, as well as a plan for a road system.[61]

For reasons unknown, Juvarra did not return, nor did the Lombard masons ever go to Lisbon. John V did not build his palatine complex meant to rival Saint Peter's. Instead, as already stated, he gave new priority and resources to the building of Mafra. The convent there was considerably enlarged, and a royal palace was added with new features such as a royal hunting lodge and a monumental library.

The opening of cultural channels and the architectural debate on the Lisbon complex were obviously essential to Mafra's architecture. The king's architect, Frederico Ludovice, incorporated details that were obvious quotations from Juvarra, as well as themes and motifs of many other architects, whose drawings and models poured into the royal collections until the end of the reign. How else to explain the stairs of the convent wing of Mafra, whose only parallel is found in stairs that Juvarra executed in many of his buildings in Turin?[62]

Ludovice merely took advantage of the cultural ambience in which Rome's architects moved and worked. Fortunately it was not only he who did so. Some researchers have cited the extraordinary importance of the Mafra construction site as the school of the eighteenth-century Portuguese baroque. It was there that tradition merged with cosmopolitanism and military engineers developed or updated their architectural sensibilities. But it was also in the "Mafra studio atmosphere"[63] that the architectural and engineering professions began to diverge.

Undiscouraged, John V continued to pursue his policy of close contact with the real Rome. His commitment to artistic patronage in the pope's city grew, especially in relation to the Accademia dell'Arcadia.

Juvarra's visit to Lisbon had other effects that cannot be discussed or even enumerated in the compass of this essay. In Lisbon he did not merely design a new royal palace and patriarchal cathedral; he was in fact John V's most important and valuable consulting architect for the project of establishing the main urbanistic choices for a renewed capital city. If his projects for Lisbon had been built, they would have been brilliantly innovative. Juvarra understood that territorial definition and planned urban spaces are essential to architecture. The same may be said of his *pensieri* for Messina. His importance as a capital builder in Turin (not to mention Madrid) is well known.[64] Any attempt to comprehend Juvarra's achievement must take into account his performance in Lisbon.

Juvarra's stay allowed John V to fashion a clear image of his plans for a new Lisbon: a true stage setting for power. That image involved three major decisions: to expand the city westward, to concentrate the temporal and spiritual symbols of Portuguese imperial power on a plateau overlooking the river, and to redevelop the riverfront as Lisbon's real face and urban center.

Lisbon aristocrats were quick to understand the implications, and many immediately built palaces along the roads linking Lisbon's center to the west, mainly on those bordering the river. Juvarra himself could have conceived at least one of these—the palace of Monteiro-Mor (Marim-Olhão)—although its construction was obviously under a Portuguese builder's control. The house is incomplete and deteriorated, but it is impressive enough in plan, overall conception, and details to recall Juvarra's later design for the Palazzo in Villa of the marchese Carron di San Tommaso, at Pozzo Strada.[65] The stairs are similar to those of the convent wing of Mafra, another example of the recurrence of this design in Juvarra's work (figs. 10 and 11).

If we can consider the development of west Lisbon as a district of aristocratic residences to be the continuation of an earlier trend, the definitive shift of the city in that

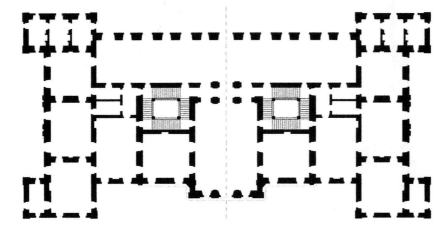

10. Comparison of the plans of the palace of Monteiro-Mor (top) and the Palazzo Carron di San Tommaso, CAD drawing by Fernando Sequeira Mendes, 2000

direction also conditioned the conception and location of new infrastructure, monastic buildings, and royal residences.[66] The shift may be seen in the famous Lisbon aqueduct (started in 1728), the industrial complex of Rato (built in 1734), the planned naval facility of Alcântara (designed around 1727), and the new Oratorian convent at Necessidades (started in 1742). The convent was part of a complex that incorporated a royal palace and the zoological garden that had been planned by John V as part of his grandiose scheme for the royal palace and patriarchal church at Buenos Aires—not far from the Necessidades site.[67]

Outside the city limits but on the same side of the river and closer to the sea, Belém became the leisure retreat of the court. Between 1726 and 1729 the king bought six *quintas* (country estates) near the Hieronymite monastery of Our Lady of Belém, which he consolidated, remodeled, and often used

11. Palace of Monteiro-Mor, Lisbon
Author photograph

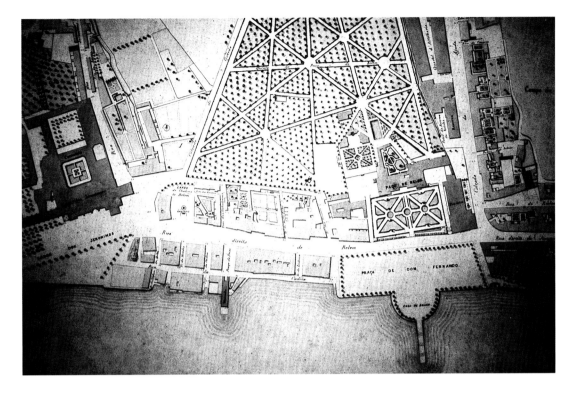

as a royal residence. The monastery was the pantheon of King Manuel I (r. 1495–1521), whose sponsorship of its construction was inspired by the messianic and imperial ambitions that he shared with other Portuguese monarchs. Some courtiers followed the king's example and built houses nearby, mainly on the river, at Pedrouços (to the west) and Junqueira (to the east). The area between Belém and central Lisbon became a truly palatial riverfront (fig. 12).

When John V bought the estates, the French consul in Lisbon reported to his government that the king was seriously considering transforming the monastery into a patriarchal palace and church and moving the Hieronymite monks to Mafra.[68] Only seven years had elapsed since the first projects for the Terreiro do Paço and the Buenos Aires site. The expense of John V's many building campaigns, especially at Mafra, is frequently cited as the most probable reason for this change of plans. I think the explanation is not so simple, and I propose that we should also pay attention to other clues, for instance, whether the pope's opposition may have been a factor.

The idea of a royal palace at Belém had been considered since the time of Philip II and would be considered again by Manuel da Maia and the marquis of Pombal after the destruction of the city in the earthquake of 1755.[69] At that time, a site near the one selected by John V and Juvarra was chosen, but it was not until 1795 that the new royal palace was finally begun, near Belém, on the Ajuda Hill.

Notwithstanding an opposite ideological and political orientation and the change to a more French than Roman tendency in the court's taste, the urban planning strategy of John V and his architects, which was impossible to realize in full in their time, was validated after the earthquake of 1755. The complex urbanistic and architectural debate triggered by the catastrophe inherited many themes and ideas from the first half of the century, primarily through the personality and work of Manuel da Maia, by then the king's chief engineer, who had worked with Juvarra. In Maia's activity, before and after the earthquake, we can detect a synthesis of the urbanism of the Portuguese military school[70] and the new ideas brought by John V's Italian masters from Carlo Fontana's studio.

Besides expanding some city functions to the west following Juvarra's plan, in the late 1720s John V began a profound transformation of the Terreiro do Paço complex. The

13. Jacques Philippe Le Bas
after Paris and Pedegache,
*View of the Opera House
after the Earthquake of 1755*,
1757, engraving
Museu da Cidade, Lisbon

14. Carlos Mardel, *Elevation
for a Fountain at Saint
Catherine's Gate, Lisbon*,
c. 1745, ink and watercolor
Museu da Cidade, Lisbon

15. Triumphal arch,
Amoreira, Lisbon (designed
by Carlos Mardel, c. 1745),
photograph c. 1925
Photograph Arquivo Fotográfico da
Câmara Municipal de Lisboa

Here and there the old city acquired new monuments and streets. Curiously, all attempts to erect a statue to John V seem to have failed.[73] In fact, although his death preceded the earthquake by five years, he was, as Eduardo Lourenço remarked, its greatest victim.[74]

In the mid-1740s, although seriously ill, John V once again tried to resurrect his life's obsession. The building of Mafra had reached an end, and the results of alterations to the old royal palace still did not please him. He ordered from Ludovice a project for a new patriarchal palace and cathedral, to be sited at the top of Cotovia Hill, facing the river. Yet again, Ludovice was to design something of "the dimensions of Rome's Saint Peter's."[75] Officially because of opposition from powerful neighbors—the Jesuits, who would have lost a pleasant view to the river—the idea did not reach fruition.

I think the three drawings identified by Paulo Varela Gomes as a project for the patriarchal cathedral on Cotovia Hill[76] are neither by the architect to whom he attributes them nor of a date some years after the earthquake, but instead are from the project John V ordered from Ludovice in the 1740s.[77] In them we can see the freshness of the reign's first decades being relinquished to quotations from the former palatine chapel.

The aqueduct triggered the building of several fountains which entailed the transformation of the public spaces in which they were located. The arches of the aqueduct also provided a monumental pretext in two places where they spanned streets. One was masked as a double-sided entry, or, more exactly, a triumphal arch, in honor of John V and his patronage. Other public structures were built and rebuilt under the crown's direction or by initiative of the city council, including a tobacco customhouse, a powder house, a slaughterhouse, docks, and a lazaretto (figs. 14, 15, and 16).

These improvements also addressed one of the key concepts of the age: mobility. Facilitating the circulation of coaches became an obsession that led to the demolition of medieval city gates and the widening of streets and roads. As early as 1718 Manuel da Maia had drafted a plan for a road connecting, according to the title of the document, "the cities of west and east Lisbon to the town of

royal chapel was radically transformed into a large and sumptuous patriarchal cathedral,[71] and a clock tower with a belfry was built. The tower, a new water supply system, and a complete remodeling of the royal apartments were the work of Antonio Canevari,[72] but Ludovice directed the renovation of the cathedral.

Behind the palace and in front of the church and other structures, a large number of houses were bought and demolished to allow the laying out of a new square, facing Saint Francis Hill. At the beginning of the reign of John V's son, Joseph I, an opera house, designed and built under the direction of Giovanni Carlo Sicinio Bibiena (1717–1760), opened its doors on that square (fig. 13).

16. Carlos Mardel, *Plan and Elevation of a Dock and Tobacco Customhouse*, 1746, ink and watercolor
Arquivo Histórico da Câmara Municipal de Lisboa

Mafra."[78] Some years later a similar road was planned along the Tagus bank, from Lisbon to the royal estates in Belém, linking the royal palaces of Necessidades and Alcântara. Before the 1720s the only way to travel this route with relative speed and comfort was by boat. But now the king and his courtiers dreamed of a promenade with pleasure gardens along the river.

A survey was made in 1727,[79] and a few years later the overall project for a riverbank promenade about twelve kilometers long was ready.[80] It would have been an intervention forceful enough to unify the urban image of Lisbon. Some parts of this promenade were actually built, but the earthquake and subsequent renovations of the riverfront destroyed what was left of the design (figs. 17 and 18). In this case the initiative had a clear French inspiration. The idea of promoting the "règne de la nature et l'ordre monarchique"[81] in a promenade by

the river could have come from newcomers to the court, one of whom was the Slovakian architect and engineer Carlos Mardel (1695–1763), the designer of the project and one of the principal figures of Portuguese architecture in the eighteenth century.[82]

The promenade project gave birth to one of the more interesting new views of Lisbon, truly representative of the ideas of John V, the marquis of Fontes, Juvarra, Manuel da Maia, and other architects, engineers, and courtiers, as expressed in the projects of 1717–1719. The view is depicted on panels of tiles made for the four walls of the cloister of the Third Order of Saint Francis in Salvador, Brazil, as a memento of the distant European capital of the kingdom.[83] With Lisbon's cityscape as a backdrop, the panels show the marriage procession that took place on 12 February 1729 for the wedding of John V's son, Joseph, to the Spanish princess Maria Ana (figs. 19 and 20).

17. Carlos Mardel, *Plan of the New Embankment and Promenade between the Terreiro do Paço and Belém*, 1733, ink and watercolor
Arquivo Histórico do Ministério das Obras Públicas, Lisbon

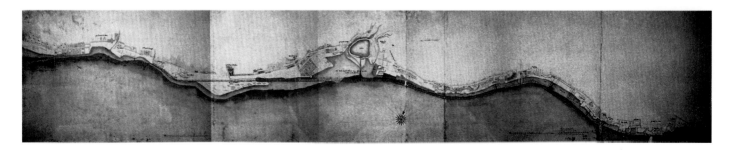

18. Carlos Mardel, *Plan of the New Embankment and Promenade between the Terreiro do Paço and Belém*, detail showing the area of Alcântara, 1733, ink and watercolor
Arquivo Histórico do Ministério das Obras Públicas, Lisbon

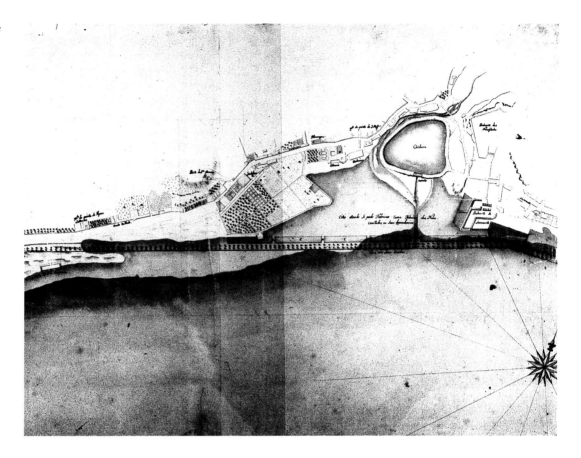

19. Anonymous, *Entry into Lisbon on 12 February 1729*, detail showing the landing at Belém, anonymous artist, second quarter of the eighteenth century, painted ceramic tile
Convent of the Third Order of Saint Francis, Salvador, Brazil

The marriage was celebrated at the Portuguese-Spanish border at the same time as that of Joseph's sister, Maria Barbara, to Maria Ana's brother, Ferdinand. The episode is known to history as the "exchange of the princesses." The newly married royal couple, the king, and all the court, along with their retinues,[84] arrived in the small village of Aldeia Galega on the south bank of the Tagus on the day before. Early the next morning the procession started as a fleet of festive boats. It crossed the river and passed along all of Lisbon's riverfront, from Xabregas, on the east, to Belém, on the west. The flotilla landed at a dock especially built for the occasion in front of the royal palace at Belém and then began the land procession by coach and foot to its destination, the royal palace on the Terreiro do Paço. It passed slowly under twenty ephemeral arches.

A description published immediately afterward is full of comparisons with events from mythology and classical antiquity and the procession, the festivities, the decorations, and the city's image.[85] To the writer, Lisbon was the equal of a long list of very different cities, including Rome and Venice. The entry itself was likened to the triumph of a Caesar.

For the first time since the sixteenth century, a festive entry into Lisbon took the form not of a ceremonial landing at the Terreiro do Paço, but of an arrival at Belém followed by a procession along the riverbank. The choice can be explained only in light of the transformations that John V envisaged and planned for Lisbon. This is what the tile panels show, a view not of Lisbon but of a Lisbon to be. In its place in a Franciscan monastery in the capital of the largest Portuguese possession, it was an allegory addressed to the entire Portuguese empire, an allegory of a modern city that also aspired to be a maritime Rome, the seat of the king's metropolitan patriarchy by the sea.

20. Anonymous, *Entry into Lisbon on 12 February 1729*, detail showing the Arco dos Italianos, anonymous artist, second quarter of the eighteenth century, ceramic tile
Convent of the Third Order of Saint Francis, Salvador, Brazil

NOTES

1. The most recent treatments of this subject are Walter Rossa, *Beyond Baixa: Signs of Urban Planning in Eighteenth Century Lisbon*, trans. Richard Trewinnard (Lisbon, 1998), and Walter Rossa, "The 1755 Earthquake: A Town under the Sign of Reason," *Rassegna* 59 (1994), 28–43. Both are references for much of the content of this paper.

2. See Renata de Araujo, *Lisboa, a cidade e o espectáculo na época dos descobrimentos* (Lisbon, 1990), and José Augusto França, "Images of Lisbon through the Centuries," *Rassegna* 59 (1994), 28–43. For a comprehensive comparison with the imagery of cities in other countries, see Lucia Nuti, *Ritratti di città: Visione e memoria tra medioevo e settecento* (Venice, 1996).

3. Published in modern translation as Damião de Góis, *Descrição da cidade de Lisboa*, ed. and trans. José de Felicidade Alves (Lisbon, 1988), 51–58.

4. Reprinted as Francisco d'Holanda, *Da fábrica que falece à cidade de Lisboa*, ed. José de Felicidade Alves (Lisbon, 1984).

5. Góis in fact visited Italy for an extended period, but it was in the economic and cultural centers of northern Europe that he stayed the longest, establishing important contacts and friendships (see Góis ed. Alves 1988, 55–58).

6. Walter Rossa, "Lisboa quinhentista, o Terreiro e o Paço: Prenúncios de una afirmaçao da capitalidade," in *D. João III e o imperio* [proceedings of an international conference commemorating the 500th anniversary of the birth of King John III] (Lisbon, 2004), 947–967.

7. It seems likely that Francisco d'Holanda tried to influence Philip II's ideas about Lisbon. In fact, when he was writing his book on Lisbon, he made considerable efforts to join Philip II's court. It is also probable that when the new Portuguese monarch first visited Lisbon and proposed architectural and planning improvements, d'Holanda was with him. See Sylvie Deswarte Rosa, *Les "De Aetatibus Mundi Imagines" de Francisco de Holanda* (Paris, 1983), chap. 6.

8. Judite Nozes, ed., *The Lisbon Earthquake of 1755: Some British Eye-Witness Accounts* (Lisbon, 1987), 18 and 90.

9. George Kubler, *Portuguese Plain Architecture: Between Spices and Diamonds, 1521–1706* (Middletown, Conn., 1972); José E. Horta Correia, *Arquitectura portuguesa: Renascimento, maneirismo, estilo chão* (Lisbon, 1991); José E. Horta Correia, "A arquitectura: Maneirismo e estilo chão," in *O Maneirismo*, vol. 7 of *História da arte em Portugal*, ed. Vitor Serrão, 15 vols. (Lisbon, 1986), 93–135; José Fernandes Pereira, "Resistências e aceitação do espaço barroco: A arquitectura religiosa e civil," in *O limiar do barroco*, ed. Carlos Moura, vol. 8 of *História da arte em Portugal* (Lisbon, 1986), 9–65.

10. See Eduardo Brasão, *A restauração: Relações diplomáticas de Portugal de 1640 a 1668* (Lisbon, 1939), and Brasão, "A importância da diplomacia na restauração de Portugal em 1640," *O Instituto* 96 (1940), 341–356.

11. On the weddings, see the following works by Eduardo Brasão: *O casamento de D. Pedro II com a princesa de Neuburg: Documentos diplomáticos* (Coimbra, 1936); "A recepção de uma raínha," *Boletim cultural e estatístico da Câmara Municipal de Lisboa* 1–2 (1937), 185–203; and *O casamento de D. João V* (Lisbon, 1937).

12. Maia's request to the marquis of Pombal, dated 16 February 1756, is the second part of his "Dissertações," first published in Christovam Ayres, *Manuel da Maya e os engenheiros militares portugueses no terremoto de 1755* (Lisbon, 1910), 33–40.

13. For a brief English-language survey of the Padroado, see Charles Ralph Boxer, *The Portuguese Seaborne Empire, 1415–1825* (New York, 1969), chap. 10.

14. Rossa 1994, 1998; Helena Murteira, *Lisboa: Da restauração às luzes* (Lisbon, 1999), 79–113 and 165–174. The latter is based on Eduardo Freire de Oliveira, *Elementos para a história do município de Lisboa*, 17 vols. (Lisbon, 1884–1911).

15. Angela Delaforce, "Lisbon, 'This New Rome': Dom João V of Portugal and Relations between Rome and Lisbon," in *The Age of the Baroque in Portugal*, ed. Jay Levenson [exh. cat., National Gallery of Art] (Washington, 1993), 49–80. This essay is a good English-language treatment of John V's aspirations. For a more extensive study of the connections between the establishment of John V's court and his ecclesiastical policy, see António Filipe Pimentel, *Arquitectura e poder: O real edifício de Mafra* (Coimbra, 1992), part 2.

16. Rossa 1998, 160–161.

17. Curiously, an arch from the time of Hadrian, which stood by the church of San Lorenzo in Lucina in Via del Corso in Rome, became known as the Arch of Portugal. It was demolished in 1665 but was known by that name for some decades afterward (Delaforce in Levenson 1993, 49).

18. Sandra Vasco Rocca and Gabriele Borghini, eds., *Giovanni V di Portogallo (1707–1750) e la cultura romana del suo tempo* [exh. cat., Istituto centrale per il catalogo e la documentazione] (Rome, 1995); Delaforce in Levenson 1993.

19. The expression is from Fernando António da Costa de Barboza, *Elogio funebre do Padre João Baptista Carbone da Companhia de Jesus* (Lisbon, 1751), 15.

20. For Portuguese politics and diplomatic activities in this period, the most important references are the following works by Eduardo Brasão: *Subsídios para a história do patriarcado de Lisboa: 1716–1740* (Porto, 1942); "A Secretaria de Estado dos Negócios Estrangeiros criação de D. Joao V," *Revista portuguesa de história* 16 (1978), 51–61; *Relaçoes diplomáticas de Portugal com a Santa Sé*, 2 vols. (Lisbon, 1973); *Relaçoes externas de Portugal: Reinado de D. Joao V*, 2 vols. (Porto, 1938); and *Dom Joao V e a Santa Sé:*

As relaçoes diplomáticas de Portugal com o Governo Pontifício de 1706 e 1750 (Coimbra, 1937). The latter includes the king's instructions to Fontes and other documents relating to his mission to Rome.

21. The correspondence is in Archivo di Stato di Torino, sez. I, Lettere Ministri Roma; quoted by Aurora Scotti in "L'Accademia degli arcadi in Roma e i suoi rapporti con la cultura portoghese nel primo ventennio del 1700," in *Bracara Augusta* 27, no. 63 (1973): 115–130. Usually it is only the role of the marquis of Fontes that is stressed, but Melo e Castro was also of great importance. In fact it was he who established the platform for the success of the Portuguese diplomatic strategy in Rome, including close contacts with the Accademia dell'Arcadia and its patron, Cardinal Pietro Ottoboni, whose private theater Fontes seldom visited (Brasão 1938, 2: 7–23). Melo e Castro's first official entry into Rome in 1709 established an important precedent for the famous entry of Fontes in 1716; see De Bellebat, *Relation du voyage de Monseigneur André de Mello de Castro à la Cour de Rome, en qualité d'Envoyé Extraordinaire* (Paris, 1709).

22. Pressure to obtain concessions from the papacy was constant until the end of John V's reign. An example is the granting to John of the title Most Faithful King on 23 December 1748. Such favors were considered essential to raising the Portuguese monarchy to the level of those that were most respected next to the papacy: the French and the Spanish.

23. The principal issue at that time was the so-called Chinese rites controversy. It resulted from the attempt of Jesuit missionaries to reconcile Chinese Confucian observance with the liturgy of the Catholic Church in order to facilitate the conversion of the Chinese people, especially among the upper classes. The defender of this initiative of the Propaganda Fide was the patriarch of Antioch, thus a prelate of the same status that John V sought for his church.

24. "He who practiced architecture with such grounding in science that few master architects could compete with him" (il quale dilettavasi di architettura con tal fondamento di scienza, che pochi architetti professori potevano stargli a lato). "Vita del Cavalieri don Filippo Juvarra," in *Mostra di Filippo Juvarra architetto e scenografo,* ed. Vittorio Viale [exh. cat., Università di Messina, Istituto di disegno] (Messina, 1966), 26. Viale (16–17) considers several possibilities for authorship of the biography, including Francesco Juvarra, Filippo Juvarra's brother, but favors Filippo himself.

25. On the patronage role of the Portuguese crown in Rome circa 1700, see Scotti 1973; Vasco Rocca and Borghini 1995; Levenson 1993.

26. See accounts in Francesco Valesio, *Diario di Roma,* ed. Gaetana Scano, 3 vols. (Milan, 1977), 3: 827, 881, 884–887.

27. The drawing is in the Biblioteca Nazionale, Torino, Ris. 59/4, fol. 104.

28. The dedicatory publication is *Funerale celebrato nella chiesa di Santo Antonio della Nazione Portoghese in Roma per la morte del Ré di Portogallo, don Pietro Secondo l'Anno MDCCVII* (Rome, 1707), with engravings by Giovanni Girolamo Frezza and Domenico Franceschini.

29. In theme and iconography, the entry was a direct evocation of another famous Portuguese entry into Rome, that of the ambassador of King Manuel I to Leo X in 1514, the year of the last of the papal bulls granting the Portuguese crown the rights that constituted the Eastern Padroado.

30. The theme has been widely studied. For a recent treatment, see Marco Fabio Apolloni, "Wondrous Vehicles: The Coaches of the Embassy of the Marquês de Fontes," in Levenson 1993, 89–100. For a contemporary chronicle, see L. Chracas, *Ragguaglio del sontuoso treno delle carrozze con cui ando all'audienza l'Illustrissimo ed Eccellentissimo Signore Don Rodrigo Annes de Saa Almeida e Meneza, Marchese de Fontes . . .* (Rome, 1716).

31. Valesio ed. Scano 1977, 3: 885. See also A. Ayres de Carvalho, *D. João V e a arte do seu tempo,* 2 vols. (Lisbon, 1960–1962), 2: 307–308.

32. *Funerale* 1707, 2.

33. The projects for the Vatican sacristy are among the most studied subjects in Roman architecture in modern times and have generated a vast bibliography. Juvarra's proposals are among the most interesting moments in this history. For an extended analysis of the entries in the competition of 1715, including those of Mattei and Canevari, see Hellmut Hager, "The Precedents of Clement XI's Competition of 1715," in *The Triumph of the Baroque: Architecture in Europe, 1600–1750,* ed. Henry A. Millon [exh. cat., National Gallery of Art] (Turin, 1999), 568–569. On Mattei's and Canevari's projects see also Hellmut Hager, *Filippo Juvarra e il concorso di modelli del 1715 bandito da Clemente XI per la nuova sacrestia di S. Pietro* (Rome, 1970).

34. Scotti 1973, 121.

35. José Fernandes Pereira, "Ludovice, João Frederico," in *Dicionário da arte barroca em Portugal* (Lisbon, 1989), 265–269. Ludovice, born in Hohenhart (Germany), was in Rome between 1697 and 1701, before he went to Lisbon as a goldsmith in the Jesuits' service. He soon managed to free himself from that contract and gradually established himself as John V's preferred architect. In fact, against the strong opposition of the establishment of military architects and engineers, he designed and supervised construction of the principal projects realized during the reign of that monarch, with the exception of the Lisbon aqueduct.

36. "Vita," in Viale 1966, 26.

37. Francisco Vieira de Matos (Vieira Lusitano), *O insigne pintor e leal esposo* (Lisbon, 1780).

38. Palazzo Reale di Caserta, inv. nn. 204, 131. The drawings were published in Walter Vitzthum, "Gas-

par van Wittel e Filippo Juvara," *Arte illustrata* (May–June 1971): 5–9; Aurora Scotti, "L'attività di Filippo Juvarra a Lisbona alla luce delle più recenti interpretazione critiche della sua architettura con una appendice sui rapporti Roma-Lisbona," *Colóquio-Artes* 28 (1976), 51–63; and in Jörg Garms, "Luigi Vanvitelli (1700–1773): Studi per vedute di Lisbona," in Rome 1995, 54–55. They are also discussed and cataloged in Cesare de Seta, *Luigi Vanvitelli* (Naples, 1998), 179, and Jörg Garms, ed., *Disegni di Luigi Vanvitelli nelle collezioni pubbliche di Napoli e Caserta,* [exh. cat., Palazzo Reale] (Naples, 1974). In the opinion of those two scholars, the young Luigi participated in the project as his father's assistant. Vitzthum insisted that the drawings were from nature and so could not have been the work of Juvarra or of Gaspare or Luigi Vanvitelli. Garms doubted that the drawings could have been the work of Luigi Vanvitelli at that time, when he was only seventeen.

39. Emilio Lavagnino, *Gli artisti in Portogallo,* volume 7 of *L' opera del genio italiano all'estero* (Rome, 1940), plate LII.

40. Musei Civici di Torino, Inv. 1859/DS, vol. I, foglio 97, disegno 157; Inv. 1860/DS, vol. I, foglio 98, disegno 158; Inv. 1706/DS, vol. I, foglio 4, disegno 7. On these drawings and Juvarra's later stay in Lisbon, see, among others, Scotti 1973, 1976; and Gianfranco Gritella, *Juvarra: L'architettura,* 2 vols. (Modena, 1992), 1: 462–469. Curiously, scholars have connected these *pensieri* to projects he had in hand at the time in Turin: the Superga, the castle of Rivoli, and the Palazzo Madama.

41. See M. Viale Ferrero, *Juvarra architetto e scenografo teatrale* (Turin, 1970).

42. See Adreina Griseri, "Itinerari Juvarriani," *Paragone* 93 (1952): 40–59.

43. *Cópia da Carta q foi ao Marq.s de Fontes no Corr.º de 22 de Junho . . . ,* Biblioteca Nacional (Lisbon), Col. Pombalina, cod. 157, fols. 214–215. The reference to the project appears just at the end of the letter. The document is devoted entirely to matters related to the Lisbon patriarchate and makes no reference to Mafra.

44. On 2 March 1717 the nuncio in Lisbon, Vicenzo Bichi, reported to Rome that John V was considering building a new patriarchal church and palace of magnificent proportions for the patriarch, "the drawings being already in hand" (havendone di già nelle mani i disegni). Archivio Segreto Vaticano, Rome (hereafter ASV), Portogallo, Seg. 74, fol. 44r). Tomasso Mattei's project was sent three months later.

45. See Ayres de Carvalho 1960–1962; Robert C. Smith, "The Building of Mafra," *Apollo* 134 (1973): 359–367; José Fernandes Pereira, *Arquitectura e escultura de Mafra: Retórica da perfeição* (Lisbon, 1994); and Pimentel 1992.

46. Francisco Xavier da Silva, *Elogío funebre, e histórico do . . . D. João V* (Lisbon, 1750). For a discussion of the Roman architecture museum, see Delaforce in Levenson 1993, 61–62.

47. Marie Thérèse Mandroux-França has documented the importance of John V's print collection in "La Collection d'estampes du roi Jean V de Portugal: Une relecture des notes manuscrites de Pierre-Jean Mariette," *Revue de l'art* 73 (1986): 49–54, and "Les Collections d'estampes du roi Jean V de Portugal: Un Programme des 'Lumières Joanines' en voie de reconstitution," in *Portugal no século XVIII, de D. João V à Revolução Francesa,* ed. Maria Helena Carvalho dos Santos (Lisbon, 1991), 281–293.

48. The nuncio in Lisbon wrote to Rome on 31 January 1719: "They say that the reason this person was invited is not so much the building of the convent at Mafra and its church or [of] the royal palace, since construction is so far advanced that his arrival will be too late, but to build a new church and patriarchal palace, because the old royal chapel, although renewed and enlarged, is still too small for [liturgical] functions, given the magnificence with which they are now celebrated and the large number of clergy who officiate there" (Dicesi che non sia stato tanto per la grand'opera del Convento di Mafra e sua chiesa, e Palazzo Reale, quale essendo di già molto avanzata saria stato tardo il suo arrivo, ma per fabricare una nuova chiesa, e Palazzo Patriarcale, mentre l'antica capella reale, benchè rimodernata, et accresciuta, riesce angusta per le Funzioni, stante la magnificenza, con la quale hora si fanno, et il Clero tanto numeroso, che vi offizia.) ASV, Portogallo, Seg. 75, fol. 18; published in Scotti 1973, 125. Records of Juvarra's stay in Lisbon are few and scattered. Perhaps the most revealing and complete are in the series of letters from the nuncio to Rome published in Scotti 1973, 125–130.

49. ASV, Portogallo, Seg. 75, fol. 47 (1719/03/14); Scotti 1973, 126.

50. In a letter of 14 February, the nuncio reported that the king was having "various meetings with the most intelligent at this court . . . with the participation of doctors, chemists, and other professors, as many as seventeen people" (varij congressi da soggetti il più intelligenti di questa corte . . . con l'intervento di Medici, Chimighi, et altri professori sino al numero di 17 persone). ASV, Portogallo, Seg. 75, fol. 26 (1719/02/14); Scotti 1973, 125.

51. João Baptista de Castro, *Mapa de Portugal antigo, e Moderno,* 3 vols. (Lisbon, 1762), 3: 193.

52. ASV, Portogallo, Seg. 75, fol. 47 (1719/03/14); Scotti 1973, 126.

53. "Poi ordinògli che facesse un disegno del palazzo reale, della chiesa patriarcale, del palazzo per il patriarca e della canonica, con questa ingiunzione che quella fabbrica dopo la rinomata gran mole di S. Pietro di Roma, tenesse il primo posto. Per trovare un sito adeguato a tanto edificio si durò fatica tre mesi; ma finalmente . . . andato in persona il re co' grandi del suo regno, il signor marchese di Fontes e don Filippo, tutti in una gondola si portarano lontano alcune miglia da Lisbona per vedere un sito poco distante del mare, bello e di molta amenità . . . e questo scelto per fare la fabbrica." "Vita," in Viale 1966, 27.

54. " . . . uno nuovo dissegno adattato al detto sito nuovamente eletto."ASV, Portogallo, Seg. 75, fols. 63–63v (1719/03/28); Scotti 1973, 126.

55. " . . . una fabbrica non pure seconda, ma uguale alla gran mole di S. Pietro, e degna della grandezza di quel re." "Vita," in Viale 1966, 27

56. The information is, again, from the nuncio: "Giardino e Zappada per animali silvestri." ASV, Portogallo, Seg. 75, fol. 63–63v (1719/03/28); Scotti 1973, 126.

57. "La prima ordinazione che ricevette fu quella di un disegno per il fanale del porto; per il quale avendo ideato una colonna sullo stile antico ad imitazione di quelle che si vedono in Roma, con l'arme del re in mezzo retta da due fame, ed in cima un gran fanale . . . per imitare le opere degli antichi imperatori." "Vita," in Viale 1966, 27.

58. It is known that Juvarra also made decorations for Holy Week for the church of Loreto, an Italian congregation in Lisbon (Scotti 1973; Delaforce in Levenson 1993, 63). A magnificent Corpus Domini procession was organized, but nothing allows us to connect Juvarra to it.

59. Scotti 1976; Gritella 1992.

60. ASV, Portogallo, Seg. 75, fols. 208v–209 (1719/09/12); Scotti 1973, 130.

61. The nuncio reported: "His Majesty, persisting in the plans for the great patriarchal complex, he solicited various designs to open long and wide streets around the city that would lead directly to it" (Persisitindo Sua Maestà nell'intenzione della gran Fabrica della Patriarcale, fa prendere varij disegni per aprire per la città lunghe strade, e larghe che conduchino direttamente sino al sito di essa). ASV, Portogallo, Seg. 75, fol. 208v (1719/09/12); Scotti 1973, 130.

62. See Paulo Varela Gomes, "O caso de Carlo Gimach (1651–1730) e a historiografia da arquitectura portuguesa," *Museu* 4, no. 5 (1996): 141–156. Among other problems, the author considers hypotheses about foreign models (from southern Italy, Sicily, and Malta) and evolution of the Mafra stair design.

63. The term was first used in a brief survey in Paulo Varela Gomes, *O essencial sobre a arquitectura barroca em Portugal* (Lisbon, 1987). Later Gomes developed the idea in other publications on Portuguese architectural culture in the eighteenth century: *A cultura arquitectónica e artística em Portugal no séc. XVIII* (Lisbon, 1988) and *A confissão de Cyrillo* (Lisbon, 1992).

64. Andreina Griseri and Giovanni Romano, eds., *Filippo Juvarra a Torino. Nuovi progetti per la città* (Turin, 1989); Antonio Bonet Correia and Beatriz Blasco Esquivias, eds., *Filippo Juvarra: De Mesina al Palacio Real de Madrid* (Madrid, 1994); Vera Comoli Mandracci and Andreina Griseri, eds., *Filippo Juvarra: Architetto delle capitali da Torino a Madrid, 1714–1736* [exh. cat., Palazzo reale, Turin] (Milan, 1995).

65. The architect recently charged with directing the restoration of Monteiro-Mor has put forth a detailed argument for attributing it to Juvarra. See Fernando Sequeira Mendes, '"Palácio do Monteiro-Mor, Bairro Alto, Lisboa: Um raro cenário urbano," *História* 27 (2000): 32–39. Given Juvarra's virtuosity and productivity and the enthusiasm for his work among the court, it was very likely that during his stay in Lisbon he produced sketches for buildings other than those for John V.

66. The thesis of my book on the planning of Lisbon's expansion (Rossa 1998) is based on a debate about this issue. An example of evidence of the westward shift is the aqueduct distribution plan, by which all the new fountains were to be located to the west of the city's dense (and thirsty) center.

67. Leonor Ferrão, *A real obra de Nossa Senhora das Necessidades* (Lisbon, 1994).

68. Letter of 26 February 1726, quoted in Manuel Francisco de Barros e Sousa, Visconde de Santarém, *Quadro elementar das relações políticas e diplomáticas de Portugal . . .* , 18 vols. (Paris, 1842–1860), 5: cxvi.

69. See the first part of Maia's "Dissertações," in Ayres 1910, 33–40.

70. For a survey of Portuguese urbanism, see Walter Rossa, "A cidade portuguesa," in *História da arte portuguesa*, 3 vols. (Lisbon, 1995), 3: 233–323. On Portuguese urbanism in the period under discussion, see José E. Horta Correia, "Urbanismo," in *Dicionário da arte barroca em Portugal* (Lisbon, 1989), 507–513.

71. Marie Thérèse Mandroux-França, "La Patriarcale du roi Jean V de Portugal," *Colóquio-Artes* 83 (1989); Marie Thérèse Mandroux-França, "La patriarcale del re Giovanni V di Portogallo" in Vasco Rocca and Borghini 1995, 81–92. See also Paulo Varela Gomes, "Três desenhos setecentistas para a basílica patriarcal," *Boletim cultural da Póvoa do Varzim* 26 (1989): 663–687.

72. As mentioned earlier, Antonio Canevari was one of the pupils of Carlo Fontana who worked for John V. Before he went to Portugal he collaborated on models and drawings of Roman monuments that were sent to Lisbon. He also designed and supervised construction of the Bosco Parrasio, the new meeting place for the Accademia dell'Arcadia on the slope of Gianicolo, a benefaction of the Portuguese monarch, built in land given by the king of Spain. Canevari stayed in Portugal from 1727 to 1732. He worked in many places and was in charge of building the patriarch's summer estate, fountains, and gardens at Santo Antão do Tojal; the palace of Correio-Mor near Loures; and the tower of the University of Coimbra. On the former, see two works by José Fernande Pereira: *Arquitectura barroca em Portugal* (Lisbon, 1986) and *A acção artística do primeiro patriarca de Lisboa* (Lisbon, 1991). The tower has only been attributed to Canevari, but his role can now be confirmed on the basis of an official document: Arquivo Nacional da Torre do Tombo (Lisbon), Mesa da Consciência ę Ordens, Universidade de Coimbra,

Maço 60, Doc. 33. See also Paola Ferraris, "Antonio Canevari a Lisbona (1727–1732)," in Vasco Rocca and Borghini 1995, 57–66.

73. A. Ayres de Carvalho, "Lisbona romana all'epoca di João V," in Vasco Rocca and Borghini 1995, 3–17.

74. "Il re Magnanimo fu indubbiamente la maggiore vittima tra tutte quelle causate dal famoso terremoto di Lisbona del 1755." Eduardo Lourenço, "Tra l'oro e l'incenso," in Rome 1995, 1.

75. See Ludovice's account, published in José da Cunha Saraiva, *O aqueducto das Águas Livres e o arquitecto Ludovice* (Lisbon, 1938).

76. See Gomes 1989. The drawings are in the Museu Nacional de Arte Antiga, Lisbon, Fundo Antigo Inv. 1682, 1682A and 1862B. They consist of an overall plan, a plan detail, and a cross section. The drawings show what would have been an extremely long and narrow church. The footprint could be explained by the desire of the architect and the king to build on the existing foundations of a palace that the Count of Tarouca had begun some decades before.

77. The only known project for the patriarchal cathedral from the period after the catastrophe is by João Pedro Ludovice (1701–1760), the son of Frederico Ludovice. Two plans are known to exist, one in the Museu Nacional de Arte Antiga (Lisbon), Fundo Antigo Inv. 1652, and the other in the Biblioteca Nacional, Lisbon, D14R. The church was quickly (and badly) built in wood, then destroyed by fire in 1769. Gomes stressed the relationship between the wooden patriarchal church and the anonymous project, but I do not think that it is possible to see an evolution from the first to the second. It is impossible to include an extended discussion here, but the only conclusion to be drawn from the research of this eminent scholar of the period is that the anonymous project was in many details very closely connected to John V's architectural patronage and to Frederico Ludovice's work, specifically at Mafra. Notwithstanding his father's support, João Pedro Ludovice had an obscure career, with no relevant commission or even independent authorship. The marquis of Pombal or Manuel da Maia would have assigned the patriarchal church project to him only because it was to be a temporary building and he could respond quickly by adapting the decade-old project designed by his father, on which João Pedro may even have worked as an assistant.

78. Manuel da Maia, *Carta topografica que compre-hende todo o terreno desde as cidades de Lisboa Occidental e Oriental té a vila de Mafra, com todos os lugares, q. contem na sua extenção*, Real Academia de la Historia de Madrid, R. 196, Sign. C/Ic2p.

79. *Planta Topographica da marinha de Lisboa Occidental, e Oriental, desde o Forte de S. Joseph de Ribamar té o Convento do Grilo feita no anno de 1727*, Museu da Cidade (Lisbon), cota 1387.

80. Carlos Mardel, "Projecto do cais novo de Belém ao cais de Santarém," Arquivo Histórico do Ministério das Obras Públicas, D27C. On Mardel, see note 82.

81. Daniel Rabreau, "La Promenade urbaine en France aux XVIIe et XVIIIe siècles: entre planification et imaginaire," in *Histoire des jardins, de la Renaissance à nos jours*, ed. Monique Mosser and Georges Teyssot (Paris, 1991), 301–312.

82. Carlos Mardel worked in many places in central Europe but was never in Italy. In addition to his native Pressburg (now Bratislava, then in Hungary), his stay in France and England was the most important influence on his development as an architect. Rossa 1998, 138–139.

83. José M. dos Santos Simões, "Iconografia lisboeta no azulejos no Brasil: Vistas de Lisboa em painéis de azulejos na cidade do Salvador," *Oceanos* 36–37 (1998): 20–50. From the reign of Manuel I (r. 1495–1521) to that of John V, the Franciscans played a decisive role in encouraging the messianic obsession of some Portuguese monarchs with the myth of the so-called Fifth Empire. In this context King Manuel I was none other than the biblical Emmanuel, the Messiah. Over the centuries some of Portugal's leading intellectuals, among them António Vieira (1608–1697) and Fernando Pessoa (1888–1935) imagined the return of King Sebastian I (r. 1557–1578), who disappeared in a battle against the Muslims in Morocco in 1578, bringing an end to the Avis dynasty and consequently the beginning of the rule Spanish kings over Portugal (1580–1640). The Fifth Empire would be characterized by a spiritual civilization based on human genius and sacred authority, not on temporal power, as were the four empires of antiquity (Babylon, Persia, Greece, and Rome) and those of modern times (Ottoman, Austro-Hungarian, Napoleonic, Russian, and British). In the context of the restoration of independence from Spain in 1640, António Vieira, a Jesuit, in his *Esperanças de Portugal, V império do mundo* of 1659 and his *Livro ante-primeiro da história do futuro* of 1666 developed the idea that the Portuguese monarchy met all the conditions for building the Fifth Empire: Christ's global empire with Portugal at its center and its civilization as its main instrument. He based his arguments on Nebuchadnezzar's biblical dream, revealed by the prophet Daniel. For a general approach see Joaquim Domingues, *De Ourique ao quinto império: Para uma filosofia da cultura portuguesa* (Lisbon, 2002).

84. The ceremonial protocols for the wedding implied an extraordinary program of patronage in which a number of architects were involved (Frederico Ludovice, Canevari, and Mardel, among others). A palace was built in Vendas Novas just for an overnight stay of the wedding party. John V also committed to important architectural projects along the party's itinerary, including remodeling of the chancel of the cathedral at Evora.

85. Manoel Coelho da Graça, *Breve noticia das entradas que por mar, e terra fizeraõ nesta Corte Suas Magestades com os Serenissimos Principes do Brazil, e Altezas que Deos guarde, em 12 de Fevereiro de 1729* (Lisbon, 1729); Silva 1750.

MARC GRIGNON

Université Laval

Robert de Villeneuve and the Representation of Quebec City at the End of the Seventeenth Century

Research on urban images has shown that the relationship between views or plans and the cities they represent varies considerably according to historical and topographical context. For example, Louis Marin has argued that, in contrast to contemporary plans intended to help people find their way around a city, the Gomboust plan of Paris (1652) included representations of churches and aristocratic hôtels not to enable viewers to identify those buildings, but rather to fill the map with familiar references.[1] Examples could be multiplied, but this one is enough to establish, at the beginning of this essay, that representations can support a wide variety of uses and meanings.

In the case of Quebec City during the French colonial period (1608–1759), the function of views and plans conforms to Marin's example only partially. Images of Quebec City were not meant to enable travelers to identify buildings and streets in the city; they were conceived and produced to allow identification of buildings within the images themselves. These images, however, were usually made in the colony for the French royal administration and represented a city that the intended viewers could not see for themselves. King Louis XIV and the marquis de Seignelay, secretary of state for the navy, had to rely on correspondence, reports, and images provided by the local governor, intendant, or military engineer to gain an idea of their capital in New France.

An analogy may be found in a distinction Michael Baxandall makes with regard to the description of works of art. Art historians' written descriptions of objects such as paintings are usually accompanied by visual reproductions. In this sense, the descriptions are made *in the presence* of the objects described, and therefore their primary function is *ostentive*. Art historical descriptions are meant to point out significant features in objects that everyone can see. In contrast, other kinds of descriptions, such as literary ones, are usually not accompanied by their objects, or by reproductions of their objects, so their function is *supplemental*. They are meant to enable readers to imagine objects that they cannot see.[2]

The views and plans of Quebec City made during the French regime fulfilled an important supplemental function for intended viewers on another continent. In the colony, however, the situation was different: members of the local elite, insomuch as they were aware of the making of city views and plans, could try to recognize in them their visions of the city and could even try to influence image makers so that buildings they owned would be portrayed in the way they wished them to be seen by the royal administration. Quebec City, being so dependent on the way it was represented in official documents because of its colonial situation, may have developed a certain awareness of its own image.

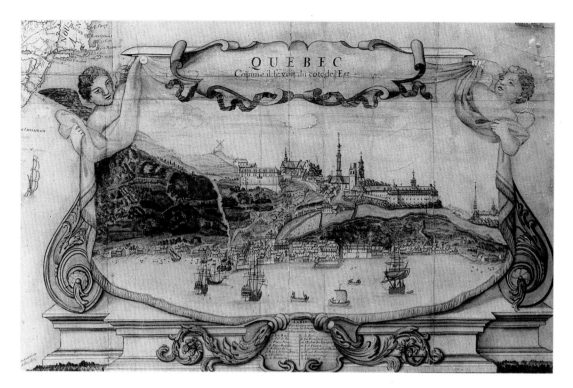

1. Jean-Baptiste-Louis Franquelin, *Québec comme il se voit du côté de l'est* (Quebec as seen from the east), 1688, detail of a manuscript map of North America, pen, ink, and washes on paper
Service historique de la Marine, Vincennes, recueil 66

Typical Views and Plans of Quebec City

A typical view of Quebec City at the end of the seventeenth century or at the beginning of the eighteenth looks west from the vantage point of the Saint Lawrence River and shows the city as a profile against an empty background.[3] As seen in a view of 1688 by Jean-Baptiste-Louis Franquelin (fig. 1) and an engraving of 1722 published in Claude Le Roy's *Histoire de l'Amérique septentrionale* (fig. 2), the city is split into the commercial Lower Town, on the bank of the Saint Lawrence, and the institutional Upper Town, situated above an abrupt cliff, the two parts linked by a single winding street. In both images, religious institutions, visible mostly by their spires, occupy prominent positions in the Upper Town. The Governor's Palace, also named the Fort Saint-Louis or the Château Saint-Louis, is the most important secular building in the drawing itself and in the legend that identifies the various structures.

City plans convey the same perception of the city, as they were consistently oriented with west at the top, thus suggesting the same eastern vantage point. Jean Bourdon's *Vray plan du haut & bas de Québec comme il est en l'an 1660* (fig. 3) is one of the early

plans that show the entire city in this manner. The Saint Lawrence River is along the lower edge of the plan, so that the subjective relationship between someone arriving by ship and the eastern aspect of the city is preserved in the image.[4] The other limits of the plan also correspond to those found in city views: the city is framed on the left-hand side by the hill known as Cap-aux-Diamants and on the right-hand side by the Saint Charles River. At the top, the plan extends approximately to the depth assumed in the city views.

Another plan using similar conventions is the *Plan de la ville de Québec capitale de la Nouvelle France* of 1693, by Josué Dubois Berthelot de Beaucours (fig. 4). As indicated by the compass rose in the upper left corner, this plan is also oriented with west at the top, presenting the shore of the Saint Lawrence along the lower edge of the sheet. The limits on the left and right sides of the sheet are the same as in Bourdon's plan, except that both shores of the Saint Charles River are drawn.

These few examples show the close coordination between views and plans of Quebec City in this period, a coordination that can be compared to that between the elevation and the plan of a building displayed one

above the other on a single sheet. In views as well as in plans, the side of the city on the Saint Lawrence River is presented as the most significant one. As far as individual buildings are concerned, these views and plans translate into visual terms a hierarchical structure of the city. As John Brian Harley has argued, the "visual hierarchy of signs in early modern maps is often a replica of the legal, feudal, and ecclesiastical stratifications."[5] The importance that city views give to the Governor's Palace also finds a parallel in city plans.[6] Despite the comparatively limited means of emphasis available in the latter mode of representation, Bourdon and Beaucours have both managed to give a certain degree of importance to that building. In Bourdon's plan, where it is labeled "Fort S Louis," it is the first building to be identified in the legend. In Beaucours' plan, the label "Le fort" is inserted directly on the map, as is also the case for the most important religious institutions—indicated as "Le Séminaire" and "L'Evesché"—and, in con-

trast to the Intendant's Palace, relegated to the letter *m* in the legend.

Robert de Villeneuve's Plan

In pursuing this examination of the role of images in the development of Quebec City at the end of the seventeenth century, instead of commenting on other typical examples, I shall focus on the most important exception to the tendency I have just described: Robert de Villeneuve's first plan of Quebec City, made in 1685 (fig. 5), which is significant because it provides the most detailed survey of the city up to that time. As substantiation for what I have said about the more typical ones, its singular character should make it the exception that proves the rule. I will proceed by examining a series of features in which this plan differs from those mentioned previously, to see whether they support my hypotheses or whether they call for qualification.

When he arrived in New France, Robert de Villeneuve was not a fully qualified military

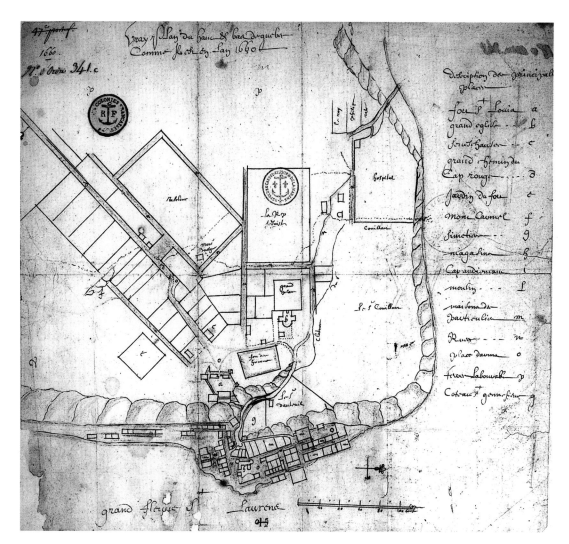

3. Jean Bourdon, *Vray plan du haut & bas de Québec comme il est en l'an 1660* (True plan of the Upper Town and Lower Town of Quebec as it is in the year 1660), 1660, pen and ink on paper
Centre des archives d'outre-mer, Aix-en-Provence, Archives nationales, France, Dépôt des fortifications des colonies (DFC), Amérique septentrionale, 341C

engineer, but merely a good surveyor selected by Louis XIV's commissioner of fortifications, Sébastien le Prestre de Vauban, in response to a request from the marquis de Seignelay. For the very first military engineer to be sent to New France, Seignelay would have preferred someone with better qualifications, capable of developing fortification projects and overseeing their construction.[7] Vauban, however, explained that he would design these fortifications himself, continuing: "[I]f you are willing to limit yourself to having plans and vertical sections made of the places that the king intends to fortify in Canada . . . , the man I sent will be appropriate."[8]

After his arrival in Canada in May 1685, Villeneuve accordingly began a detailed survey of Quebec City.[9] Completed during the fall, the plan follows the general conventions used by French military engineers for pre-senting their work, such as showing extant buildings in red and projected ones in yellow, and indicating topography by gradations in the intensity of gray washes. It emphatically displays a concern for objectivity in the last two words of its title, *Plan de la ville et chasteau de Québec, fait en 1685, mezurée exactement.* The plan is accompanied by two intersecting sections showing the vertical profile of the site. The first (fig. 6)—which follows an east-west line marked on the plan by the letters *A*, *B*, and *C*—shows one side of Sous-le-Fort Street and cuts through the "Maison du S[ieu]r Joliet" at the foot of the cliff and through the Governor's Palace at the top.[10] The other section (not reproduced), identified by the letters *D*, *E*, and *F*, intersects with the first in the court of the Governor's Palace, showing the main facade of the building. Although there is no external evidence to support this

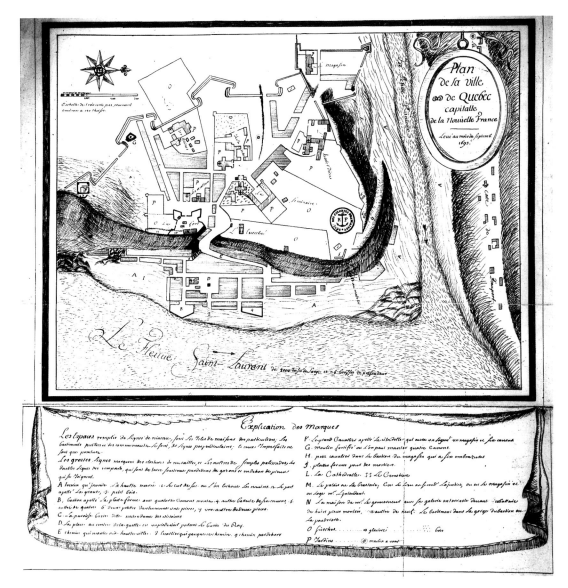

hypothesis, the precision of the plan may have been motivated by a desire to make a three-dimensional model, or relief map, of the city.

In addition to fulfilling a documentary function quite effectively, Villeneuve's plan includes features consistent with a rhetorical function, if we recall Aristotle's definition of rhetoric as the art of persuasion, an art that can sway decisions when dialectic, or pure argumentation, alone cannot.[11] Choices Villeneuve made in preparing his drawings reveal a point of view that may have contributed to the difficulties he soon began to have with colonial officials. In 1687, the governor of New France, the marquis de Denonville, called him "a fool, a libertine, a debauchee," and he continued to complain

about him until Villeneuve was summoned back to France in 1689.[12]

As Bourdon did in 1660 and as Beaucours would do a few years after him, Villeneuve identified religious institutions by putting their names directly on the plan, in contrast to secular buildings, which are identified by numbers keyed to a legend in the upper right-hand corner of the sheet. Indeed, religious buildings ("Le Séminaire," "les Jésuites," "les Urselines," and so on) are labeled on the plan in the same way as topographical features: "le Sault au mathelot," "Cap aux Diamants" (figs. 7 and 8). However, for the church under construction next to the seminary, Villeneuve chose the label "paroisse," or parish church (fig. 8). While not exactly false, this designation refers to the

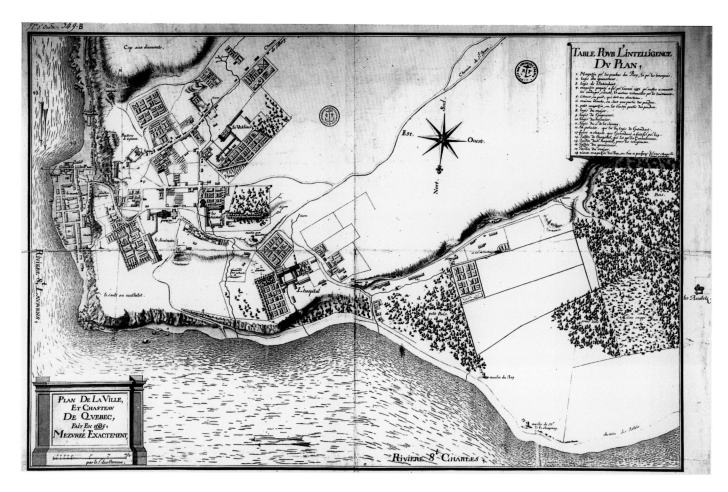

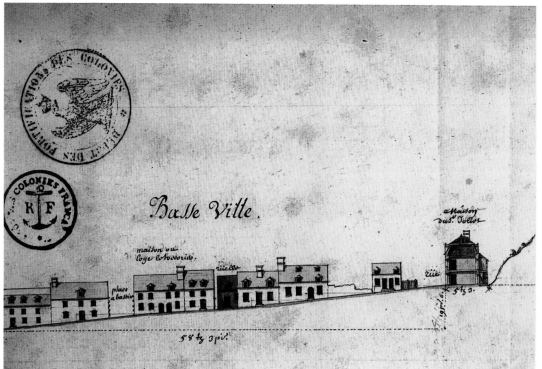

5. Robert de Villeneuve, *Plan de la ville et chasteau de Québec, fait en 1685, mezurée exactement par le s[ieur] de Villeneuve* (Plan of the city and palace of Quebec, made in 1685, measured accurately by the sieur of Villeneuve), 1685, pen, ink, and washes on paper
Centre des archives d'outre-mer, Aix-en-Provence, Archives nationales, France, DFC, Amérique septentrionale, 349B

6. Robert de Villeneuve, *Couppe sur la ligne A, B, C marquée sur le plan de Québec* (Section along the line A, B, C indicated on the plan of Quebec), 1685, detail of Sous-le-Fort Street, pen, ink, and washes on paper
Centre des archives d'outre-mer, Aix-en-Provence, Archives nationales, France, DFC, Amérique septentrionale, 352C

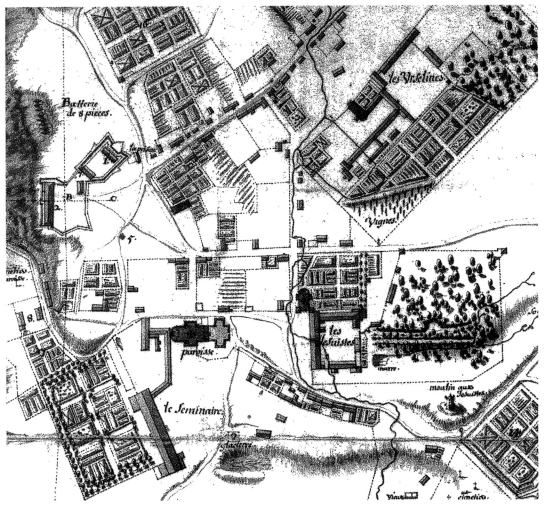

7. Robert de Villeneuve, *Plan de la ville et chasteau de Québec*, 1685, detail of the Upper Town with the Ursuline convent, the Jesuit monastery, the Seminary, and the "parish church," pen, ink, and washes on paper

Centre des archives d'outre-mer, Aix-en-Provence, Archives nationales, France, DFC, Amérique septentrionale, 349B

less lofty of the two ecclesiastical functions attributed to the building, the other being that of cathedral. This choice provides a clue about the tensions between Villeneuve and some colonial officials: the church was elevated to the rank of cathedral in 1674, but it also continued to serve as parish church. When Villeneuve arrived in New France, Bishop François de Montmorency-Laval had an important project under way to replace the church with a three-story facade based on early-seventeenth-century Parisian models and flanked by twin towers (fig. 9). Villeneuve, however, decided to keep the designation of parish church, even though his plan shows the new building under construction.

The Récollet Monastery

Another peculiarity of Villeneuve's plan is the way in which the monastery of the Récollet friars, a branch of the Franciscan order, is represented by a building drawn in the margin, outside the frame of the image, on the right-hand side of the sheet (fig. 10). The monastery was actually located a little farther west than the reach of the plan, in an area called Notre-Dame-des-Anges, in the valley of the Saint Charles River, and Villeneuve had to invent some kind of device in order not to leave the monastery out. In doing this, he was again making a significant choice, since the Récollets owned another, smaller building situated within the city, a hospice on Place d'Armes, which could also have represented them on the map. In its location, next to the gardens across from the fort in the Upper Town, the map shows a small, unidentified structure (fig. 7).

Villeneuve's decision to show the monastery outside the town, rather than the hospice in the Upper Town, puts him squarely on the side of the friars in their ongoing conflict with Bishop Laval. The bishop had

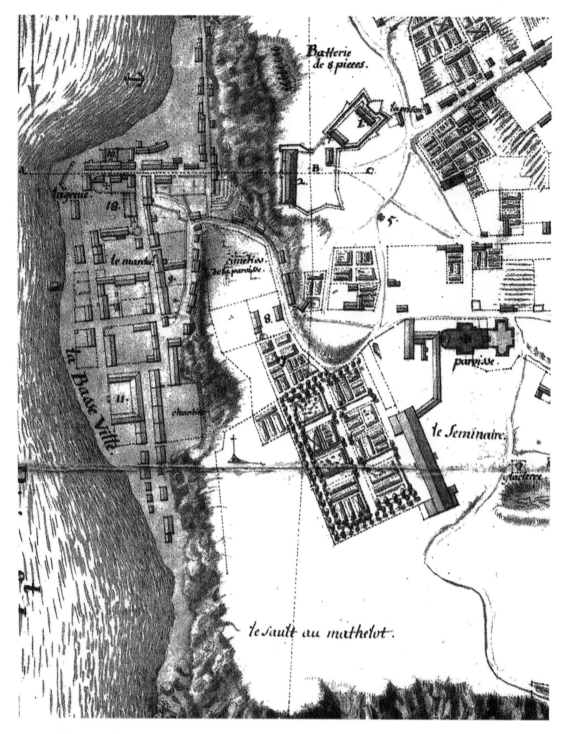

8. Robert de Villeneuve, *Plan de la ville et chasteau de Québec,* 1685, detail of the Lower Town and the Upper Town, pen, ink, and washes on paper
Centre des archives d'outre-mer, Aix-en-Provence, Archives nationales, France, DFC, Amérique septentrionale, 349B

originally agreed to the construction of a modest infirmary, but, after the friars erected a belfry on the roof in June 1683 and declared their building a hospice, he wrote to King Louis XIV, asking that the friars be expelled from the city, arguing that they were using his original authorization as a pretext to create a new institution intra muros against his will.[13] For the Récollets, on the other hand, the hospice did not constitute a distinct establishment, but merely a small dependency of their monastery, "in a lonely place in the middle of the forest" (dans une solitude au milieu des bois).[14]

In 1684 the king refused the bishop's request to expel the friars, but he did order the Récollets to destroy their belfry and to keep the hospice chapel closed to the

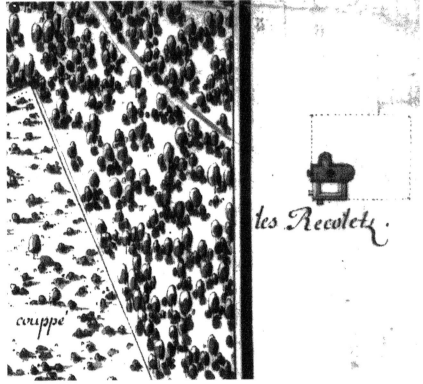

public.[15] The Récollets, dissatisfied, continued to send reports arguing that these restrictions were profoundly unjust. Thus a report prepared in 1686 for the superiors of the order in France gives a complete list of the Récollet establishments in New France but omits mention of the hospice in Quebec City, so that it would not be taken for an independent entity.[16] By not putting the name of the order next to the hospice and by situating the monastery in the margin next to the wooded area west of the city, Villeneuve's representation emphasizes the distance between the monastery and the city and represents the relationship in a way that corresponds exactly to the Récollets' argument about the relative importance of their own buildings. It is not clear how significant Villeneuve's plan was to the events that followed, but the Récollets won their case in 1691, when Bishop Saint-Vallier, who had replaced Laval a few years earlier, allowed the construction of a complete monastery on Place d'Armes.[17]

A Chapel in the Lower Town

If we turn to the Lower Town, Villeneuve's plan continues to show interestingly peculiar elements. Among the projected buildings shown on the plan is a church identified as number 18, which the legend describes as "Vieux magazin du roy, ou l'on a proposé faire une chapelle l'année prochaine" (Old 'King's warehouse,' where the construction of a chapel has been proposed for next year) (fig. 11 and fig. 19). Bishop Laval had wanted to open a chapel in the Lower Town, where most of the population was established, since 1680, and he claimed the abandoned *magasin du roi* to that end. Fearing that the building might be given to the Récollets, he had made his own plea to the king, arguing that masses must be celebrated in that area of town since the way to the cathedral was too difficult for elderly people during the winter. In 1681 he also had an altar installed in the abandoned building in order to begin holding masses on the site. Seeing the irregularity of these procedures, the comte de Frontenac, governor of New France—who was not particularly favorable to Bishop Laval in general[18]—explained in a letter that he had to protect the *magasin du roi* by posting a guard next to it, so that the bishop could not have masses celebrated in the building before the site was officially turned over to a new owner.[19]

In 1682, the sieur de La Barre, who was being sent to replace Frontenac as governor, was instructed by Louis XIV to ascertain whether the old *magasin* could be of any utility to the state. Should it be demonstrated otherwise, he could accept the bishop's request and grant the land to the seminary:

Monsignor the Bishop . . . has claimed the lot of the old warehouse in order to build a chapel of ease. His Majesty wishes that Sieur de La Barre consider that proposal and, should there be no inconvenience and the warehouse be deemed useless, grant it to him for the erection of the aforesaid chapel.[20]

Considering that there would be enough space to rebuild the *magasin du roi* on land next to the marketplace should it ever become desirable, de La Barre saw no difficulty with the bishop's request, and in October 1683 he granted the seminary the land on the edge of Sous-le-Fort Street, where the project is located in the plan (fig. 11).

After learning of the grant, however, the king felt that de La Barre had acted too much on his own and had failed to send him proper information about the usefulness of the land on which the *magasin* stood. In a letter dated 10 April 1684, addressed to de La Barre, Louis XIV wrote, "Before granting the old warehouse in the new town of Quebec for the creation of a chapel, you should have waited for my order, and informed me whether the warehouse was actually useless to my service."[21] In addition, it turned out that de La Barre had made the grant without the approval of the colony's intendant, who also had authority over the matter.

The king therefore considered the grant invalid and ordered the marquis de Denonville, whom he had sent to Canada as governor in 1685, to examine the question all over again:

His Majesty learned that Sieur de La Barre had made the grant all by himself, which was contrary to his orders, according to which the governor should only make a grant of land together with the Intendant. It is His Majesty's wish that Sieur Denonville examine, together with Sieur De Meules, whether anything would be prejudicial to his service, and only then gives the authority to confirm the grant.[22]

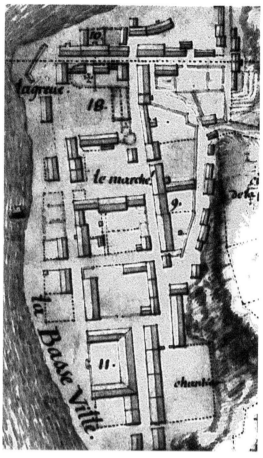

11. Robert de Villeneuve, *Plan de la ville et chasteau de Québec,* 1685, detail of the Lower Town, with the marketplace ("le marché") and the projected chapel, pen, ink, and washes on paper
Centre des archives d'outre-mer, Aix-en-Provence, Archives nationales, France, DFC, Amérique septentrionale, 349B

Denonville confirmed that the land was indeed useless to the state, and in August he once again made a grant of the property, this time extending it all the way to the marketplace.[23] This enlargement would allow the projected church to be turned ninety degrees and to face the square as it does today. The king's official approval, however, was given only the following spring, at the end of May 1686.[24] Thus, in the summer of 1685, Villeneuve may still have been in the dark about Governor Denonville's intentions, or he may have judged that the dispute was not quite settled. In any case, his plan sides with de La Barre's earlier decision about the church, and, as we will see, Villeneuve was envisaging a completely different type of square.

The "Place de Québec"

In January 1685 Governor de La Barre and Intendant Jacques De Meulles granted Claude Baillif, an architect in Quebec City, a piece of land situated within the marketplace. On

12. Robert de Villeneuve,
Place de Québec, 1685, pen,
ink, and washes on paper
Centre des archives d'outre-mer, Aix-
en-Provence, Archives nationales,
France, Atlas Moreau de Saint-Méry,
F-3 290, no. 68

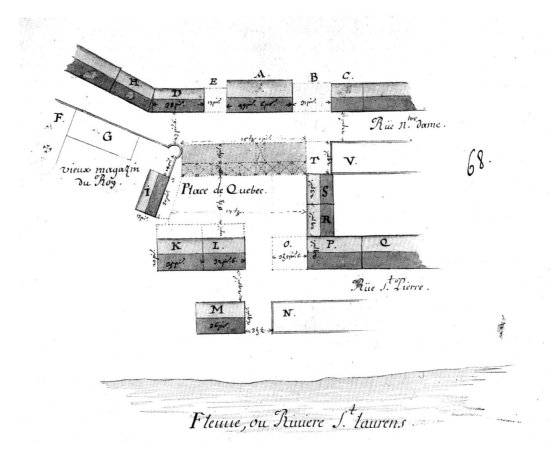

this land, Baillif wanted to erect a building that would transform the market of the Lower Town into a formal city square, to be called Place de Québec. The precise arrangement between Baillif and the authorities is not known, but it must have been similar to those by which royal squares were then being created in France. The building may also have included a new warehouse for the king.

As can be seen in the drawing that Villeneuve included in a report explaining the project (fig. 12), the property extended along Notre-Dame Street, from one corner of the square to the shell of the old *magasin du roi* on the next corner. The projected building occupies the entire property, thus closing the square entirely on that side. At ground level, the building has an open arcade facing the square, in addition to a vaulted passage connecting the square to Notre-Dame Street. The passage, slightly off center in the building, lines up with a street that runs from the harbor into the square.

The overall design of the proposed square recalls the Place Royale in Paris, which has continuous facades on three sides, an open arcade at ground level, vaulted passages that set off the square from the surroundings while providing access under the buildings, and secondary access from the streets at two corners. Similar features are clearly recognizable in the Quebec project, despite the small scale and the compromises that had to be made to accommodate the surrounding buildings.[25]

The project, however, ran into difficulties in June 1685, when Baillif started measuring the site and the merchants of the Lower Town realized what was going on. The merchants immediately mounted strong opposition to the transformation of the marketplace, and in the fall several reports and other documents making a case against the project were sent to the king.

Villeneuve's report, meant as documentation on which the king could base his decision, counters to the merchants' objections in a subtle manner. The drawing shows the projected square and puts the church in the same position as in his city plan, where it would have to be for Baillif's project to be

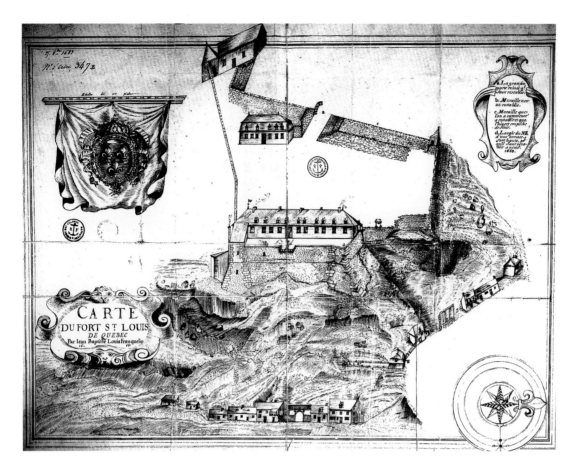

13. Jean-Baptiste-Louis Franquelin, *Carte du Fort St Louis de Québec* (Map of Fort Saint-Louis in Quebec), 1683, pen and ink on paper

Centre des archives d'outre-mer, Aix-en-Provence, Archives nationales, France, DFC, Amérique septentrionale, 347B

feasible. The letter *F* marks the "square where it is proposed to build a church in 1686" (place ou l'on propose faire une chapelle dans l'année 1686) and the letter *G*, next to it on the plan, indicates the location reserved for the presbytery. Villeneuve enhances Baillif's reputation by presenting him as "Le Sieur Renaud, architecte" (his full name being Claude Baillif dit Renault). The title "Place de Québec" draws attention to the square rather than to the projected building, and the explanations do likewise: "[T]he yellow wash shows the area where the Sieur Renaud, architect, intends to build an arcade of nine feet in depth, and a passage with porte-cochère, to allow circulation between Notre-Dame Street and the square."[26] In none of these comments is the building itself explicitly mentioned.

The merchants expressed their opposition to the project in a document titled "Mémoire pour les bourgeois habitant la basse-ville de Québec."[27] Identifying Baillif with the less flattering title "master mason and contractor," it focuses on the building itself and argues that no part of the public

space should be alienated in the interests of an individual.

Louis XIV approved the project, and his choice of words reflects the point of view suggested in Villeneuve's presentation:

Today, on the 31st day of May 1686 at Versailles, the king was notified of the awarding to a certain Bailly, architect at Quebec, of a plot of land situated in the Lower Town of that city. His Majesty has confirmed the award, thereby granting the land to the aforesaid Bailly.[28]

The king's identification of Baillif as an architect is a clue to his agreement with Villeneuve's way of presenting the situation. Recognizing, however, that he might not be thoroughly familiar with the local situation, the king left the final decision to Bochart de Champigny, the new intendant whom he was sending to New France that year, and who was to hand-deliver the royal response. In the end, Champigny gave in to the merchants and canceled the royal grant, as indeed he was authorized to do.[29]

Champigny's original intention, however, may have been different, since he had also brought with him a bronze copy of Bernini's bust of Louis XIV. The bust was meant for the new square, to be redefined as a *place royale*, since Louis XIV had instructed his intendants to create royal squares in the most important cities and towns of his kingdom just a year earlier.[30] Because the withdrawal of the land grant meant the cancellation of Baillif's project, however, a few months later only the bust was installed in the center of the marketplace. It appears, situated in the axis of the street connecting the marketplace with the harbor, in Franquelin's 1688 view (fig. 1), identified as "Effigie du roy" in the legend. In Beaucours' 1693 plan, the square is neither a *place royale* nor a marketplace, but ambiguously described as "the square at the center of which is a pedestal for the bust of the king" (la place au centre de laquelle est un piedestal pour le buste du Roy) (fig. 4).[31]

The Visibility of the Intendant's Palace

The last peculiarity of Villeneuve's plan that I wish to discuss is not a specific detail, but rather its orientation, which, as indicated by the compass rose, is south, with the Saint Lawrence River on the left-hand side (fig. 5). It is the only known document to show Quebec City in this way. Its orientation cannot be explained entirely, as some historians

have suggested, by the need to show the area close to the Saint Charles River where the city could be expanded.[32] Indeed, as can be seen in Beaucours' plan, other military engineers had no difficulty preserving the customary cartographic orientation while including the land in the vicinity of the Saint Charles considered for an expansion of the fortified enclosure. The explanation for Villeneuve's decision, I contend, has to do, once again, with the politics of representation and constitutes an attempt to give more weight to the symbolic representation of the intendant, the second most important administrator in the colony.

The Château Saint-Louis, official residence of the governor, already had a strong visual presence in the eastern face of Quebec City, and it was consequently a dominant feature in city views. The *Carte du Fort St. Louis de Québec* of 1683, by Jean-Baptiste-Louis Franquelin, is a partial view of the eastern side of the city that focuses on the governor's residence (fig. 13). The hybrid character of this "view" is underlined by the word *carte* (map) in its title and by the inclusion of a compass rose in the lower right corner. The compass rose shows that the orientation is that of Bourdon's and Beaucours' plans, with west at the top. These cartographic features of Franquelin's view make explicit, in a single document, the strong connection between views and plans in that period.

In contrast to the governor, the intendant had no official residence until 1685, and the first two incumbents to occupy this post, Jean Talon and Jacques Duchesneau, had to live in existing buildings rented for them and of little architectural significance in the city. In 1685, however, Intendant Jacques De Meulles was authorized to transform a brewery established by Talon on the Saint Charles River into a suitable residence for himself.[33] Villeneuve readily acknowledged the ongoing transformations, and, for the first time, the "Logis de l'intendant" is identified in the legend of a plan or a city view (fig. 14 and fig. 19, number 3).

In this context, the orientation chosen by Villeneuve provides a way of emphasizing the visibility of the residence—and, consequently, that of the intendant—by relating the building to a new vantage point on the city. Because it is oriented south, the plan

14. Robert de Villeneuve, *Plan de la ville et chasteau de Québec*, 1685, detail of the intendant's residence (number 3), pen, ink, and washes on paper

Centre des archives d'outre-mer, Aix-en-Provence, Archives nationales, France, DFC, Amérique septentrionale, 349B

15. Attributed to Jean-Baptiste-Louis Franquelin, *Québec vue de l'est* (Quebec seen from the east), 1699, detail of a manuscript map of New France, pen, ink, and washes on paper
Service historique de la Marine, Vincennes, recueil 66

16. Attributed to Jean-Baptiste-Louis Franquelin, *Québec vue du nord ouest* (Quebec seen from the northwest), 1699, detail of a manuscript map of New France
Service historique de la Marine, Vincennes, recueil 66

suggests a vantage point that privileges the intendant's new residence on the Saint Charles River. It is not possible to determine whether the intendant chose this site because it was visible from the Saint Charles or whether, since the date of the map and that of the building's conversion are the same, the new vantage point was developed in order to show the intendant's palace. The best hypothesis is probably that there was some kind of agreement between De Meulles and Villeneuve. Indeed, one could take into consideration the solidarity that De Meulles and Villeneuve showed in supporting Baillif's project for the transformation of the marketplace. De Meulles, for example, imposed a fine on everyone who publicly contested the validity of the grant he had made to the architect.[34]

It took about fifteen years for the new vantage point implicit in Villeneuve's plan to be fully recognized, at least if we judge from the views that can be found today. A large map of New France made in 1699 by Jean-Baptiste-Louis Franquelin incorporates two vignettes with views of Quebec City. The larger view (fig. 15), presenting the city from the east, is dominated by the Governor's

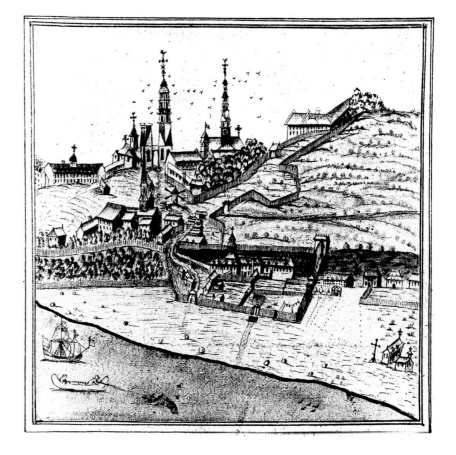

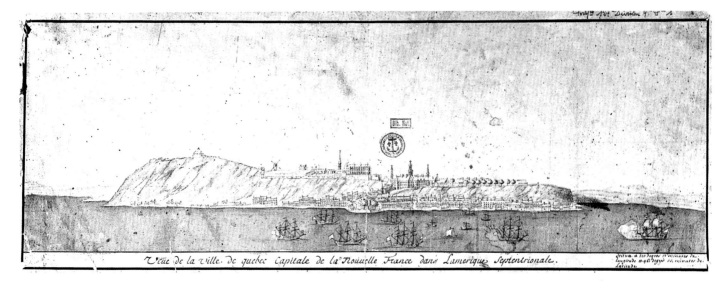

Vëüe de la ville de quebec Capitale de la Nouvelle France dans Lamerique Septentrionale.

17. Anonymous, *Veue de la ville de Québec capitale de la nouvelle France dans l'Amérique septentrionale* (View of the city of Quebec, capital of New France in North America), c. 1720, pen, ink, and washes on paper
Bibliothèque nationale de France

18. Anonymous, *Veue de la ville de Québec capitale de la nouvelle France dans l'Amérique septentrionale. Veue du côté de la rivière St Charles* (View of the city of Quebec in North America. View from the Saint Charles River), c. 1720, pen, ink, and washes on paper
Bibliothèque nationale de France

Palace and religious institutions. The other (fig. 16), a bit smaller and placed in a secondary position on the map, shows the city from the north—the vantage point suggested in Villeneuve's 1685 plan—and includes the remodeled brewery as one of its major features. This new vantage point remained the only contender to that of the Saint Lawrence River until the British conquest of 1759. After both the Governor's Palace and the Intendant's Palace were rebuilt at the beginning of the eighteenth century, the two viewpoints were often given the same importance. For example, the Bibliothèque nationale in Paris preserves two views of Quebec City that are clearly conceived as a pair: one represents the city as seen from the Saint Lawrence River and is dominated by the

Governor's Palace (fig. 17), and the other one shows the city from the Saint Charles River, with the Intendant's Palace equally in evidence (fig. 18).

This explanation for the peculiar orientation of Villeneuve's plan is also supported by the way numbers are used to identify buildings in the city. It is noticeable that these numbers are not laid out in a logical sequence, from left to right or from top to bottom. They appear to be thrown like dice on the sheet, their random arrangement forcing the eye to move constantly from one corner of the map to the other. They nevertheless follow a clear order that appears only in the legend: number 1 refers to the king (in fact, the "Magazin pour les poudres du Roy"), number 2 to the governor and his palace, number

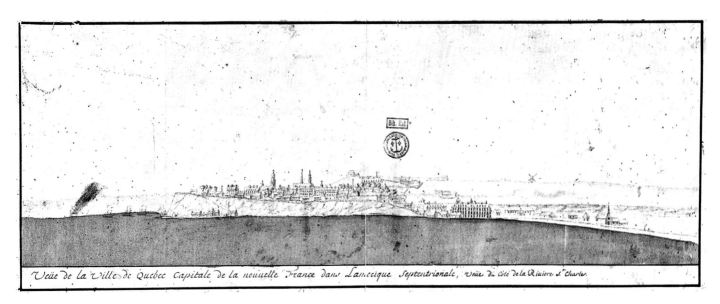

Vëüe de la ville de Quebec Capitale de la nouuelle France dans Lamerique Septentrionale, vëüe du côté de la Riuiere S.t Charles.

3 to the intendant, and so forth (fig. 19). The buildings are listed in the legend according to the sociopolitical hierarchy they represent, and this consideration explains the dispersal of the numbers across the plan: orderliness *on the plan* would have led to disorder *in the legend*, something that would have been so much contrary to what Jürgen Habermas calls "the publicity of representation" that it seems here almost unthinkable.[35] And since this is the first time the intendant's residence is acknowledged in a city plan, there is little doubt that Villeneuve had to make a personal decision about the best way to give that building an appropriate place in the image of the city.

After being recalled to France in 1689 and then returning to Canada in 1691, Villeneuve made a second large plan of Quebec City in 1692 (fig. 20). This time, however, he was under the authority of Franquelin, who was officially entrusted with the responsibilities of a military engineer.[36] Throughout the rest of his military career, Villeneuve in fact seems never to have held the same level of responsibility he had in New France between 1685 and 1689.[37] The 1692 plan is also much more conventional (although no less rhetorical) than that of 1685, with its western orientation, the old Récollet monastery left out of the map altogether (even though it had become the Hôpital général in 1691), and the cathedral more properly identified as "Église Notre-Dame."

In the end, the peculiarities and biases of Villeneuve's 1685 plan of Quebec City reveal something quite typical of the period. Villeneuve's plan is perhaps exceptional in its biases and its rhetoric, but it fills the same role as other images of the colonial capital during the French regime—especially if we consider the perception of the city that it suggests. The representation of the Récollet monastery in one of the margins, the placement of the projected chapel of the Lower Town on Sous-lc-Fort Street, or the ordering of buildings in the legend reveal Villeneuve's personal opinions. At the same time, however, these features provide us with clear indications of what conferred symbolic power on a building in Quebec City at that

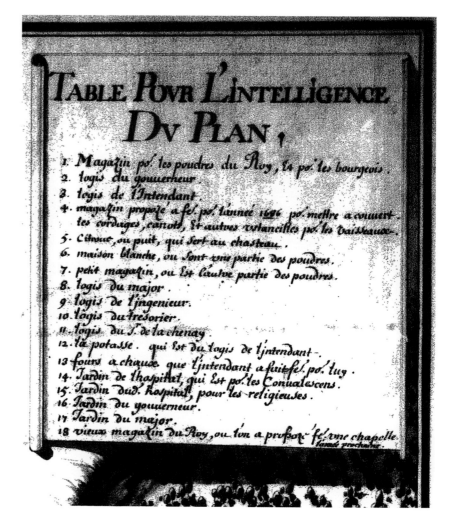

19. Robert de Villeneuve, *Plan de la ville et chasteau de Québec*, 1685, detail of the legend, pen, ink, and washes on paper

time. Similarly, the unusual orientation of Villeneuve's plan does not disrupt the direct correspondence between the orientation of city plans and the choice of vantage point in city views that is common practice in other images. By proposing a new orientation, Villeneuve suggests a new perspective on the city, and he supports the intendant's desire for a stronger architectural presence, both in the city and in its image. As Louis Marin has demonstrated in *Le Portrait du roi*, the reality of the king and the image of the king were completely integrated during the reign of Louis XIV.[38] Villeneuve's 1685 plan suggests that this argument is also valid for the king's representatives and their buildings in the city of Quebec. It reveals the importance given to the visibility of these buildings in the perception of the city.

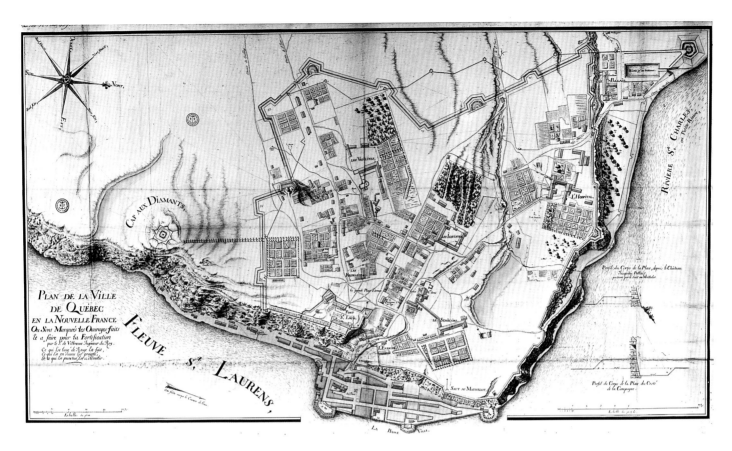

20. Robert de Villeneuve,
*Plan de la Ville de Québec en
la Nouvelle France* (Plan of
the city of Quebec in New
France), 1692, pen, ink, and
washes on paper

Centre des archives d'outre-mer, Aix-
en-Provence, Archives nationales,
France, DFC, Amérique
septentrionale, 439A

NOTES

1. Louis Marin, *Le Portrait du roi* (Paris, 1981), 213.

2. Michael Baxandall, *Patterns of Intention: On the Historical Explanation of Pictures* (New Haven, 1985), 33–35.

3. See Marc Grignon, "Comment s'est faite l'image d'une ville," in *Ville imaginaire, ville identitaire: Echos de Québec,* ed. Lucie K. Morisset et al. (Quebec City, 1999), 99–117.

4. Ships arriving in Quebec City followed the northern channel around the Ile d'Orléans and then turned to starboard in order to approach the southern shore, where the city is located (actually facing east because of an angle in the river). The city thus appeared to the traveler rather suddenly at the exit of the channel and presented itself from the side that is generally shown in city views during the French period such as that by Franquelin and the engraving published by Le Roy (figs. 1 and 2).

5. John Brian Harley, "Maps, Knowledge, and Power," in *The Iconography of Landscape: Essays on the Symbolic Representation, Design, and Use of Past Environments,* ed. Denis Cosgrove and Stephen Daniels (New York, 1988), 292.

6. As mentioned earlier, religious buildings are obviously the most prominent structures. I am purposely leaving them aside here as the questions they raise about "representational hierarchies" are discussed in Marc Grignon, *Loing du Soleil: Architectural Practice in Quebec City during the French Regime* (New York, 1997), chaps. 1–3.

7. Jean-Baptiste Colbert, marquis de Seignelay, to Sébastien Le Prestre, marquis de Vauban, 19 March 1685, in Louise Dechêne, ed., *La Correspondance de Vauban relative au Canada* (Quebec City, 1968), 9.

8. "[S]i vous voulez vous contenter de me faire envoyer des plans et profils des lieux que le Roy voudra faire accomoder au Canada . . . l'homme que j'ay fait envoyer conviendra." Vauban to Seignelay, 29 March 1685, in Dechêne 1968, 10.

9. See Gérard Morisset, "Villeneuve, Robert de," *Dictionary of Canadian Biography,* vol. 1, ed. Frances G. Halpenny and Jean Hamelin (Toronto, 1966), 663–664.

10. This is the house that Louis Jolliet, the explorer of the Great Lakes and the Mississippi, Wisconsin, and Illinois rivers, had built for himself in 1684–1685.

11. Lane Cooper, trans., *The Rhetoric of Aristotle* (Englewood Cliffs, N.J., 1960), section 1.1.

12. Morisset 1966, 664.

13. Bishop François de Montmorency-Laval to Louis XIV, Quebec City, 10 November 1683, Archives nationales de France, Paris (hereafter AN), Colonies, F-3 (collection Moreau de Saint-Méry), vol. 6, fol. 59; Bishop Laval to Seignelay, Quebec City, 10 November 1683, AN, Colonies, F-3, vol. 6, fol. 73–74.

14. The Récollets to Bishop Laval, Quebec City, 4 June 1683, AN, Colonies, F-3, vol. 6, fol. 37–38.

15. Louis XIV to Governor de La Barre, Versailles, 10 April 1684, AN, Colonies, F-3, vol. 6, fol. 84–85.

16. "Estat de la Mission des PP. Recolets de Canada," [1686], in [Inventory of the documents concerning the Récollets in Canada preserved in the Archives des Yvelines, Versailles], appendix to Sixte Le Tac, *Histoire chronologique de la Nouvelle-France,* ed. Eugène Réveillaud (Paris, 1888), 216.

17. Grignon 1997, chap. 2.

18. About the conflicts between Laval and Frontenac, see William John Eccles, "Buade de Frontenac et de Palluau, Louis de," *Dictionary of Canadian Biography,* 1:137–138.

19. "M. l'Evesque ayant fait dresser un autel pour faire une chapelle dans le magasin de la basse-ville sans en parler, le major y a mis une sentinelle pour en empêcher l'entrée." Extrait des lettres de 1681, Frontenac, Quebec City, AN, Colonies, C-11A (Correspondance à l'arrivée, Canada et colonies du nord de l'Amérique, série générale), vol. 6, fol. 106v.

20. "Le S[ieu]r Evesque . . . a demandé un emplacement appelé le Vieux magazin et d'y faire une chapelle succursale. Sa Ma[jes]té veut que le d[it] S[ieu]r de La Barre examine cette proposition et en cas qu'il n'y trouve aucun inconvénient et que le magazin soit inutile il luy remette pour y establir la d[ite] chapelle." Louis XIV to the sieur de La Barre, Versailles, May 10, 1682, AN, Colonies, B (correspondance au départ), vol. 8, fol. 102.

21. "[V]ous auriez deub avant que de faire la concession du vieux magasin de la nouvelle ville de Québek pour y bastir une chapelle en attendre un ordre de ma part et m'informer si ce magazin est inutile à mon service." Louis XIV to Governor de La Barre, Versailles, April 10, 1684. AN, Colonies, B, vol. 11, fol. 6v.

22. "Sa Ma[jes]té a appris que le d[it] S[ieu]r de La Barre en avoit fait la concession seul, ce qui estoit cont[air]re à ses ordonnances qui portent que le gouverneur ne doit faire aucune concession qu'avec l'Intendant, Elle veut que le d[it] S[ieu]r de Denonville examine avec le S[ieu]r de Meules s'il n'y a rien de préjudiciable à son service, Et en ce cas elle lui donne pouvoir de la confirmer." Louis XIV to the marquis de Denonville, Versailles, March 10, 1685, AN, Colonies, B, vol. 11, fol. 86r–v.

23. Grant of the land of the "Vieux magazin," Denonville and De Meulles to Bishop Saint-Vallier, Quebec City, 12 August 1685, Musée de l'Amérique française, Archives du Séminaire de Québec (hereafter ASQ), Séminaire 1, no. 42.

24. "Elle approuve aussy, qu'il ayt accordé a l'église la place du vieux magazin de la basse ville pour en faire un paroisse succursale." Louis XIV to Denonville, Versailles, 31 May 1686, AN, Colonies, B, vol. 12, fol. 28.

25. I have argued elsewhere that Baillif, trained as a mason and stonecutter in Paris before leaving for New France in 1675, usually relied on Parisian models from the first half of the seventeenth century. See Marc Grignon, "La Pratique architecturale de Claude Baillif," *Journal of Canadian Art History* 15 (1992): 6–30.

26. "[C]e qui est lavé en jaune est la place où le Sieur Renaud architecte prétend bastir et faire des porches de neuf pieds de profondeur, et un passage à porte cochère, pour communiquer de la rue Notre-Dame à la place." Robert de Villeneuve [Plan of the market-place in the Lower Town of Quebec City], 10 November 1685, Centre des Archives d'outre-mer, Aix-en-Provence, Atlas Moreau de Saint-Méry, F-3, 290, no. 68.

27. "Mémoire pour les bourgeois habitant la basse-ville de Québec," 1685, AN, Colonies, C-11A, vol. 7, fols. 241–147.

28. "Aujourd'huy dernier may 1686, le Roy estant a Versailles s'estant fait representer la concession faite au nommé Bailly architecte de la ville de Québec . . . d'une place size dans la basse-ville du dit Quebec . . . Sa majesté a confirmé la dite concession et en conséquence a accordé et fait don au dit Bailly de la dite place." Brevet, Louis XIV to Claude Baillif, 31 May 1686, AN, Colonies, B, vol. 12, fol. 24r.

29. Champigny was instructed to examine the situation and either deliver the *brevet* to Baillif in order to confirm the grant, or return it to the king in order to cancel it (Louis XIV to Champigny, Versailles, 3 June 1686, AN, Colonies, B, vol. 12, fol. 41). The document was actually returned to the king with a note explaining that the square was too small to be subdivided (Champigny to Louis XIV, Quebec City, 16 November 1686, AN, Colonies, C-11A, vol. 8, fol. 250v).

30. Jean-Marie Pérouse de Montclos, *Histoire de l'architecture française: De la Renaissance à la Révolution* (Paris, 1989), 355. The period coincides exactly with the creation of numerous *places royales* in France. See also Richard L. Cleary, *The* Place Royale *and Urban Design in the Ancien Régime* (New York, 1999).

31. In 1699 or 1700 the bust was removed from its original location because of the obstruction it created to circulation on the square. The intention was to place it against a merchant's house on the west side of the square, but this may never have been done. The last mentions of the royal bust indicate that it was displayed inside the Intendant's Palace. Afterward, Champigny may have brought it back to France at the end of his mandate in 1702, or it may have been destroyed when the building burned in 1713. In 1931 France offered to the province of Quebec a new copy of Louis XIV's bust, which was installed in its original location in Quebec City. See *The Canadian Encyclopedia Online*, s.v. "Place Royale" (by Marc Grignon), http//:www.thecanadian encyclopedia.com (2002; accessed 1 February 2005); see also Pierre-Georges Roy, "Le Buste de Louis XIV à Québec," in *La ville de Québec sous le régime français*, 2 vols. (Quebec City, 1930), 1: 469–470.

32. See, for example, Luc Noppen and René Villeneuve, *Le Trésor du Grand Siècle* (Quebec City, 1994), 152.

33. John Hare, Marc Lafrance, and David-Thiery Ruddel, *Histoire de la ville de Québec, 1608–1871* (Montreal, 1987), 66.

34. The fine of 50 livres is mentioned in "Mémoire pour les bourgeois," fol. 241v.

35. Jürgen Habermas, *The Structural Transformation of the Public Sphere* (Cambridge, Mass., 1989), 5–14. John Brian Harley also observes that the map legends clearly express social hierarchies during this period; see Harley 1988, 294.

36. Morisset 1966, 664.

37. His limited ability in the design of fortifications may have been a determining factor in the outcome of his career.

38. Marin 1981, 267.

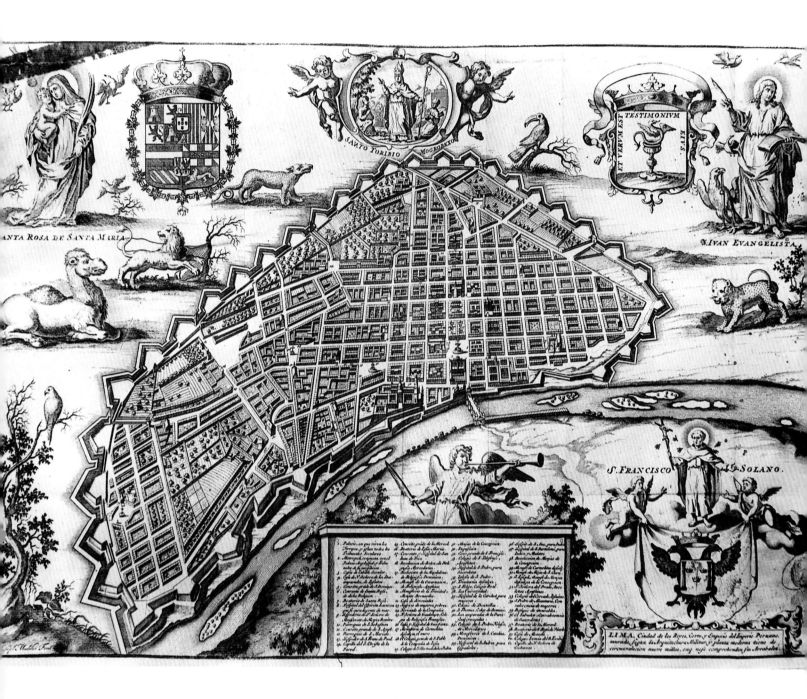

SANTA ROSA DE SANTA MARIA

SANTO TORIBIO MOGROBEXO

ET VERVM EST TESTIMONIVM EIVS

S. IVAN EVANGELISTA

S. FRANCISCO S.º SOLANO

LIMA, Ciudad de los Reyes, Corte, y Emporio del Imperio Peruano murada, segun las Arquitectura Militar, y planta moderna tiene de circumvalacion nueve millas, cuy, mesi comprehenden sus Arrabales.

FRANCISCO STASTNY
Universidad Nacional Mayor de San Marcos, Lima

From Fountain to Bridge: Baroque Projects and Hispanism in Lima

Lima was founded by Francisco Pizarro in January 1535 and named the City of Kings, in honor of the three Magi. From the beginning, it was designed as the capital of a viceroyalty that encompassed most of South America. Its location in an isolated valley near the sea guaranteed both security and ease of communication with its metropolis. By this choice of site, Pizarro thus established a precedent of aloofness from the empire he had conquered and a distancing of the city from the social realities of the New World while maintaining ties with Spain. It was the opposite of the course Hernán Cortés chose in Mexico. In Lima, Spanish and criollo populations were thus predominant in number and influence.[1] Next to the many government officials and ecclesiastical dignitaries stationed in the city, with time there developed an important stratum of merchants of Sevillian, Basque, and Navarrese origin who formed ties to local families and dominated intercolonial commerce through a growing maritime network. In the unusual urban society that resulted, Spanish and Moorish traditions were reinterpreted in the context of the colonial New World and at the same time were influenced by those of other culturally dominant European countries such as Italy and Flanders. From time to time, the political or ecclesiastical authorities encouraged the artistic environment that developed under these circumstances to imitate metropolitan fashions, in an effort to keep abreast of modern European achievements. This paper will examine two such cases, both of which had their origins in the desire of newly arrived viceroys to accommodate the capital entrusted to them to baroque urban ideals.[2]

Following the tradition of Roman and medieval military settlements and the ideals of humanist utopias,[3] Lima, like many early American towns, was laid out on a grid plan whose modular and regular design satisfied the rational spirit of the day (fig. 1).[4] Years later, in 1573, the experience of the founding was codified by the crown in the Leyes de Indias (Laws of the Indies), which regulated all aspects of urban organization in the New World.[5] Occasionally this system can also be found in some of the rare European cities founded in the sixteenth century, among them Valetta, on Malta, which, established some thirty years later than Lima, followed a similar urban evolution.

The orthogonal plan was a totally different urban structure from that which was common in the old capitals of Europe, where the occasional Renaissance chef-d'oeuvre did not alter the medieval weblike network. When the need for change arrived in Europe with the Counter-Reformation, New World cities such as Lima required no drastic transformation. Not only did the prevalent geometric design combine ease of orientation and circulation with strategic advantages and centralized social control; it also possessed the aesthetic virtue of affording long

1. Joseph Mulder, copy of Pedro Nolasco de Mere, *Lima, Ciudad de los Reyes, corte y emporio del Imperio Peruano*, 1685, engraving
From Francisco de Echave y Assu, *La estrella de Lima convertida en sol* ... (Antwerp, 1688); Library of Architect Juan Gunther Doering, Lima

vistas, in some cases of more than seven hundred meters, which were easily adaptable to the baroque purpose of creating a sense of finality and of fulfillment in harmony with the ambitious goals of the colonial system.

That is one set of reasons why Lima's grid plan was kept unaltered throughout the period, even though frequent earthquakes provided opportunities for renewal. It could also be argued that the relative security offered by wide, straight streets, even in cases of major telluric movements, was a reason to preserve the grid. Another, no less important, was the psychology of the colonial mentality. The transformations brought about by the baroque requirement of a strong rhetoric usually applied to an external formal enrichment that did not touch the inner urban core and its layout. In most cases the prototypes were established in the second half of the sixteenth century, under the prestige of the Renaissance and of early Counter-Reformation stylistic choices, and did not change from then on. One perceives that a predominant feature of colonial art throughout history is the selective accumulation, rather than successive substitution, of styles. Cities as well as buildings and objects preserved the early tectonic modules and transformed only the outer vestment of decoration in order to adapt to the demands of changing formal and spatial concepts of the times.

The superimposed baroque decoration that covered the classical structures of colonial America sometimes went to extremes for powerful formal effects. Addressed to a population with a high percentage of native inhabitants attached to pre-Christian practices and habits of thought, the ornamental language tended, in some regions, to take on a hypnotic character of intoxicating visual effect.

Something similar happened in urbanism: orthogonal structure was preserved while buildings were transformed in external appearance in the search for a new grammar to transmit the colonial version of absolutist convictions. The seventeenth-century retable facades of New World churches served this purpose (fig. 2). As Erwin Walter Palm first observed, by imitating in stone or stucco the appearance and vocabulary of wooden altars, the churches, repeating the accomplishment of Gothic cathedrals, became virtually transparent. Long, straight streets

were transformed into the prolongation of the nave, giving to the faithful a blessed feeling of anticipation of the encounter with the high altar and with the divine mystery of the Eucharist.[6] The whole city was thus sacralized and converted into an open area where domes and towers provided the axial elevations that led believers to imagine a vision of celestial domains.

2. Retable facade of the Church of San Francisco, by Constantino Vasconcelos and Ascencio Salas (?), Lima, 1657–1672
Author photograph

3. Fountain of Lions and Dragons, by Pedro Noguera, Plaza Mayor, Lima, inaugurated 1651, bronze
Author photograph

This process was helped, from the seventeenth century on, by extending churches and convents with front or lateral atriums. They created a series of small collateral squares whose presence did not affect the pattern of straight streets but gave breathing room to the retable facade and its implicit message, as well as to other types of church fronts.[7] A particular baroque experience of mysticism and artistic exaltation was thus created in these structures, so different from the Roman or French counterparts of the period and yet so similar in the intended persuasive effects.

Initial Baroque:
The Fountain of Lions and Dragons

The situation just described explains the importance assumed by woodcarving and cabinetwork in the early stages of the baroque in Lima. The battle for souls and for the victory of the colonial system was first fought with the interior decoration of the nave; only later did it emerge in exterior architecture. Experimentation with a new organization of space was easier in such works as choir stalls and carved altars. The first place where such new unifying motifs were used was the choir stalls of the Lima cathedral (1624–1636). Pedro de Noguera (Barcelona, 1592–c. 1655), head of that project and *maestro mayor* of the cathedral, was called in 1649 by the recently arrived viceroy, Sarmiento de Sotomayor, count of Salvatierra, to design a new fountain for the main square, the Plaza Mayor (fig. 3).

In it, he incorporated old and new decorative ideas to fulfill an iconographic program dedicated to celebrating the definitive victory of Spain over the Andean world. The moment seemed ripe for such a commemoration. Internal wars were over, the mines were yielding a large quantity of silver, and the natives and other "castes" accepted in daily practice the moral and military superiority of Europeans. However, the conservation of ancestral pagan practices in the native daily cults, a practice that the Spanish religious authorities had fought energetically from the early seventeenth century, had not diminished. The year the fountain was commissioned (1649), Bishop Pedro de Villagómez of Lima launched a new campaign of "extirpation of idolatry," which involved searching out and burning old Inca cultic sites and punishing clandestine priests. The presence of this clandestine religious restlessness among the Indians was a further reason for a public display of the symbols of Spanish triumph.[8]

High on top of Noguera's fountain, an image of Fame displayed the coat of arms of Castille and León and of the City of Kings. Nearer eye level were escutcheons of the viceroy. Between the two, a grotesque ornamentation of acanthus leaves alternating with green masks, mermaids with vegetal bodies, and veiled female heads creates a wild and bizarre atmosphere. Particularly disturbing are the tongues protruding slightly from the mouths of the female figures, which seem to mock the beholder (fig. 4). Such heads (with the lips closed) have been related symbolically to Roman vestals and, by extension, according to Sebastiano Serlio, to the Virgin Mary. The way in which their meaning is twisted in the fountain is a clear indication of a paradoxical message.[9] The impression one receives from the combination of natural, monstrous, and human figures is that of a reconstruction of the New World's idolatrous civilization, half wild and incongruous, as seen in the fantasy of seventeenth-century Limeños. This perception is strengthened by a double row of winged cherubs, which seem to provide a supernatural protection for the coats of arms on top and, below, for the names of the viceroy and the members of the town hall, isolating them from pagan chaos.[10]

Finally, on the outside rim are eight groups of emblematic animals. Victorious on top of each is the Spanish lion, symbol of Christ, virtue, and strength. Underneath, forcibly subdued, are dragon serpents, representative of evil in Christian iconography and of the Inca people in the colonial context (fig. 5).[11]

This monument, inaugurated in 1651, was the first to introduce into urban space the decorative ideas that transformed late Renaissance themes into baroque experiments. Placed on the highest level of the shaft are protruding handlelike ornaments that prepare the eye for the diagonal thrust of the statue of Fame (fig. 6).[12] These curved motifs, whether flat or volumetric, became one of the main decorative supports of the baroque grammar developed in Lima's architecture and decorative art (fig. 7). The principal contribution of the Fountain of Lions and Dragons to urban renovation, however, was its effect on the organization of space in the Plaza Mayor. More than ten meters high, it stood out in the vast, flat expanse of the square as a "crystal obelisk," according to the description of Pedro Peralta y Barnuevo, published in 1732.[13] The axial effect of this monument was crucial to a renewed perception of the square as a dynamic political and religious center. Fragmented space earlier defined by buildings of different heights and volumes such as the long, flat viceroy's palace, the towered cathedral, and the town hall, was now unified into a meaningful dimension. Anyone entering the square would be attracted to the focal point of the brightly gilded fountain, whose mysterious arguments

would reflect the messages of domination of the colonial powers distributed around it, while homogenizing the space through its central presence. The symbolic importance the monument achieved is clearly stressed in two orthogonal plans of the town. One, designed in 1674 by Fray Bernardo Clemente Príncipe and shown in a watercolor, now in the Library of Congress in Washington, is the earliest preserved and most detailed general plan of Lima. The other, of 1685, in the Archivo de Indias, Seville, was drawn by Fray

4. Fountain of Lions and Dragons, by Pedro Noguera, Plaza Mayor, Lima, detail of veiled female heads, 1650, bronze
Photograph by Mylene d'Auriol.

5. Fountain of Lions and Dragons, by Pedro Noguera, Plaza Mayor, Lima, detail of lions and dragons, 1650, bronze
Author photograph

6. Fountain of Lions and Dragons, by Pedro Noguera, Plaza Mayor, Lima, detail of handlelike volutes on the upper shaft, 1650, bronze
Photograph by Mylene d'Auriol

Pedro Nolasco de Mere (fig. 8). The two authors were friars of the Convent of La Merced in Lima.[14] In both plans, the three buildings surrounding the square seem to be dwarfed and to rotate around a monumental fountain.

It is worth mentioning that by the time Noguera's work was being completed in Lima, Gian Lorenzo Bernini had developed, in a grander style and with much wider and dynamic scope, similar obelisk-fountains for Roman sites: one for the Piazza Navona (1648–1651) and another as part of the first project for the square of Saint Peter's (1656) in Rome, where he proposed to place the old fountain, remodeled by Carlo Maderno, in front of the obelisk in order to create a centralized axis for the open space facing the basilica. This scheme was transformed the following year in the famed Piazza Obliqua with oval arms and a symmetrical arrangement of twin fountains. The evolution of Bernini's ideas is best illustrated in the series of commemorative medals struck for the occasion.[15]

Noguera, born in Barcelona and in Lima from 1619, probably had no knowledge of contemporary Roman baroque; he was more familiar with the language of the late Renaissance and the ornamental vocabulary of mannerism. The search for a more fluid, expressive, and emotional language was an evident, though slow, process in his work. The turning point, which meant taking his experiments in woodcarving outdoors, can be more easily understood in light of the presence in Lima of the count of Salvatierra, who governed as viceroy from 1648 to 1655. Before his appointment in Peru, he spent years at the court in Madrid, where he witnessed the construction of early baroque buildings (Plaza Mayor, 1617–1619; Alcazar, 1619–1627) and the transformation of the city by a series of fountains with mythological subjects (1600–1635), which were designed by Italian artists.[16] In Madrid, he learned about the effectiveness of a fountain as an active urban modifier. The idea was not wasted on Noguera, who quickly

7. Retable facade of the Church of San Francisco, by Constantino Vasconcelos and Ascencio Salas (?), Lima, 1657–1672, detail of handlelike volutes
Photograph by Mylene d'Auriol

grasped the possibilities of the work he was commissioned to design. He not only made it a focal point of ideological convergence, but transformed it into an experimental baroque "total work of art" in which all senses and arts were combined: sculpture and sense of volume; painted ceramic tiles and colorful design (in allegorical depictions of the Months of the Year); the incorporation of a tamed *opera di natura* in the running water among the bronzes; and the roaring melody of the water rushing through the many spouts.

Two Exceptions

The direct involvement of officials or artists arriving from Europe was not the only stimulant to the creation of exceptional works that challenged the underlying structures of colonial architecture. For various reasons some bold and innovative works broke openly with convention. The most notable are the circular cloister of the College of Saint Thomas Aquinas, designed in 1665 by the Dominican architect Fray Diego Maroto (1617–1696), and the eighteenth-century church of Corazón de Jesús (also known as Los Huérfanos).

The chancellor of the College of Saint Thomas Aquinas, Fray Francisco de la Cruz, who took great interest in the building of his institution, was born in Granada, and it has been assumed that he suggested to the architect a design for the cloister based on his memory of the palace of Charles V (Pedro Machuca, 1525), which is in the Alhambra, in his home city. This source might indicate a confluence of Serlio's Renaissance designs with an experimental interest in new baroque volumes.[17] While Franciscans and Jesuits tended to develop the artistic skills of native peoples and tried to incorporate their works into ecclesiastical decoration, the Dominican order was more attached to Spanish artists and classical models, preferring in some cases to import entire retables from the metropolis or marble statues from Italy.[18] That the cloister was built at all, however, clearly confirms the experimental mood of the second half of the seventeenth century, when a new feeling for the distribution of space and decorative grammar emerged in all fields. The use of consoles as a transition

between piers and entablature is an element of this original vocabulary applied by the innovative Dominican architect Diego Maroto (figs. 9 and 10).

The only church in Peru with an elegant elliptical plan, Corazón de Jesús was built in 1758–1766 (fig. 11). Its decoration and conception belong to the rococo. The interior is harmoniously constructed with sweeping, curved lines with a high molded cornice that seems to lead the movement. The most original solution is the baptistery. Pairs of caryatids, two stories tall, lend an exotic note in the corners, and an oculus set in a large rococo shell permits incoming light. Though small in size, the nave produces the effect of a wide, undulating space modulated on one end by the dynamic molding of the tall choir (figs. 11 and 12).[19]

8. Pedro Nolasco de Mere, *Lima, Ciudad de los Reyes, corte y emporio del Imperio Peruano*, 1685, engraving (see fig. 1), detail showing the fountain in the Plaza Mayor
From Francisco de Echave y Assu, *La estrella de Lima convertida en sol . . .* (Antwerp, 1688); Library of Architect Juan Gunther Doering, Lima

9. College of Saint Thomas, circular cloister, by Diego Maroto, Lima, 1665
Author photograph

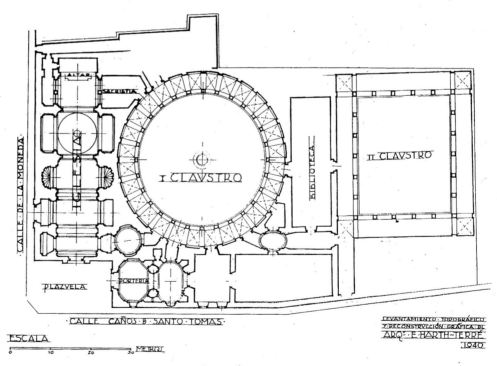

10. Plan of the College of Saint Thomas, by Diego Maroto, Lima, 1665, after Emilio Harth-Terré

From Antonio San Cristóbal Sebastián, *Fray Diego Maroto, alarife de Lima* (Lima, 1996), 93, fig. 7.3

11. Baptistery of the church of Corazón de Jesús, oculus in shell surround, anonymous, Lima, 1758–1766
Author photograph

The Equestrian Statue: Withdrawal toward Hispanism

As time went by, the optimism of the 1650s confronted more serious matters. In the early decades of the eighteenth century members of the surviving pre-Hispanic nobility of the north coast sent one of their members to Spain to represent their interests to the king. Once in Madrid, the Inca noble (cacique) Vicente Mora Chimo Capac, of Chicama, published several documents protesting against the injustice and exploitation his people were suffering (1721–1729). In 1736 caciques from Paita sent a strongly worded memorial to Madrid denouncing the king for not taking measures to correct the situation. Nothing changed, and the next year the first important signs of rebellion appeared in the south (Azángaro, 1737; Oruro, 1738–1739). By the middle of the century, Juan Santos Apu Inca led a widespread revolutionary

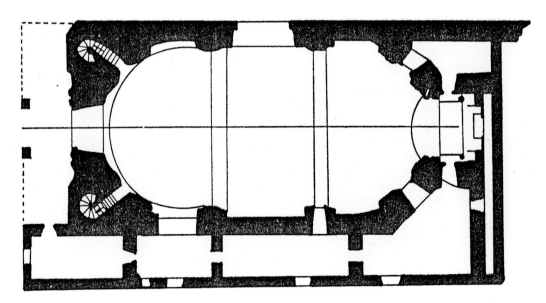

12. Plan of the church of Corazón de Jesús, anonymous, Lima, c. 1758
From Antonio San Cristóbal Sebastián, *Lima: Estudios de la arquitectura virreinal* (Lima, 1992)

movement from Peru's central Amazonic region. In the meantime, from the 1720s, caciques in Lima began to discuss the situation and consider what measures should be taken. By 1750 they conspired to start an armed rebellion, which was aborted.[20]

The troubled social climate greeted the new viceroy, Don José Mendoza Caamaño, marquis of Villagarcía, in 1736. The marquis, appointed, unusually, at the age of seventy, was the last of the grandes de España (the exclusive nobility of Spain) to attain the Peruvian viceroyalty. From then on, the high position was entrusted only to professional military officers. His reaction to the unrest was a primary reflex: to demonstrate a visible assertion of the power of the crown. For this purpose he commissioned his first and only artistic work, an equestrian statue of King Philip V. The artist in charge of the project was Baltasar Gavilán (or Baltasar Meléndez, hereafter Baltasar; active 1738–1760), the most distinguished sculptor of the time, several of whose works are preserved.[21]

The statue, destroyed only seven years after its inauguration by the violent earthquake of 1746, became an empty reference in local art history. It was known to be the earliest equestrian monument of the New World, erected more than a half century before the famous *Caballito* portraying Charles IV (model, 1796; bronze version, 1803) of Manuel Tolsá in Mexico City.[22] All other details were long unknown: How did the artist decide on the position of the horse and its relation with the rider? Was it made of bronze, stone, or wood? Apparently no drawing, engraving, or printed description exists.[23]

Most of these questions, however, have now been answered. Chance has recently brought to my attention two small eighteenth-century Spanish paintings on copper.[24] Their reverses show an engraved plate, which was cut in half to make the two ovals for the paintings. One represents the top of a monument that holds an equestrian statue, with two rampant lions and the coats of arms of Castile and León on the pedestal, set next to a balustrade and flanked by two large pinnacles. The other shows an arch sustained by two pillars and an inscription dated in Lima in 1739 referring to the viceroy, who had "this arch crowned by putting on

it the statue of the King Our Lord Philip V." (figs. 13 and 14).[25]

The normal setting for a statue of a Bourbon king would have been the politically dominant position in the center of the Plaza Mayor, following the model of the French *place royale*. The famous exemplar was the Place des Vosges in Paris, started in 1606 and decorated in 1639 with the now lost equestrian monument to Louis XIII, the king's statue by Pierre Biard and the horse by Daniel de Volterra.[26] That solution, which was used much later in the Zócalo of Mexico City for Santiago Sandoval's and Manuel Tolsá's statues of Charles IV (1786, 1796), was not possible in Lima, where the center of the square was already occupied by an equally important earlier viceregal commission, the Fountain of Lions and Dragons. A new site near the Casas Reales, the palace of the viceroy, had to be found.

Pedro José Bravo de Lagunas y Castilla, appointed a year earlier (1737) as general advisor of the viceroyalty and a cultivated art amateur, most likely devised the project and the bold new placement. The idea developed by Bravo de Lagunas was a subtle combination which blended Iberian and classical Roman traditions. It looked back to the equestrian monuments characteristic of parks surrounding Spanish royal palaces instead of following the French fashion of the public *place*. At the same time, it referred to the Roman custom of commemorative arches built over bridges.[27]

Behind the palace was an open space overlooking the river Rímac, which had been partially occupied since the seventeenth century by the church of Desamparados, a prestigious Jesuit church decorated by the best artists of the time. Next to it was a space in front of a bridge and an arch, used as the north city gate. The sixteenth-century viceroys made their ceremonial entrances into the capital there. The chronicler Bernabé Cobo, writing before 1629, described the arch as "of carved stone," and in the eighteenth century, with apparent exaggeration, Juan José Cevallos, count of Torres, compared its strength and beauty to the arch of the royal palace of Madrid.[28]

By installing the equestrian statue on the bridge, Bravo de Lagunas exalted the monument, bestowing on it the prestige of

13. Anonymous, *Equestrian Statue of Philip V*, 1739, engraved plate showing the statue by Baltazar Gavilán or Baltazar Meléndez
Valery Taylor Gallery, New York

14. Anonymous, *Arch over the Stone Bridge of Lima*, 1739, engraved plate with inscription
Valery Taylor Gallery, New York

15. Arco del Cavallo (equestrian statue of Niccolò d'Este), by Leon Battista Alberti, c. 1443, Piazza del Duomo, Ferrara, plan and elevations
From Franco Borsi, *Leon Battista Alberti: The Complete Works* (New York, 1989), fig. 6

a triumphal arch. Though none are extant, Roman precedents are documented graphically on coins and medals from Augustan times, several from Spain and others from Gallia.[29] During the early Renaissance, Leon Battista Alberti supervised construction of, and most likely designed the setting for, an equestrian sculpture of Niccolò d'Este (c. 1443), which was placed on top of an arch in the Piazza del Duomo in Ferrara (fig. 15). It thus established a prestigious revival of the classical prototype of an honorary arch that, however, did not find immediate followers. A similar idea was taken up in late baroque works in several European cities, for instance, in François Blondel's project for the Porte Saint-Martin in Paris.[30]

The most original aspect of the short-lived Lima monument, however, is the location Bravo de Lagunas envisioned for it. The unusual setting combines the concept of a triumphal arch with an extended view over a body of water in an open, mountainous landscape. The Pont-Neuf in Paris is the well-known prototype of an equestrian monument overlooking a river (1614) that becomes a conceptual *place royale*, dominating the river and the "whole city as well."[31] However, it does not share the notion of an elevated triumphal arch. No other existing permanent monument, in my knowledge, combines the three conditions in the way they were re-created, following vanished Roman examples, in the statue of Philip V in Lima.

In the early twentieth century, historians assumed the lost statue to have been made of bronze. At least one eighteenth-century description says, however, that the horse was made of wood.[32] Some doubts about the material may remain, but the later example in Mexico City, where the equestrian statue of Charles IV was twice carved in wood before its laborious and costly casting in metal, may be considered a good indication of how the work in Lima was executed.[33]

It is clear that Bravo de Lagunas must have provided the sculptor, Baltasar, with an engraving of the statue of Philip IV in Madrid, by the Italian sculptor Pietro Tacca with features based on a portrait bust of the king by the Sevillian sculptor Juan Martínez Montañés, to use as a model.[34] Except for the wig and the face, the two statues are quite similar. The king dressed in armor, one arm extended holding a baton (in the position of the classical Marcus Aurelius), the horse prancing and the tail touching the ground for stability, all are consistent with the Madrid model. The arch itself is a combination of plain pilasters and a Roman Doric entablature with characteristic frieze decorated with bucrania.[35] It is surmounted by a balustrade, marked on either side by prominent pinnacles (derived from Juan de Herrera) and recalling as well Juan Gómez de Mora's central facade of the lost Alcazar of Madrid.[36]

What this unusual monument achieved in terms of a symbolic definition of space relates both to the urban fabric and to its relation to the surrounding territorial extension. In the city, it was a way of recognizing the prominent ideological significance of the viceroy's palace and the adjacent streets toward the north. Their importance lies in their placement leading to the bridge and to the traditional ceremonial entranceway followed by the highest authorities representing the crown to the South American viceroyalty.[37]

It also stressed the power of a martial king, on horseback and surrounded by rampant lions, who, stationed at the edge of the town, acted as its permanent defender against a potentially hostile population.

The Equestrian Statue and Tamed Nature

Beyond the northern gate was an ambiguous open space, which assumed a particular symbolic significance in the colonial context. Being outside the walls, it was open to a marginal population of fisherman and other, less fortunate people, where victims of leprosy (in the hospital of Saint Lazarus), runaway slaves, and other outcasts could hide. It also led, however, to the outskirts of the city, which needed only the dedication of saintly men of penitence and contemplation or the urban improvements of a viceroy of vision to become a place of rest and solace for the city's population. This process began in 1592 with an initiative of the barefoot Franciscans, to build a convent for religious retirement (*recoleta*). It was completed when the viceroy, the marquis of Montesclaros, after building a stone bridge (the Puente de Piedra), in 1610, created a tree-lined avenue,

the Alameda de los Descalzos (1611), to aid access to the Franciscans and to provide a rural boulevard for Lima's inhabitants. The design followed, at a larger scale, the idea of the Alameda de Hércules (begun c. 1574) in Seville, probably the earliest promenade of its kind in Europe.[38]

The colonial world of Ibero-America had strong medieval components, which, even in the late seventeenth century, kept alive the archaic urban conception of a walled, safe city; an urban *hortus conclusus* protected from hostile nature, pagan Indians, and pirates. That is why the plan of Lima drawn by Pedro Nolasco de Mere in 1685 shows an encircled town with a bridge that leads nowhere. The marginal district of Saint Lazarus was entirely ignored. By 1739, when Baltasar's statue was erected, members of the elite made an effort to reject old notions and to endorse baroque concepts of urban space, which tended to link an open town to its natural surroundings and to create expanded perspectives for its heroic axes.[39]

The region beyond the river held a small urban population, scattered churches, and the Franciscan retirement convent in a setting of stony terrain, mountains, and distant

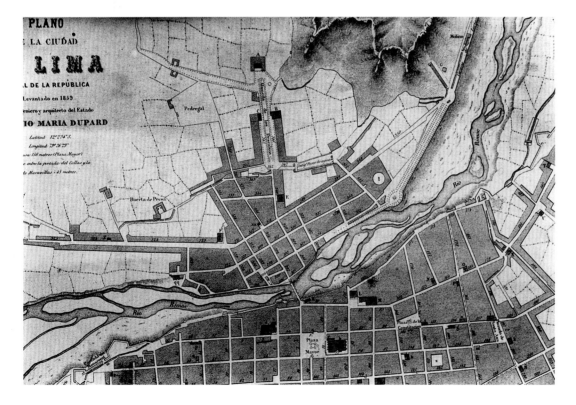

16. Antonio María Dupard, *Plano de la Ciudad de Lima*, 1859, lithograph, detail showing the Alameda de Acho (1) and the Alameda de los Descalzos (A)

From Mariano F. Paz Soldán, *Atlas geográfico del Perú* (Paris, 1865); Library of Architect Juan Gunther Doering, Lima

17. Anonymous, *Alameda de los Descalzos*, 1865, lithograph

From Mariano F. Paz Soldán, *Atlas geográfico del Perú* (Paris, 1865), plate 36; Library of Architect Juan Gunther Doering, Lima

roads. The statue high on the bridge was a beacon for these extensions, a way of absorbing and organizing the natural energy of these distant spaces to link them to the internal dynamic of the dominant city. For that specific purpose Bravo de Lagunas had a new tree-lined avenue, the Alameda de Acho, built on the opposite bank of the Rímac when he had the statue installed. This rural avenue followed the river in a long, perpendicular line, east of the bridge.[40] It was a pendant to the Alameda de los Descalzos, mentioned earlier, which followed the north-south orientation of the bridge. Together these two boulevards projected the visual presence of the king's monument to a wide horizon (fig. 16).

There is, however, a visible distinction between the European and the American experience in this respect. While in Europe the urban transformations started by planting green areas on ramparts, thus neutralizing them, in Peru the wooded avenues were laid out on the far side of the river, respecting the encircling wall. The *alamedas* thus appeared as civilizing entries into the wilderness of nature and alien societies. They followed the pattern of viceregal dealings with the New World; the residue of long habits of promoting expeditions of discovery, conquest, and evangelization.

The rural avenues were, therefore, a way of relating the highly organized structure of Lima's urban design with reclaimed parts of the natural surroundings. They served as theaters for ceremonial promenades, where people would go during the long *limeño* summers in carriages and on horseback to enjoy the natural setting and the breeze coming from the river. While they circulated

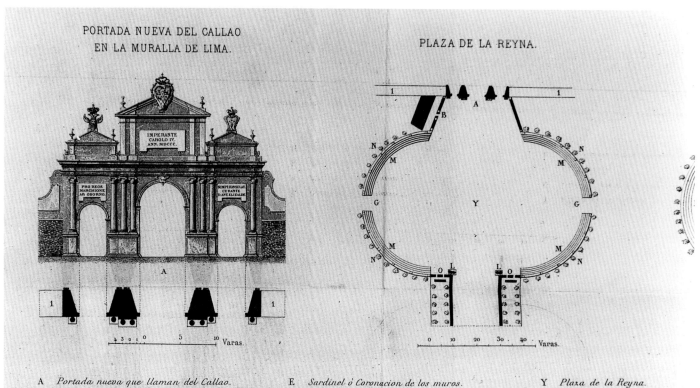

PORTADA NUEVA DEL CALLAO
EN LA MURALLA DE LIMA.

PLAZA DE LA REYNA.

A   Portada nueva que llaman del Callao.
B   Casa del Guarda de la Portada.
C   Camino nuevo en terraplen, ò Calzada Rᶦ sobre la haz del terreno.
D   Muros de Cal y canto, ò estrivos de la Calzada.

E   Sardinel ò Coronacion de los muros.
F   Escarpe empedrado.
K   Paseos de a pie.
H   Lineas de arboles y sus azequias.

Y   Plaza de la Reyna.
G   Salidas para los contornos e. la Muralla.
L   Dos Leones sobre pedestales.

Nota. Las tres Plazas ultimas de esta explicacion, son de construccion igual a la del Marques de Osorno, y la obra del Camino, se.

leisurely among the trees, they could see, or imagine, the figure of the vigilant king with his lions in the distance. The meaning of this presence was not wasted on any member of the society, high or low, European or Indian, free or slave. The king and his army were there to stay. In that sense, the open space beyond the river with its mountainous prospects, marginal population, and possibly hostile hinterland was taken as a symbol of the territory of the viceroyalty, whose rebellious Indians were the ultimate recipients of the stern military message.

The viceregal project to raise a statue of Philip V based on the model of Philip IV's statue in Madrid was also the earliest example in Lima of a regressive artistic trend that sought a revival among amateurs and artists of the former glories of Spanish art. Some twenty years later, this archaic tendency was fully established in one artistic sector. Copies of famous works by the mas-

ters of the "golden age," in the line of Zurbarán, Giuseppe Ribera, El Greco, and Murillo, were produced for churches and collectors, among them Pedro Bravo de Lagunas. Even at the end of the eighteenth century new avenues were built, such as one leading to the port of Callao (1800). It incorporated a sumptuous triumphal arch installed in the city wall in honor of Charles IV. The front of the arch was surrounded by an open plaza, the Plaza de la Reyna (Plaza of the Queen), and the way proceeded in a sequence of oval spaces that projected the monument's message into the landscape (fig. 18).[41]

But while the Spanish and criollo elite of Lima took refuge mentally in the art of the past, history continued on its course. Indian rebellions continued to stir the country. A military commander (1745) replaced the elderly marquis as viceroy, and the crown prepared itself for war. Then in 1746 the most disastrous earthquake and tsunami in the his-

18. Augustin François Lemaitre, *Triumphal Arch for Charles IV on the Road to Callao*, 1874, after an engraving by Marcelo Cabello, 1801
From Manuel Odriozola, ed., *Documentos literarios del Perú* (Lima, 1874), 6: 350; Library of Architect Juan Gunther Doering, Lima

tory of Lima destroyed most of the city and its port. The triumphal arch and the statue of Philip V fell and were ruined. It might be concluded, in consequence, that both parts of the sculpture—king and horse—were made of wood after all, and that the monument was as ephemeral as the viceregal colonial system itself, which only some decades later (1821) came to an end.

NOTES

1. Criollos were the descendants of Spanish settlers born in America.

2. High-ranking officials or members of the Spanish and criollo nobility of Lima tried to re-create the artistic conditions they experienced in Spain. Apart from the viceroys here mentioned, other famous cases are the bishop of Cuzco, Juan Mollinedo y Angulo (in office 1673–1699), and the viceroy Manuel Amat (in office 1761–1776). The commercial ties of Lima with the northern region of Spain (Navarre-Basque) were particularly strong in the eighteenth century. In the case of silverwork, the tendency was reversed: Peruvian objects were proudly sent back to Spain. See Alberto Flores Galindo, *La ciudad sumergida: Aristocracia y plebe en Lima, 1760–1830* (Lima, 1991), 48–69; Horacio Villanueva, "Los Mollinedo y el arte del Cuzco colonial," *Boletín del Instituto Riva Agüero* 16 (1989): 209–220; Francisco Stastny, "Platería colonial, un trueque divino," in *Plata y plateros del Perú* (Lima, 1997), 199–206. For a comparison between Peru and Mexico, see Tom Cummins, "A Tale of Two Cities: Cuzco, Lima, and the Construction of Colonial Representation," in *Converging Cultures. Art and Identity in Spanish America,* ed. Diana Fane [exh. cat., Brooklyn Museum of Art] (New York, 1996), 157–170.

3. Medieval and fifteenth-century military settlements in France and Spain, which can be appreciated in the plan of Santa Fe de Granada (1491), followed the tradition of the Roman castrum. On the other hand, from the early days in Mexico, Franciscans followed the utopian ideals of Thomas More, of Leon Battista Alberti's treatise based on Vitruvius, and of other classic writers. See George Kubler, "El problema de los aportes europeos no ibéricos en la arquitectura colonial latinoamericana," *Boletín del Centro de Investigaciones Históricas y Estéticas* 9 (1968): 104–116; Jorge Enrique Hardoy, "Las formas urbanas europeas durante los siglos XVI y XVII y su utilización en América Latina," in *Urbanización y proceso social en América* (Lima, 1972).

4. Actually the Lima plan has two deviations from the geometric grid, corresponding to an old Inca road and a small river that run on either side of the city. They show how the conquerors adapted to the realities of America. See Leopoldo Torres Balbás, Fernando Chueca, and Julio González, *Planos de ciudades iberoamericanas y filipinas existentes en el Archivo de Indias,* 2 vols. (Madrid, 1951); Leonardo Benevolo, "Las nuevas ciudades fundadas en el siglo XVI en la América Latina," *Boletín del Centro de Investigaciones Históricas y Estéticas* 9 (1968): 117–136. For Lima, see Juan Bromley and José Barbagelata, *Evolución urbana de Lima* (Lima, 1945), and Juan Gunther Doering, *Planos de Lima (1613–1983)* (Lima, 1983).

5. See a summary of the principal provisions in Benevolo 1968, 127–128.

6. Erwin Walter Palm, "The Art of the New World after the Spanish Conquest," in *Heimkehr ins Exil: Schriften zu Literatur und Kunst* (Cologne, 1992), 199–201; also Humberto Rodríguez Camelloni, "The Retablo-Facade as Transparency: A Study of the Frontispiece of San Francisco, Lima," *Anales del Instituto de Investigaciones Estéticas* 62 (1991): 111–122.

7. See a different interpretation in Antonio San Cristóbal Sebastián, "Las plazuelas en el urbanismo limeño," in *Lima: Estudios de la arquitectura virreinal* (Lima, 1992), 135–150.

8. Pierre Duviols, *La Lutte contre les religions authoctones dans le Pérou colonial: "L'Extirpation de l'idolatrie" entre 1532 et 1660* (Paris, 1971), 165; Kenneth R. Mills, *Idolatry and Its Enemies: Colonial Andean Religion and Extirpation, 1640–1750* (Princeton, 1997), chap. 5, esp. 143–149.

9. The paganism of the New World was frequently interpreted as a diabolic mockery of the true faith. Thus the Spanish authors sometimes wrongly compared Inca *acllacuna* or *mamacona* to Catholic nuns. The irreverent maidens represent such an allusion. In Europe the veiled heads are a common motif of grotesque decoration. They have been associated with the goddess Vesta. Serlio related the Corinthian order, inspired by the proportions of maidens, to the virgin Vesta and recommended that in modern times this order be used in buildings related to the Virgin Mary. In Francisco Villalpando's Spanish translation: "El orden corintio, se debe consagrar . . . a la Virgen Sacratísima. . . . " Sebastiano Serlio, *Tercero y Cuarto libro de arquitectura, Traduzido por Francisco de Villalpando* (Toledo, 1563), bk. 4, chap. 8, fols. 4–5, quoted in José de Mesa and Teresa Gisbert, *Arquitectura andina, 1530–1830: Historia y análisis* (La Paz, 1985), 33; Rodríguez Camelloni 1991, 116, fig. 11. On demoniac mystification, see Duviols 1971, 67–72; Sabine MacCormack, *Religion in the Andes: Vision and Imagination in Early Colonial Peru* (Princeton, 1991), 44, 47.

10. Francisco Stastny, "Naturaleza, arte y poder en una fuente barroca," *Iconos* 3 (August 2000): 10–19.

11. The double serpent was an Inca divinity associated with the supernatural *amaru*, a powerful hybrid combination of puma (American lion), snake, and deer. In colonial times the *amaru* acquired the iconography of a dragon as represented in the Old World. It is frequently depicted as such in *qero* paintings. After the Spanish conquest, serpents were added to the coat of arms conceded to Inca nobility and became a generalized symbol of the Indian population. Enrique Gammarra y Hernández, *Nobiliario de las ciudades del Perú* (Lima, 1938), 5; John H. Rowe, "Colonial Portraits of Inca Nobles," offprint, *Twenty-Ninth International Congress of Americanists* (Chicago, 1951).

12. The present-day statue of Fame is a modern copy, which lacks the movement and the meaning of the original sculpture, lost in 1903. M. Haydeé di Doménico Suazo, *La fuente de la Plaza Mayor de Lima* (Lima, 1945), 7–8; Stastny 2000, 12–13, figs. 4 and 5.

13. Pedro de Peralta Barnuevo, *Lima fundada, o, Conquista del Perú*, 2 vols. (Lima, 1732), 1: 323.

14. Fray Pedro Nolasco de Mere designed, in 1685 and 1687, two plans of Lima in bird's-eye perspective. The one reproduced here (figs. 1 and 8) is a nearly exact copy of the plan of 1685 made three years later by the Flemish artist Joseph Mulder. A small difference can be observed, however, in the fountain itself. In the original the jets of water run all the way down, creating the impression of a larger volume than in the copy published here. The copy was included in Francisco Echave y Assu's *La estrella de Lima convertida en Sol sobre sus tres coronas: El beato Toribio Alfonso de Mogrovejo . . .* (Antwerp, 1688), 5, pl. 1. This version belongs to the library of architect Juan Gunther Doering, of Lima, whom I thank sincerely for allowing me to reproduce it and other prints illustrated here. See Juan Gunther Doering, ed., *Planos de Lima, 1613–1983* (Lima, 1983); A. San Cristóbal, "Los planos de Lima de Pedro Nolasco (1685)," in *Lima: Estudios de la arquitectura virreinal* (Lima, 1992), 113–134.

15. Though Bernini's first proposal for the square of Saint Peter's, which he presented to Alexander VII in 1656, is no longer extant, it is known to have consisted of a trapezoidal space that would later be the Piazza Obliqua. This early design, inspired by Michelangelo's Campidoglio, stressed the central axis by placing the old fountain, redesigned by Carlo Maderno (1613), in front of the obelisk. Only later did Bernini adopt the symmetrical solution with two fountains. The first (August 1657) and the second foundation medals for the piazza clearly illustrate these changes. See Timothy K. Kitao, *Circle and Oval in the Square of Saint Peter's: Bernini's Art of Planning* (New York, 1974), 9 and figs. 9, 18, 20, and 21; Augusto Roca De Amici, "The Piazza," in Antonio Pinelli et al., *The Basilica of Saint Peter in the Vatican*, 4 vols. (Modena, 2000), vol. 3, *Texts*, 292, 445; and Cesare D'Onofrio, *Le fontane di Roma* (Rome, 1986), 285–289. On the drawings and medals, see Heinrich Brauer and Rudolf Wittkower, *Die Zeichnungen des Gianlorenzo Bernini*, 2 vols. (Berlin, 1931), 74, notes 4 and 5.

16. María Elena Gómez-Moreno, "Escultura del siglo XVII," *Ars Hispaniae* 16 (1963): 312.

17. Harold Wethey, *Colonial Architecture and Sculpture in Peru* (Cambridge, Mass., 1949), 251–253; Antonio San Cristóbal Sebastián, *Fray Diego Maroto, alarife de Lima, 1617–1696* (Lima, 1996), 98–100.

18. The retable of the Virgin of the Rosary arrived in Lima from Seville in 1585. Although the tendency to favor work by European artists diminished in the second half of the seventeenth century, the greatest glory of the Dominican order in the New World, the canonization of Saint Rosa of Lima, the first saint of the Americas (1669), was also celebrated by importing from Rome a marble statue of the saint by Melchiore Caffà, a distinguished follower of Bernini. At the same time, however, local painters were commissioned to finish the decoration of the cloister of the College of Saint Thomas Aquinas, begun by two Sevillian artists. See José Torre Revello, "Obras de arte enviadas al Nuevo Mundo en los siglos XVI y XVII," *Anales del Instituto de Arte Americano e Investigaciones Estéticas* 1 (1948): 87–96; Francisco Stastny, *Las pinturas de la vida de Santo Domingo en el Convento de la Orden de Predicadores de Lima*, Banco de Crédito del Perú (Lima, 1998), 57; José Flores Araoz et al., *Santa Rosa de Lima y su tiempo* (Lima, 1995), 156; Antonio San Cristóbal Sebastián, *Estructuras ornamentales de la arquitectura virreinal peruana* (Lima, 2000), 353–366.

19. Wethey 1949, 253–254.

20. The official in charge of judging and punishing the participants in the rebellion was Pedro Bravo de Lagunas. About this personage and his involvement in Lima's urbanism and in the royalist cause, see farther on and note 27. See also José Antonio Lavalle, "Don Pedro José Bravo de Lagunas y Castilla (Apuntes sobre su vida y sus obras)," *El Ateneo de Lima* 3 (1887): 336–337; John H. Rowe, "El movimiento nacional Inca," *Revista Universitaria [Universidad Nacional San Antonio Abad del Cusco]* 107 (1954): 17–47; and Scarlett O'Phelan Godoy, *Rebellions and Revolts in Eighteenth-Century Peru and Upper Peru* (Cologne, 1985).

21. The last name of this artist is not documented. An alternative name, Baltasar Meléndez, has been suggested. Rubén Vargas Ugarte, *Ensayo de un diccionario de artífices de la América Meridional*, 2d ed. (Burgos, 1968), 428; personal communication of Luis E. Wuffarden.

22. Two wooden statues of Charles IV were carved in Mexico before Tolsá's equestrian monument was founded in 1803. The first, of 1789, was by Santiago Cristóbal Sandoval; the second was carved by Tolsá himself in 1796. See Manuel Toussaint, *Colonial Art in Mexico*, trans. Elizabeth Wilder Weissman (Austin, 1967), 434–435; Rogelio Ruiz Gomar, "La escultura académica hasta la consumación de la Independencia," in *Historia del arte mexicano*, vol. 7, ed. Jorge Alberto Manrique (Mexico City, 1982), 77, 80.

23. Much literature was published in Mexico for the monument of 1803. The engraving discussed here is the only printed commemoration of the inauguration of the Lima statue in 1739. The British Library has a large collection of such publications about Tolsá's monument. Some are mentioned in Clara Bargellini, "La lealtad Americana: El significado de la estatua ecuestre de Carlos IV," in *Iconología y sociedad: Arte colonial hispanoamericano*, XLIV Congreso Internacional de Americanistas (Mexico, 1987), 207–220, notes 17 and 21. See the collection of materials in the British Library under the number [1145.bbb.44].

24. The paintings were some years ago in the hands of Valery Taylor Gallery, New York.

25. The inscription reads: "El Exmo. Sr.Marqués de Villa García, / siendo virrey, mandó coronar este arco, y poner en / el la estatua del rey nuestro Señor Don Phelipe Quinto / (que Dios guarde) / Cometió la obra al Sr.Marqués de Cassaconcha, oydor decano de esta Real Audiencia, de / Lima año de 1739." A scale between the arch and the inscription indicates a width of 20 *baras*, or 16.71 meters.

26. The concept of the piazza as a politically charged symbol exhibiting the image of the monarch was developed in Rome and Tuscany following Michelangelo's Piazza di Campidoglio (1540). In the early seventeenth century Marie de Médicis took it to France where, later, under Louis XIV, it was applied in grand style in the Place des Victoires (1685) and the Place Vendôme (from 1688). See Claude Mignon, "Urban Transformations," in *The Triumph of the Baroque: Architecture in Europe, 1600–1750*, ed. Henry A. Millon [exh. cat., Palazzina di Caccia di Stupinigi] (Turin, 1999), 329; Anthony Blunt, *Art and Architecture in France, 1500–1700* (Harmondsworth, 1957), 94–96, 110, and 256, note 3; Christian Norberg-Schulz, *Baroque Architecture* (Milan, 1986), 32.

27. Pedro Bravo de Lagunas had a lively interest in the arts. The painter Cristóbal Lozano, with whom he shared an attachment to the order of Saint Camille, was his protégé. In his will he left a detailed inventory of his personal collection, which included some hundred paintings. See Lavalle, 1887: 329–346, 361–381.

28. The first viceroy to make his entry into Lima from the north, over an earlier bridge and through an adobe arch, was the count of Nieva, in 1561. That bridge was replaced in 1610 by the one that stands today. Bernabé Cobo wrote that it had a "most sumptuous arch and gateway as of a city, of carved stone that can be seen from the square." Bernabé Cobo, *Historia de la fundación de Lima*, vol. 1 of *Monografías históricas sobre la ciudad de Lima* (Lima, 1935), 58. Juan J. Cevallos wrote about it in Madrid, as quoted in Domingo Angulo, *El barrio de San Lázaro de la Ciudad de Lima*, vol. 2 of *Monografías históricas sobre la ciudad de Lima* (Lima, 1935), 96, note 12. See also Ricardo Mariátegui Oliva, *El Rímac, barrio limeño de Bajo el Puente: Guía histórica y artistica* (Lima, 1956), 43–45, and Bromley and Barbagelatta 1945, 64.

29. In Rome the triumphal arches of Titus (82) and Septimius Severus (203) were crowned with quadrigas. The evolution of typologies from a single rider to a complete quadriga is illustrated in Marina Pensa, "Genesi e sviluppo dell'arco honorario nella documentazione numismatica," in *Studi sull'arco onorario romano* (Rome, 1979), 19–27, plates 1–4. See also Sandro di Maria, *Gli archi onorari di Roma e dell'Italia romana* (Rome, 1988), and A. García Bellido, "Arcos honoríficos romanos en Hispania," in *Coloquio italo-spagnolo sul tema: Hispania romana*, Accademia Nazionale Lincei (Rome, 1974).

30. Adolfo Venturi, "Un opera sconosciuta di Leon Battista Alberti," *L'Arte* 14 (1914): 153–156; Franco Borsi, *Leon Battista Alberti: The Complete Works* (London, 1989), 19–24, figs. 6 and 7. In later periods the idea was extended to city gates in several European towns. For Blondel's project see Millon 1999, 530, catalogue entry 372; Damian Dombrowski, "Das Reiterdenkmal am Pirnischen Tor zu Dresden. Stadtplanung und Kunstpolitik unter Kurfürst Christian I von Sachsen," *Münchner Jahrbuch* 50 (1999): 107–146. I thank Jennifer Montagu for calling my attention to this recent publication.

31. Norberg-Schulz 1979, 34.

32. T. J. C. y P., "Carta sobre la Música," *Mercurio Peruano* 4 (Lima, 1792), 109, mentions that the statue of the king was pressing "a un animado bruto de madera" (an animated piece of rough timber). Though technically difficult to imagine, these words could suggest that the king's statue was bronze. Emilio Gutiérrez de Quintanilla, in *Algo sobre bellas artes* (Lima, 1920), 82, referred to it as bronze (*estatua ecuestre broncínea*), a description repeated by Domingo Angulo (Angulo 1935, 2: 95).

33. Even more so, as while Tolsá's horse is walking, in the Lima statue, Philip V's mount copies the rearing position of the horse in the statue of Philip IV in Madrid. The Madrid sculptor, Pietro Tacca, achieved that depiction with great difficulty thanks to the help, it is said, of mathematical calculations made by Galileo. See Gómez-Moreno 1963, 312.

34. Juan Martínez Montañés was called from Seville to Madrid to carve a bust of the king, in order to send a model of Philip IV's features for the equestrian portrait being prepared by Pietro Tacca in Florence. Diego Velázquez took the opportunity to paint a portrait of the famous Sevillian sculptor at work. For the history of the statue and reproductions of engravings, see Jonathan Brown and John H. Elliot, *Un palacio para el rey: El Buen Retiro y la corte de Felipe IV* (Madrid, 1981), 117–120, figs. 11, 58, 60; Beatrice G. Proske, *Juan Martínez Montañés, Sevillian sculptor* (New York, 1967), 121–123, 165, n. 366.

35. Even for Europe the date is early for an experiment in neoclassicism. Neoclassicism arrived in Lima around the year 1800 with the Spanish architect and decorator Matías Maestro. See José García Bryce, "Del Barroco al Neoclasicismo en Lima: Matías Maestro," *Mercurio Peruano* 488 (1972).

36. The same type of Spanish pinnacle had already appeared in Lima in the middle of the seventeenth century, on the portal of the convent and on the church of San Francisco. See Wethey 1949, 81; Humberto Rodríguez Camelloni, "El conjunto monumental de San Francisco en Lima en los siglos XVII y XVIII," *Boletín del Centro de Investigaciones Históricas y Estéticas* 14 (1972): 39, fig. 50; George Kubler, *Arquitectura de los siglos XVII y XVIII*, Ars Hispaniae, vol. 14 (Madrid, 1957), 57, fig. 66. I wish to thank Fernando Marías for the reference to the Alcázar and the information that the statue of Philip IV was placed for a time behind the balustrade in the Alcazar, in a setting that recalls the design of the arch in Lima.

37. On the emblematic value of the north gateway to the city, see Rafael Ramos Sosa, *Arte festivo en Lima virreinal, siglos XVI–XVII* (Seville, 1992), 69–70.

38. Mignot 1999, 329–330.

39. Norberg-Schulz 1986, 14–18.

40. The name of the avenue was related to that of an ephemeral bullring located in the same area. It was the predecessor of the large Plaza de Acho, built in 1761–1776, one of the earliest still existing. See Mariátegui Oliva 1956, 114–115.

41. The elevation and plan of the arch were originally engraved by Marcelo Cabello in 1801 for Hipólito Unánue, *Discurso histórico sobre el nuevo camino del Callao, construído del orden del Excmo. Señor Marqués de Osorno, Virrey Gobernador y Capitán General del Perú, . . . Lima 1801*. It was copied in Paris by A. F. Lemaitre for publication in Manuel de Odriozola, ed., *Documentos literarios del Perú*, 10 vols. (Lima, 1874), 6: 350. See also Vargas Ugarte 1948, 390.

Contributors

Elisa Debenedetti is professor of the history of modern art at the Università di Roma "La Sapienza." She edited the series Quaderni sul Neoclassico (1973–1980). In 1980 she founded the series Studi sul Settecento Romano, which she still directs. She has also written on contemporary art (*I Miti di Chagall*, 1962; awarded the Premio della Cultura del Consiglio dei Ministri), later switching to eighteenth-century architecture (*Valadier diario architettonico*, 1980; *Valadier segno e architettura*, 1985; *L'Architettura neoclassica*, 2003). She is completing a volume on the Sforza-Cesarini family art collection in the seventeenth and eighteenth centuries, as well as preparing an exhibition on Roman neoclassical architecture.

Marc Grignon is professor in the history department and the Centre interuniversitaire d'études sur les lettres, les arts et les traditions (CELAT) at Université Laval (Quebec City). He teaches the history of architecture in the art history program, specializing in Canadian architecture, the representation of cities, and the theory of architecture in Canada and France from the seventeenth through the nineteenth century. His publications include *"Loing du Soleil": Architectural Practice in Quebec City during the French Regime* (1997) and articles in journals such as *Architecture and Ideas, Journal of Architectural Education*, and *Journal of the Society for the Study of Architecture in Canada.*

Hellmut Lorenz is professor and head of the Institute of Art History at the University of Vienna. His main fields in research, teaching, and publishing are history of Renaissance and baroque architecture, baroque art in central Europe, and history of architectural theory. He is preparing a book about the baroque palaces of Vienna.

Fernando Marías is professor of art history at the Universidad Autónoma de Madrid (Spain) and editor of *Annali di architettura.* He has written widely on Renaissance and baroque architecture and architectural theory and Spanish painting. His other publications include *El largo siglo XVI* (1989), *Otras Meninas* (1995), and, written jointly with Felipe Pereda, editions of *Diego de Sagredo: Medidas del romano* (2000) and *La "Pintura sabia" de Fray Juan Andrés Ricci de Guevara* (2002).

Henry A. Millon, dean emeritus, Center for Advanced Study in the Visual Arts, National Gallery of Art, has published articles on the architecture of Michelangelo, Guarino Guarini, and Filippo Juvarra, among others. He has curated three exhibitions of architecture and edited the related catalogues: *Michelangelo Architect: The Façade of San Lorenzo and* the Drum and Dome of St. Peter's (with Craig Hugh Smyth; 1988); *The Renaissance from Brunelleschi to Michelangelo: The Representation of Architecture* (with Vittorio Magnago Lampugnani; 1994), which was awarded the Prix Hercule Catenacci of the Académie des sciences morales et politiques; and *The Triumph of the Baroque: Architecture in Europe 1600–1750* (1999).

Konrad A. Ottenheym is professor of architectural history at Utrecht University, the Netherlands. He is coauthor, with Krista De Jonge, of *Unity and Discontinuity in the Architecture of the Low Countries, 1530–1700* (2005). He has also published monographs on seventeenth-century Dutch architects (Philips Vingboons, Pieter Post, and Jacob van Campen), as well as on the influence of architectural treatises in seventeenth-century Dutch architecture. He is working on a new English edition of Vincenzo Scamozzi's treatise *L'Idea della architettura universale* (1615).

Walter Rossa is professor of theory and history in the department of architecture at the University of Coimbra. He has published in Portuguese, Spanish, Italian, and English three books and numerous articles on Portuguese urbanism and land ordinance history, focusing mainly on colonial and Enlightenment issues. He has participated in several scholarly meetings and exhibitions on these topics, and has edited and co-edited related publications: most notably, the proceedings of the international conference *The Portuguese Urbanistic Universe, 1415–1822* (Lisbon, 1999).

Cesare de Seta teaches the history of architecture and directs the Center for the Study of the Iconography of the European City at the Università degli Studi di Napoli Federico II in Naples. He also directs the series La città nella storia d'Italia, published by Laterza. Among his most recent works translated into various languages are *Napoli fra Rinascimento e illuminismo* (1990); *L'Italia del Grand Tour: Da Montaigne a Goethe* (1995); *Le città europee dal XV al XX secolo* (1996); *Il secolo della borghesia*, 2 vols. (1999); *Viaggiatori e vedutisti in Italia tra settecento e ottocento* (1999); *L'Architettura della*

modernità tra crisi e rinascite (2002); *Napoli tra barocco e neoclassico* (2002); and *Le architetture della fede* (2002).

Dmitry Shvidkovsky is professor and head of the department of architectural history at the Moscow Institute of Architecture and serves as vice president for research at the Russian Academy of Fine Arts. He has written on the history of Russian architecture, urban planning, and garden history in works such as *The Empress and the Architect: British Gardens and Follies at the Court of Catherine the Great* (1996) and *Saint Petersburg* (1997) and edited *Guide du patrimoine de Moscou* (1998).

Mårten Snickare is curator of old master drawings at the Nationalmuseum, Stockholm. He has written widely on baroque and state ceremonial architecture, particularly on the Swedish court architect Nicodemus Tessin the Younger (1654–1728). His current research project is titled "Performativity in Baroque Art."

Francisco Stastny was a senior lecturer in colonial art history at the University of San Marcos, Lima, for thirty-five years. He directed the Museo de Arte in Lima from 1964 to 1970 and, in 1970, created the Museo de Arte y de Historia at the University of San Marcos, which he directed until 1986. He was a Getty Scholar in 1993–1994. He is the author of numerous publications on Peruvian art, including *Breve historia del arte en el Perú* (1964), *Maniera o contramaniera en la pintura latinoamericana* (1980), *Artes populares del Perú* (1981), and an extensive chapter titled "Platería colonial un trueque divino" in *Plata y plateros del Perú* (1997).

Giles Worsley is a senior research fellow at the Institute of Historical Research, University of London, and architecture critic for the *Daily Telegraph*. He was the founding editor of *The Georgian Group Journal*. His numerous books include *Classical Architecture in Britain: The Heroic Age* (1995) and, most recently, *The British Stable* (2004). He is currently working on a book on English baroque architecture as seen within its European context.

Index

Studies in the History of Art
Published by the National Gallery of Art, Washington

This series includes: Studies in the History of Art, collected papers on objects in the Gallery's collections and other art-historical studies (formerly Report and Studies in the History of Art); Monograph Series I, a catalogue of stained glass in the United States; Monograph Series II, on conservation topics; and Symposium Papers (formerly Symposium Series), the proceedings of symposia sponsored by the Center for Advanced Study in the Visual Arts.

[1] *Report and Studies in the History of Art,* 1967

[2] *Report and Studies in the History of Art,* 1968

[3] *Report and Studies in the History of Art,* 1969 [In 1970 the National Gallery of Art's annual report became a separate publication.]

[4] *Studies in the History of Art,* 1972

[5] *Studies in the History of Art,* 1973 [The first five volumes are unnumbered.]

6 *Studies in the History of Art,* 1974

7 *Studies in the History of Art,* 1975

8 *Studies in the History of Art,* 1978

9 *Studies in the History of Art,* 1980

10 *Macedonia and Greece in Late Classical and Early Hellenistic Times,* edited by Beryl Barr-Sharrar and Eugene N. Borza. Symposium Series I, 1982

11 *Figures of Thought: El Greco as Interpreter of History, Tradition, and Ideas,* edited by Jonathan Brown, 1982

12 *Studies in the History of Art,* 1982

13 *El Greco: Italy and Spain,* edited by Jonathan Brown and José Manuel Pita Andrade. Symposium Series II, 1984

14 *Claude Lorrain, 1600–1682: A Symposium,* edited by Pamela Askew. Symposium Series III, 1984

15 *Stained Glass before 1700 in American Collections: New England and New York (Corpus Vitrearum Checklist I),* compiled by Madeline H. Caviness et al. Monograph Series I, 1985

16 *Pictorial Narrative in Antiquity and the Middle Ages,* edited by Herbert L. Kessler and Marianna Shreve Simpson. Symposium Series IV, 1985

17 *Raphael before Rome,* edited by James Beck. Symposium Series V, 1986

18 *Studies in the History of Art,* 1985

19 *James McNeill Whistler: A Reexamination,* edited by Ruth E. Fine. Symposium Papers VI, 1987

20 *Retaining the Original: Multiple Originals, Copies, and Reproductions.* Symposium Papers VII, 1989

21 *Italian Medals,* edited by J. Graham Pollard. Symposium Papers VIII, 1987

22 *Italian Plaquettes,* edited by Alison Luchs. Symposium Papers IX, 1989

23 *Stained Glass before 1700 in American Collections: Mid-Atlantic and Southeastern Seaboard States (Corpus Vitrearum Checklist II),* compiled by Madeline H. Caviness et al. Monograph Series I, 1987

24 *Studies in the History of Art,* 1990

25 *The Fashioning and Functioning of the British Country House,* edited by Gervase Jackson-Stops et al. Symposium Papers X, 1989

26 *Winslow Homer,* edited by Nicolai Cikovsky Jr. Symposium Papers XI, 1990

27 *Cultural Differentiation and Cultural Identity in the Visual Arts,* edited by Susan J. Barnes and Walter S. Melion. Symposium Papers XII, 1989

28 *Stained Glass before 1700 in American Collections: Midwestern and Western States (Corpus Vitrearum Checklist III),* compiled by Madeline H. Caviness et al. Monograph Series I, 1989

29 *Nationalism in the Visual Arts,* edited by Richard A. Etlin. Symposium Papers XIII, 1991

30 *The Mall in Washington, 1791–1991,* edited by Richard Longstreth. Symposium Papers XIV, 1991, 2002

31 *Urban Form and Meaning in South Asia: The Shaping of Cities from Prehistoric to Precolonial Times,* edited by Howard Spodek and Doris Meth Srinivasan. Symposium Papers XV, 1993

32 *New Perspectives in Early Greek Art,* edited by Diana Buitron-Oliver. Symposium Papers XVI, 1991

33 *Michelangelo Drawings,* edited by Craig Hugh Smyth. Symposium Papers XVII, 1992

34 *Art and Power in Seventeenth-Century Sweden,* edited by Michael Conforti and Michael Metcalf. Symposium Papers XVIII (withdrawn)

35 *The Architectural Historian in America*, edited by Elisabeth Blair MacDougall. Symposium Papers XIX, 1990

36 *The Pastoral Landscape*, edited by John Dixon Hunt. Symposium Papers XX, 1992

37 *American Art around 1900*, edited by Doreen Bolger and Nicolai Cikovsky Jr. Symposium Papers XXI, 1990

38 *The Artist's Workshop*, edited by Peter M. Lukehart. Symposium Papers XXII, 1993

39 *Stained Glass before 1700 in American Collections: Silver-Stained Roundels and Unipartite Panels (Corpus Vitrearum Checklist IV)*, compiled by Timothy B. Husband. Monograph Series I, 1991

40 *The Feast of the Gods: Conservation, Examination, and Interpretation*, by David Bull and Joyce Plesters. Monograph Series II, 1990

41 *Conservation Research. Monograph Series II*, 1993

42 *Conservation Research: Studies of Fifteenth-to Nineteenth-Century Tapestry*, edited by Lotus Stack. Monograph Series II, 1993

43 *Eius Virtutis Studiosi: Classical and Postclassical Studies in Memory of Frank Edward Brown*, edited by Russell T. Scott and Ann Reynolds Scott. Symposium Papers XXIII, 1993

44 *Intellectual Life at the Court of Frederick II Hohenstaufen*, edited by William Tronzo. Symposium Papers XXIV, 1994

45 *Titian 500*, edited by Joseph Manca. Symposium Papers XXV, 1994

46 *Van Dyck 350*, edited by Susan J. Barnes and Arthur K. Wheelock Jr. Symposium Papers XXVI, 1994

47 *The Formation of National Collections of Art and Archaeology*, edited by Gwendolyn Wright. Symposium Papers XXVII, 1996

48 *Piero della Francesca and His Legacy*, edited by Marilyn Aronberg Lavin. Symposium Papers XXVIII, 1995

49 *The Interpretation of Architectural Sculpture in Greece and Rome*, edited by Diana Buitron-Oliver. Symposium Papers XXIX, 1997

50 *Federal Buildings in Context: The Role of Design Review*, edited by J. Carter Brown. Symposium Papers XXX, 1995

51 *Conservation Research 1995. Monograph Series II*, 1995

52 *Saint-Porchaire Ceramics*, edited by Daphne Barbour and Shelley Sturman. Monograph Series II, 1996

53 *Imagining Modern German Culture, 1889–1910*, edited by Françoise Forster-Hahn. Symposium Papers XXXI, 1996

54 *Engraved Gems: Survivals and Revivals*, edited by Clifford Malcolm Brown. Symposium Papers XXXII, 1997

55 *Vermeer Studies*, edited by Ivan Gaskell and Michiel Jonker. Symposium Papers XXXIII, 1998

56 *The Art of Ancient Spectacle*, edited by Bettina Bergmann and Christine Kondoleon. Symposium Papers XXXIV, 1999

57 *Conservation Research 1996/1997. Monograph Series II*, 1997

58 *Olmec Art and Archaeology in Mesoamerica*, edited by John E. Clark and Mary E. Pye. Symposium Papers XXXV, 2000

59 *The Treatise on Perspective: Published and Unpublished*, edited by Lyle Massey. Symposium Papers XXXVI, 2003

60 *Hans Holbein: Paintings, Prints, and Reception*, edited by Mark Roskill and John Oliver Hand. Symposium Papers XXXVII, 2001

61 *Italian Panel Painting of the Duecento and Trecento*, edited by Victor M. Schmidt. Symposium Papers XXXVIII, 2002

62 *Small Bronzes in the Renaissance*, edited by Debra Pincus. Symposium Papers XXXIX, 2001

63 *Moche Art and Archaeology in Ancient Peru*, edited by Joanne Pillsbury. Symposium Papers XL, 2001

64 *Large Bronzes in the Renaissance*, edited by Peta Motture. Symposium Papers XLI, 2003

65 *Tilman Riemenschneider, c. 1460–1531*, edited by Julien Chapuis. Symposium Papers XLII, 2004

66 *Circa 1700: Baroque Architecture in Europe and the Americas*, edited by Henry A. Millon. Symposium Papers XLIII, 2005

67 *Creativity: The Sketch in the Arts and Sciences*. Symposium Papers XLIV*

68 *Nationalism and French Visual Culture, 1870–1914*, edited by June Hargrove and Neil McWilliam. Symposium Papers XLV, 2005

69 *The Art and History of Botanical Painting and Natural History Treatises*, edited by Amy Meyers and Therese O'Malley. Symposium Paper XLVI*

* Forthcoming